COMING HOME AGAIN

COMING HOME AGAIN

American Family Drama
and the Figure of the Prodigal

Geoffrey S. Proehl

Madison • Teaneck
Fairleigh Dickinson University Press
London: Associated University Presses

Associated University Presses
440 Forsgate Drive
Cranbury, NJ 08512

Associated University Presses
16 Barter Street
London WC1A 2AH, England

Associated University Presses
P.O. Box 338, Port Credit
Mississauga, Ontario
Canada L5G 4L8

The paper used in this publication meets the requirements
of the American National Standard for Permanence of Paper
for Printed Library Materials Z39.48–1984.

Copyrights and Acknowledgements:

From *LONG DAY'S JOURNEY INTO NIGHT* by Eugene O'Neill. Copyright © 1956, renewed 1991. Reprinted by permission of Yale University Press.

From *A RAISIN IN THE SUN* by Lorraine Hansberry. Copyright © 1958 by Robert Nemiroff, as an unpublished work. Copyright © 1959, 1966, 1984 by Robert Nemiroff. Reprinted by permission of Random House, Inc.

Library of Congress Cataloging-in-Publication Data

Proehl, Geoffrey, 1950–
  Coming home again : American family drama and the figure of the
prodigal / Geoffrey S. Proehl.
    p.   cm.
  Includes bibliographical references (p.) and index.
  ISBN 0-8386-3547-4 (alk. paper)
  1. Domestic drama, American—History and criticism.   2. Husbands
in literature.   3. Brothers in literature.   4. Prodigal son
(Parable)   5. Family in literature.   6. Return in literature.
7. Home in literature.   8. Sons in literature.   I. Title.
PS338.F35P76   1997
812.009′355   dc20   96-13831
                                                          CIP

For Darrold and Mercedes Proehl
and
Morlie, Kristen, and Josh

Contents

Preface

Toward the end of this study, I quote Tennessee Williams to the effect that a "difficult familial background" is a prerequisite for becoming a "writer of consequence." I was not aware of Williams's opinion on this subject until I read the Spoto biography, but it expressed a perception that I had carried with me for at least twenty years, from whenever it was that I first started to think about stories of the family and becoming some sort of a writer myself. Indeed I remember describing in a journal entry written during my senior year in high school how I had to seclude myself in the bathroom at night to escape the drinking, profanity, and general squalor of my own family life. The entry was, however, a complete fabrication, an exercise in creative writing based not on my experience of family life but on a sense of what a family narrative should be about, gleaned from the literary and dramatic models to which my limited reading had exposed me.

My own experiences growing up during the fifties and sixties in a small logging town in the Pacific Northwest were, despite all the crises of childhood and adolescence, quite happy. I remember being spanked once or twice, being yelled at on special occasions, and a few silent meals when all that could be heard was the sound of other people eating, but never once did I try to run away from home or even consider it. I do not wish to romanticize or idealize this childhood time, to turn it into some kind of Arcadian pastoral in the woods of Oregon, which, of course, it was not, but as far as I can remember, I always perceived myself as fortunate to have been born into a relaxed, relatively happy, not overly demonstrative but certainly loving and supportive family. The only serious drawback was that given this relatively happy family life I could never become Williams's "writer of consequence," because I lacked an "anguished familial situation," which to my adolescent mind meant domestic fireworks: people yelling at each other; getting drunk and swearing; the breaking of dishes, hearts, and furniture. Of course this may have been happening all along and was being kept secret out of some urge to thwart a literary career, or I may have been simply too dense for any of it to register. In any event in my high school years I sensed a gap between family

9

life as I knew it and the kind of family life that was worth writing about, a gap that revealed some early sense of literary and dramatic convention: writers should write about their own lives in a realistic manner; that at the center of that narrative should be the story of their family; that dysfuntional families, to use the more current term, were the most interesting and useful for these purposes.

The point of this personal history is not, of course, the history itself or the sabotaging of a writer's career so much as to mark an initial awareness of a tension between two sets of perceptions: one of literary convention, the other of daily experience, neither one necessarily more valid than the other. This awareness eventually led to this study, to an interest in conventionality itself, in the kinds of family situations that theater audiences apparently want to see enacted again and again, in those elements, images, situations, and characters that are most recurrent within the family drama. This study addresses some of these concerns. It examines the plays of my childhood, dramas performed in the years immediately following World War II, in a search for certain patterns of representation. It tries to understand more clearly the kinds of family dramas I felt my own experiences had not prepared me to write.

If American post–World War II domestic drama has a generic form, I believe it is the one that I trace in this book: this story of a man with a bottle, a prodigal son or husband, often yoked to a brother, regularly linked to a more static figure, one who patiently waits for the prodigal's return, whether father, mother, or wife. As noted above my awareness of the conventions of family narratives is longstanding. My recognition of this paradigm is, however, more short-lived. It began with a reference in Ernest Bernbaum's *The Drama of Sensibility* to the "sorely-tried but loyal wife," the "repentant young prodigal," and the "wayward but reclaimable husband" in the sentimental comedies of the seventeenth and eighteenth centuries, and my sense, up until that point, that Miller's *Death of a Salesman* was primarily a play about a little man crushed by an uncaring system, about a tragic gap in American life between dream and realization. What struck me about this new mix of Willy, prodigality, and the reform motif was the perception, despite its talk of refrigerators and mortgages, that Miller's play was a direct descendant of the sentimental comedy, that Willy was the "wayward but reclaimable husband" (surprised by his son in a prodigal moment) and Linda, the "sorely-tried but loyal wife," that she with her stockings was an almost exact double of Cibber's Lady Easy and her steinkirk in a play appropriately titled, *The Careless Husband* (1704). My hypothesis had been that *Life with Father, I Remember Mama,* and *Ah, Wilderness!* were perhaps the twentieth-century equivalents of these earlier dramas. My reassessment, after noting this conjunction of Willy Loman and sentimental comedy, then noting the presence of so many male characters in American drama who seemed to fit within the rubric of the prodigal son or husband, was that perhaps the true heirs of sentimentalism were not these lighter works but those plays that we generally perceive as being unsentimental, serious, and problematic and that the true sons of Cibber and Steele were not Lindsay, Crouse, Van Druten, and the O'Neill of *Wilderness* but Williams, Miller, the O'Neill of *Long Day's Journey into Night*, and even in some ways, the Sam Shepard of *A Lie of the Mind*. Furthermore the link between the eighteenth century and the twentieth was the temperance melodrama of the nineteenth century. All three (sentimental comedy, temperance melodrama, American family drama) regularly represented the family as an apolitical institution strained by male sexual energy: conventionally expressed in terms of whiskey, whores, and waste; conventionally redeemed (often in the midst of tears) by the inherent goodness of the prodigal and the heartfelt benevolence of some parent or spouse.

My goal then became to see if one could profitably read a number of midcentury American domestic dramas as manifestations of this particular paradigm and if so to then explore the nature of these continuities in terms of dramatic form and function. This approach does not, of course, assume that authors consciously manipulate these conventions, although they may, or that spectators are always consciously aware of their presences. The demonstrable presence of a dramatic paradigm does, however, suggest the existence of a body of conventional expectations that play about and around both the creation of playscripts and their performances. If this study can shed some light on just what some of those expectations might be, on some of the ways in which a group of American dramas regularly perceive and manipulate the family unit, then it will have been successful.

Acknowledgments

ALTHOUGH writing a book is often a solitary process, it depends on the contributions of many other individuals. It reflects not only the works cited within a final bibliography but also many hours of classes, seminars, tutorials, and conversations. The department of drama at Stanford University provided an immensely positive place to work on the initial version of this study and to its faculty, staff, and my fellow students—too many to list in this small space—I owe a large debt of thanks. I must, however, acknowledge the work of four individuals who contributed directly to the completion of this project: Sandra Richards, Alice Rayner, Martin Esslin, and Charles Lyons—all of the drama faculty in the years I studied there. Professors Richards and Rayner offered abundant encouragement and support, but even more importantly, each led me to consider questions and resources that I would have otherwise certainly neglected. Professor Esslin gave me the gentle push I needed to take as my topic the role of the family in American drama; Professor Lyons, my principal reader and adviser, nurtured an interest in fundamental dramatic conventions, first, in the works of Eugene O'Neill, later, within the field of domestic drama itself. The intelligence, integrity, and generosity of these four scholars will always be for me a model of teaching and mentorship at its best. Whatever is good about this work owes much to their many contributions; its deficiencies are, of course, my own.

To these words of thanks, I would add these others. To Ron Davies for technical assistance in the use of computer hardware and software in the initial stages of this work's composition at Stanford University. To compose a manuscript today without the aid of a computer is almost unthinkable. Most of us, however, must rely on some mentor to guide us through the related complexities of word processing, DOS commands, and laser printing. Ron has helped me and numerous other members of the Stanford community with these complexities, sharing his expertise in a remarkably patient and generous way.

To the *George Lurcy Educational and Charitable Trust* for a dissertation fellowship during my final year of study. The generous support of the Lurcy Trust made it possible for me to focus exclusively on

13

this work for an extended period of time, a contribution that did much to make the timely completion of this project possible.

To Villanova University where I taught from 1988 to 1994 for a reduction in load that made possible a thorough revision of the original manuscript, as well as to friends and colleagues at Villanova who supported this work with their interest and encouragement: Earl Bader, James Christy, Rev. Peter Donohue, Joanna Rotté, Roxane Rix, Lon Winston, Donna Mattia, and graduate student research assistants Theresa Epp and Peggy Martinez.

To Thomas Yoseloff, Michael Koy, and Diane Burke, of Associated University Presses for their help and patience, as well as Margaret Loftus Ranald, the reader for Fairleigh Dickinson University Press who provided invaluable editorial advice at important stages in this manuscript's development.

Finally I cannot write about the representation of the family in American drama and not acknowledge the continuing presence and support of my own family. Therefore I would conclude these notes with the names of my parents, Darrold and Mercedes Proehl, two fine teachers who always made learning important; my daughter Kristen and son Joshua, who make me proud; my friend, partner, and wife, Morlie, who is as much a part of this work as I am.

COMING HOME
AGAIN

1

The Bottle

Arthur: Ma, I'm sorry. I'm sorry for what I said.
He bursts into tears and puts his forehead against her elbow.
Ma: There. There. We all say wicked things at times. I know you didn't
mean it like it sounded.
He weeps still more violently than before.
Why, now, now! I forgive you, Arthur, and to-night before you go to bed
you . . . (*She whispers.*) You're a good boy at heart, Arthur, and we all
know it.[1]

In the center of Thornton Wilder's *Happy Journey to Trenton and
Camden* (1931), two characters play a scene that evokes a set of conventions central to our perception of the family in American drama.
The Kirby family (mother, father, son, and daughter) is traveling by
car across New Jersey to visit a married daughter, who recently lost
a child at birth. On the way Mrs. Kirby and son Arthur discuss
whether he should take on a daily paper route in addition to his
Thursday deliveries of the *Saturday Evening Post*. They disagree. He
wants to work for the Newark *Daily* and get up every morning at
4:30 A.M. She will not let him "miss the sleep God meant him to
have."[2] He responds by third-personing her and treating the deity
with some jocularity: "Hhm! Ma's always talking about God. I guess
she got a letter from Him this morning."[3] The intensity of her reply,
comically violent as it is, amazes: eternal mother turns into monster
of piety in the middle of a cheerful play. She orders the husband,
docile Elmer, to stop, then tells Arthur to return to Newark, alone,
summarizing her attitude toward her son in four words, "I don't want
him."[4] But this rejection only anticipates what the mother perceives
as the end of a process on which Arthur appears to have embarked,
one that will, according to her, eventually lead to "speak-easies and
night-clubs and places like that":[5] Jimmy the Priest's, the Hell Hole,
Fat Violet's, Willy's room in Boston, "The Tarantula Arms."[6] The

father intervenes, promising a man-to-man talk later, so the journey can continue, but not before a move that exiles the son to the front seat and an isolation that encloses him like *"the shocked silence after a scandal."*[7]

Arthur does not say a word for three pages, then over a hot dog he stutters out an apology and bursts into tears. His sister cries too, and suddenly mom is *"joyously alive and happy."*[8] Parent and child reunite; the daughter rejoins her father in the front seat. Mrs. Kirby announces that she "wants to sit with her beau" and passes final judgment on his character: "You're a good boy at heart, Arthur, and we all know it." Isolated from the rest of the world in their Chevrolet, sufficient unto themselves, this American family drives on happy in their contentment, singing into the night, and wishing on stars. They drive on until they must return again to the particular, to their destination, to Trenton and Camden: the A&P store on the left, the daughter's home, two new puppies, a chicken in the oven, and a mother's song for death (a final universal), while the daughter sleeps:

> "There were ninety and nine that safely lay
> In the shelter of the fold,
> But one was out on the hills away,
> Far off from the gates of gold. . . ."[9]

So goes one version of America's favorite fairy tale.

The mother's song comes, of course, from a parable, one of three stories of loss and recovery in Luke 15. Arthur's episode—from parting to reunion—functions as *reductio* and homage to the third of these stories, that of the prodigal. The shape and function of that story in American domestic drama is the central concern of this study. My initial focus, however, will be on a simple action that is often a key to its manifestation, an action so common and banal as to be almost invisible.

THE BOTTLE

To begin with, I have chosen a handful of plays that premiered in the years immediately following World War II. They come from a period of about fifteen years, marked on one end by the baby boom and an affluent postwar economy and on the other by the assassinations of Kennedy and King, the escalation of the Vietnam War, the women's movement, and the social upheaval of the sixties. My primary reference points are the last New York premiere of an O'Neill play during that author's lifetime (*The Iceman Cometh*, 1946) and the opening of Albee's remarkable domestic drama, *Who's Afraid of Virginia Woolf?* (1962). This period coincides with the most productive years of Williams's career from *The Glass Menagerie* (1945) to *The Night of the Iguana* (1961), as well as with major periods of creativity for Miller and Inge. They also include the O'Neill revival that began in the midfifties with the Quintero/Robards production of *Iceman*. These years will serve as a frame for the exploration of a phenomenon that has played a major role in American drama from at least the middle of the nineteenth century to the present.

Here then is a cluster of plays:

The Iceman Cometh (O'Neill, 1946),
A Streetcar Named Desire (Williams, 1947),
A Moon for the Misbegotten (O'Neill, 1947),
The Country Girl (Odets, 1950),
Come Back, Little Sheba (Inge, 1950),
The Seven Year Itch (Axelrod, 1952),
Cat on a Hot Tin Roof (Williams, 1955),
Long Day's Journey into Night (O'Neill, 1956; written 1939–41),
Look Homeward, Angel (Frings, based on the Thomas Wolfe novel, 1957),
A Raisin in the Sun (Hansberry, 1959),
All the Way Home (Mosel, based on the James Agee novel, *A Death in the Family*, 1961),
The Night of the Iguana (Williams, 1961),
Who's Afraid of Virginia Woolf? (Albee, 1962).

For some these works represent the golden years of American drama; for others they will read like an inventory of old warhorses; and for still others they represent the core of a traditional canon of American drama best forgotten: three late O'Neills, a late Odets, an early Inge, two major works by Williams, the first African-American family drama to find a large White audience, two adaptations from novels, and the unlikely combination of an Axelrod and an Albee. With the exception of Hansberry and Frings, they are the works of White, male writers, produced, in most cases quite successfully, on Broadway. Most, for better or for worse, eventually found their way onto film as well. Presentationally these plays are not representatives of the theatrical avant-garde. As a group they have more in common with the work of turn-of-the-century authors (Ibsen, Strindberg, Chekhov) than that of their European contemporaries (Brecht, Beckett, Ionesco). Most are middle-class family dramas. I include *Iceman* in this category, despite its tavern setting, because of the centrality of family relationships in so many of the characters' lives, especially Hickey's and Parritt's. Hansberry's family is, at least, in transition, moving toward middle-class status. Generically they range from Axelrod's light comedy to as close as American drama has yet come to writing its own tragedies. Overall they are major and representative works of the post–World War II American theater; in most cases they are familiar even to individuals with only a passing knowledge of American drama. (Indeed, I count on this familiarity in the discussion that follows.) They are now fast becoming dramatic dinosaurs, period pieces of our recent past. As a group they are increasingly detached from our perceptions of relevance, increasingly distanced by our sense of their conventionality, by their old-fashionedness, and a healthy desire to go beyond them into different structures with different concerns. Yet in many ways, these texts are just now moving far enough away from us in time to allow some perspective on the ways in which they work.

These plays share the mimesis of a simple action: a hand carries a bottle or glass to the lips, alcohol passes over the lips, down the throat and into the bloodstream; tastes and sensations move from lips to tongue, from stomach lining to bloodstream, to the brain and back to the body's surfaces; altering, at first subtly and then more radically, the drinker's perceptions and state of being. The action of taking a drink of beer or whiskey or wine is perhaps too simple, too banal to concern most who write about American drama. Then again most of that work begins and ends within the oeuvre of a particular author, an approach that often limits our perspective. The image of a man with a bottle stretches across those boundaries. Once identified it seems like a national obsession.

Most criticism of American drama relies on a metaphor of surface and depth: it seeks out the hidden meanings of plays, which the critic decodes. This convention lies there for everyone to see and, because of its superficial presence, often ignore. My concern in examining the drinker and the drunk is not so much with hidden meanings as with how theatrical meanings are made, with this device and the conventions that surround it as a series of functions available for ready use by anyone within the culture who makes plays. My interest lies less in those profound, idiosyncratic meanings of texts, than in the ways in which certain simple conventions function within a wide range of plays and in the hegemonic values these conventions often carry, particularly within the works of relatively "mainstream" writers, in the ways in which even our most "serious" authors still seem to operate within a sentimental tradition that stretches back at least through the temperance melodramas of the nineteenth century to the reform dramas and sentimental comedies of the seventeenth and eighteenth centuries. This image is easy to push aside in favor of some more exotic motif and yet extremely important to an understanding of American drama and society, especially now, in the neotemperance era of the eighties and nineties. This simple action, which is, of course, not so simple, occurs again and again in these plays, hundreds, thousands of times, to the point of the banal and the mundane, yet still it persists as a fundamental convention of American playwriting. Indeed to create a generic American family drama at midcentury, one would almost have to begin with a bare stage, a man, and a bottle.[10]

In most of these plays, this convention is inseparably linked to our perception of one or more of the play's central characters. Productions of *Iceman* or *Country Girl* or *Sheba* or *Cat* or *Woolf* without alcohol are inconceivable. Of course in some of the other works listed above, its presence is less obvious. *Look Homeward*, for example, moves the figure with a bottle to the side of the action by making the drunken father only one of several elements in Gene Gant's coming of age. In *Raisin*, Walter's drinking and drunkenness, his visits to the local tavern, and especially his plans for investing in a liquor store are important issues (Mama Younger would feel at home in the temperance movement of the nineteenth century), but they may not be what immediately comes to mind when we think of this work. Axelrod's *Seven Year Itch* exemplifies another diminished, yet still significant presence. It focuses on a husband's infatuation with the girl next door, while his wife and son are away for a summer vacation. Still we first meet Richard Sherman, husband and father, with a bottle of raspberry soda in hand. His wife and his doctor have put him "on the wagon," which, naturally, he falls off of as soon as he sees "the girl." Sherman is a diminutive of the committed drinker: an anemic double of O'Neill's Jamie or Inge's Doc.

Some of these plays move around the mimesis of this action in a relatively tight circle; in others the action is more tangential. But in each case, drinking is integral to the structure of the play. As George says in *Woolf*, "We drink a great deal in this country, and I suspect we'll be drinking a great deal more, too . . . if we survive."[11] My primary concern is not, however, with drinking in the real world. My interest is instead with the realization that we seem to "drink a great deal" in this country's plays, not only in those listed here but in many others from the temperance melodramas of the nineteenth century such as Smith's *The Drunkard* (1844) and Pratt's *Ten Nights in a Bar-Room* (1858, based on T. S. Arthur's novel) to more recent examples such as Sam Shepard's *True West* (1980) and Eric Bogosian's *Drinking in America* (1986). Few writers are more quintessentially American than Spalding Gray, son not of a Baptist but of a devout teetotaling Christian Scientist mother, and in Gray as well, alcohol (in addition to other drugs) plays a significant role: in *Sex and Death to the Age of 14* (1982), in *Swimming to Cambodia* (1985), and in *Monster in a Box* (1990). Of course theater and Dionysus have a history perhaps as long as dramatic representation itself, but in American drama our thirst for drink seems almost insatiable. Yet in a strange way, the whole phenomenon has become almost invisible, something to be overlooked while we go on to other, more pressing critical concerns.[12]

An anecdote from an article in *The Eugene O'Neill Newsletter* concerning the 1985 Robards/Quintero revival of *Iceman* exemplifies this tendency. In a backstage conversation at Washington's National Theatre, Robards discusses Peter Sellars's suggestion that *Iceman* is actually about alcoholism:

> Peter thinks this is a play about alcohol. Now he wants to do plays about all of the American problems. Next season he wants to do a play about abortion, then he wants to do a play about suicide. But I don't know. That's why I mentioned it. I felt very funny the other night when he brought the subject up. I don't know if he believes it. But I've been thinking about it since then. I've been thinking about it my whole day off.[13]

Robards is talking here to James Greene, who was also in the original production of *Iceman,* and he is particularly concerned that O'Neill might be saying in *Iceman* that you've "got to be drunk to live," certainly not a happy thought for a recovering alcoholic. According to the author of the article (Sheila Hickey Garvey), Greene reassured Robards that there were "many ideas and issues in the play which place O'Neill's work on a grander, broader scale," that *Iceman* was indeed about those issues that Robards had always assumed were central, "about dreams and reality."[14]

Perhaps Sellars was speaking only in jest and certainly *Iceman* is not a single issue play. But in a way he was right: *Iceman* and American drama in general are often as much about the relationship between a man and a bottle as they are about anything else. This, anyway, is the point at which I would like to initiate this inquiry into the representation of the family in American drama: an image that might lead in any one of several different directions.

In encountering a recurrence of this sort, the obvious and perhaps irresistible question is why, given all the possibilities of human experience, should this particular action repeat itself so often? This is an interesting question (maybe easily answered, maybe not) and one that I hope to consider both implicitly and explicitly before this study is over, but this is not where I want to start. Instead, I would like to begin by considering the dramatic functions that this convention performs within these plays, to think about some of the ways the dramatic process appropriates, for its own purposes, the image of a man with a bottle.

THE USES OF DRINKING IN AMERICAN DRAMA

On an apparently banal level, drinking conventionally serves as just a *simple activity* in realistic dramas, as stage business that characters perform half-consciously, while they advance (usually through dialogue) what we perceive as the main action of the play. Indeed one reason for its use in this context is that—like smoking, eating, drinking coffee, or playing cards—a character can perform this activity and carry on a conversation at the same time. As such it includes as well all of the related business of offering drinks, choosing what to have, assembling the ingredients, preparing the drinks themselves, passing them out, deciding whether or not to have another, and so forth. In many of the plays listed above (e.g., Williams's *Cat*, O'Neill's *Journey*, Albee's *Woolf*), dialogue and stage directions precisely note the specifics of this business. *Journey* and *Woolf* are almost primers on the integration of these activities into a dramatic narrative. In these plays, drink may, at times, do nothing more than provide an excuse to bring a character onstage or perhaps remove one for a few moments. In other instances, as in *Woolf*, the finishing of a drink or the offer to replenish one acts as a kind of dramatic punctuation mark, indicating the end of one action and the beginning of another. For O'Neill, Williams, Albee, and others, the notations of this activity are often as significant as the pause or moment of hesitation in Pinter or Beckett. Furthermore as playscripts become performances, actors, directors, and others make numerous decisions concerning the precise nature of these activities, further appropriating drink's status as a common stage activity for their own ends in ways that range from an actor's nuance in the handling of a glass to a director's need to give an awkward performer something to do with his hands or a designer's wish to show the subscribers that they are getting their money's worth by displaying an expensive crystal set.

Ironically in the dozen plays I have listed, drinking generally has too much significance to be thought of simply as an activity. Yet in many dramas it does operate at just this supposedly innocuous level, as stage business that at most gives a rough indication of the drinker's socioeconomic status or general character: blue-collar workers drink beer; executives, martinis; Baptists, lemonade. Some individuals, however, find insidious or at least highly significant these seemingly innocuous details. On this point Roland Barthes and modern day advocates of temperance might agree, although for different reasons. The latter have objected to the casual use of alcohol and drugs, especially in films and on television. They worry that the routine, seemingly inconsequential status of these activities encourages the use and abuse of these substances, especially if the characters involved serve as role models for children. Their position, of course, goes back at least as far as Plato. Although not particularly significant to the concerns of this chapter, I mention it here, because it represents a contemporary, if somewhat minor, example of the proposition that mimesis is a potentially dangerous process.

Barthes joins the religious fundamentalists, not as a teetotaler but because he also draws our attention to the significance of potentially overlooked small details within narrative structures, details that we might otherwise not notice. He does not specifically discuss drinking, but in his essay "The Reality Effect," Barthes discusses what might be regarded as "insignificant notation" in works of realism such as those by Flaubert and Michelet.[15] He mentions, for example, seemingly superfluous details as in this reference to a barometer by Flaubert: "an old piano supported, under a barometer, a pyramidal heap of boxes and cartons."[16] In trying to account for the role of such details within the structure of a realistic story, he argues that these apparently meaningless bits of filler perform a powerful rhetorical function: they hide the conventionality of the form they inhabit. They signify to readers that they are in the presence of "the real," that life is this way. The mimesis of drinking and other "coffee cup" activities also fill this function. They belong to those conventions of dramatic realism that work to obscure its conventionality. They naturalize the insights of a play by presenting them within the reassuring and familiar context of daily life. In the first case (the temperance position), the concern is with the powers of mimesis to influence behavior subtly; in the second (Barthes's), the concern is with an art form that presents itself not as art but as *the real thing* captured onstage.

In most of these postwar plays, drinking is, however, more than a casual activity that increases a play's verisimilitude, a function any number of similar activities might perform.[17] On the contrary, in these works drinking often attracts attention to itself, because it operates in a more conspicuous fashion, obviously serving in one way or another to communicate to the spectator some information about the world of the drama: it moves from the signified of various icons (glass raised to the lips), indexes (slurred speech or staggered walk), and symbols ("Have you been drinking again?") to the role of a signifier, often as an *index* in its own right. It points the spectator toward some aspect of character or action that is not initially so readily apparent as the drinking itself.[18] Intensive drinking in particular begs to be read, but because it cannot be read in any one way, it becomes a useful dramatic device. It exists as the effect of some cause either in the present or the past, as a sign or symptom that in one way or another foregrounds itself. Axelrod's *Seven Year Itch* provides an initial example of this process. As noted above the bachelor husband begins the play with a soda, but then switches to a whiskey just after he meets the new girl next door. Exchanging soda for liquor signals a change in the present: the beginnings of an infatuation, a loosening of marital restraints.

Closely related is drinking, especially chronic drinking, which points the spectator toward an inquiry into events from the past still affecting the character in the dramatic present. Here the openness of the signifier is limited only by the convention that extreme or habitual drinking often signals pain, dis-ease, suffering or at least self-pity: the source of that suffering is, of course, almost unlimited so the flexibility of the device remains. Fundamental to this convention is the set speech in which someone explains why the drunkard became a drunkard, as in this example from Odets's *Country Girl:*

> *Unger:* Tell me—why did Frank begin to drink?
> *Georgie:* There's no one reason a man becomes a drinker. You should know that—you're a writer, Mr. Unger. Looking back, I'd say bad judgment started him off. He had some money once, but you don't know my Frank—he wanted to be his own producer—eighty thousand went in fifteen months, most of it on two bad shows. I didn't know a thing about it—he was afraid to tell me. A year later we lost our little girl. It was awesome how he went for the bottle. He just didn't stop after that.[19]

Georgie's remark at the beginning of her speech reiterates a basic feature of this convention. Drinking may have various causes in the present or past but no "one reason." Nonetheless a particular reason does emerge, and *Country Girl* uses this connection between chronic drinking and its implied origin in intense personal pain to create a degree of sympathy for its protagonist. In this instance it calls upon another stock device of domestic dramas: the death of a child.

In O'Neill's *Journey*, Edmund, like Georgie, also reflects on what drinking signifies, in this instance, his and his father's. As in *Country Girl*, alcohol points to pain and an attempt to lesson its impact. Here again, that pain comes from the loss of a family member, although this time a mother and wife, not a child.

Edmund: Well, what's wrong with being drunk? It's what we're after, isn't it? Let's not kid each other, Papa. Not tonight. We know what we're trying to forget. (*hurriedly*) But let's not talk about it. It's no use now.
Tyrone: (*dully*) No. All we can do is try to be resigned—again.
Edmund: Or be so drunk you can forget.[20]

Of course the process of trying to forget immediately directs the spectator's attention to that pain's source, to an exploration of the present or the past, just as the spectator's curiosity would be aroused if he or she saw a person run in terror from one side of the stage to the other. Similarly when we see a man with a bottle, dramatic convention invites a search for the reason behind this drinking, either in the nature of the man or the story of his past. This latter course, the invitation to explore an individual's past in an effort to understand the present is, of course, fundamental to the central convention of dramatic realism: the exploration of causality in the life of a specific individual. As Georgie's speech suggests, the past may be overdetermined, but this does not prevent the search for reasons from going on.

Drink often serves then as an *open signifier,* an effect that might have any number of causes, a wound that we puzzle over. Of course, various reasons for drinking may turn into literary or dramatic conventions themselves (e.g., marital problems, financial failure, the death of child), but this does not eliminate other possibilities. Williams's Brick, for example, tells Big Daddy that he drinks to deaden his self-disgust, a disgust anchored in a complex response to his past relationship with another man: a friend, a teammate, and a potential lover. His drinking initiates in turn an exploration of the past by Big Daddy and the members of the audience. They want to know just why Brick is consuming all this alcohol, they want to solve the mystery of this drinking man. The inquiry initiated by the image of a man with a bottle structures much of the play.

Various sorts of drinking also give dramatic realism, the predominant presentational mode of these plays, ways to *extend the range* of presentable behavior without violating dramatic conventions that demand actions be logically motivated and consistent with the audience's sense of everyday life. In this way alcohol serves not only as the effect or index of some cause, but also as the cause that justifies certain spectacular, firework-like effects. The grandfather of these behavioral alterations is the delirium tremens scene of temperance melodrama, which uses alcohol and its long term effects to justify a full blown mad scene, one so popular that it was at times performed "as a solo exhibition."[21] Of course, delirium scenes—alcohol induced eruptions of energy or violence—are still being written, although we may not necessarily think of them in these terms. Drunkenness in the more realistic plays of the immediate postwar period is frequently used to interject violence, subjectivity, madness, melodrama, humor, and various other more or less "fantastic" states of being into a form (dramatic realism) that has never quite been sure of its power to hold an audience. Under alcohol's influence a man or woman might laugh or cry or sing (see Walter's tabletop song in *Raisin*), divulge his or her deepest secrets (Jamie in *Journey* and *Moon*), try to jump high hurdles at three in the morning (Brick in *Cat*), attack someone with an ax (Doc in *Sheba*), or act in any number of ways that sobriety would not normally allow (*Woolf*).

Drunkenness allows a release of emotions (comic, violent, maudlin, and otherwise) that spectators generally seem to enjoy watching. Not long into the first act of *Look Homeward*, the father, W. O. Gant, comes crashing home. Eliza, mother and wife, tries to clear the porch of her boarders before he arrives, but to no avail: they do not want to "miss the show."[22] Their reaction reflects the attitude of most audiences: from a distance anyway, drunkenness, as either melodrama or farce, is quite entertaining. Furthermore because it enlarges the range of linguistic and emotional behavior available to a character, writers and actors may also appropriate scenes of drunkenness for their own purposes, as opportunities to display their linguistic prowess or their histrionic abilities. In other words many actors love a good drunk scene.

Alcohol enables texts to represent scenes from daily life—a life in which, as Chekhov noted, "People do not shoot themselves, or hang themselves, or fall in love, or deliver themselves of clever sayings every minute"[23]—without having to give up all of those qualities which Chekhov lists and audiences love. This enjoyment of the drunk is not, however, always as benign and as disinterested as it might seem. *Sheba*, for example, utilizes alcohol as both a cause of and justification for verbal and physical violence. (Other examples would be Albee's *Woolf* and Shepard's family dramas including *Buried Child* and *True West*.) This particular use of alcohol as a pretext for violence (e.g., Doc's verbal and physical attack on Lola) works on two levels. Within the play it justifies the husband's violent eruption of hatred and anger, while simultaneously excusing it. Within the world of stage and spectator, it permits the audience to witness a woman being brutalized, while justifying this spectacle by placing it within the logical context of a drunk scene. There resides in this strategy a potential complicity between spectator and performance: the one will not admit that he really enjoys seeing Lola berated and terrorized; the other will not admit that it really wants the spectator to enjoy this display. Consciously or not both will hide their essential misogyny behind a nominal cause, drunkenness, that may not be so much a reason for violence as its rationalization. I do not think this criticism applies to every play in which a drunk argues with his wife, but this play, in particular, seems at some level to enjoy the opportunity to attack the woman that Doc's drunken state supplies. (In an early temperance melodrama, Taylor's *The Bottle*, we find a similar scene— in this instance the wife is killed—and the same sense that the play, on one level, decries the effects of drink, while on another, it enjoys them.) In any event, the injection of violence (physical, verbal, emotional) is a central function of alcohol in many plays.

Perhaps the most important way in which alcohol opens up the realistic drama is with respect to language and communication. As an element of release, alcohol relaxes nothing so much as it relaxes the tongue. Drunks are, by convention, voluble, often in intimate and uncensored detail, almost as if they were speaking without anyone else present. As such, their longer speeches often fill a function similar to that of the monologue or the soliloquy, permitting characters to reveal themselves before others and the audience in ways foreign to their more guarded, sober selves. Steven Bloom makes this point in his essay on drinking and alcoholism in *Journey*,[24] as does Travis Bogard in describing how in O'Neill's late plays alcohol, weariness, and despair take the place of earlier, more obviously presentational devices (masks, asides, and so forth) in the revelation of outer and inner selves:

> Jamie's cynical mask is dropped as the whiskey begins to talk, permitting the defenseless child in him to be seen. In the same way, as Mary descends farther into the doped state, the young girl alive within the pain-wracked woman comes forth to haunt them all. Whiskey and morphine effectively remove all disguise.[25]

Jamie actually enunciates this "in vino veritas" convention in a drunken speech to Edmund in the final act of *Journey:*

> *Jamie:* Listen, Kid, you'll be going away. May not get another chance to talk. Or might not be drunk enough to tell you truth. So got to tell you now. Something I ought to have told you long ago—for your own good. (*He pauses—struggling with himself. Edmund stares, impressed and uneasy. Jamie blurts out.*) Not drunken bull, but "in vino veritas" stuff.[26]

Just as drunkenness may be the sign of an inner pain with its source in the individual's past, it may also be the sign of true speech, the lubricant that loosens the tongue, that allows a character to blurt out both confessions and accusations. Ironically the convention of drink as an escape from reality does not conflict with this convention of drink as a way into the inner life, the inner reality of the character. Drinking can work in two different dimensions at once: temporally and realistically (revealing former events of significance); spatially and expressionistically (revealing the internal landscape of the individual character at a given moment in time).

Alcohol's effects are not, however, confined to matters of content. It also permits, indeed demands, variations in verbal style. Jamie's reference to "drunken bull" suggests this, as well as outright lying. Drink and drunkenness provide an opportunity to introduce into the world of the drama a heightened language, often self-consciously florid, overblown, and rhetorical. It leads, for example, to the enjoyment of speech for its own sake found in Albee's *Woolf,* as verbal play that is engaging, energizing, potentially cathartic, potentially destructive. (Other examples would include Walter's drunk scene in *Raisin;* Doc's verbal attack on Lola in *Sheba,* and Hugo's tirades in *Iceman.*) In a sense drunken rhetoric serves American drama as a sort of poor man's wit and poetry. The inadequacy of this substitute is perhaps a good commentary on the state of dramatic diction in American drama, but drunken rhetoric at least suggests an enthusiasm for language, a Whitmanesque love for the sound of the human voice, for the sound of words as words, that is often absent from American theater.

The great divide in opinion over the role alcohol should play in American life also contributes to its effectiveness as a theatrical device. What at first seems like a rather simple phenomenon carries with it, at least potentially, a variety of conflicting messages that resist facile reduction. Of course spectators will not consciously register all of these various connotations or resonances when they see a performance. Furthermore what is evoked will depend on the particular nature of the drinking in any given scene, and the variations can be extreme, from tippling to delirium tremens; but drinking behaviors, at least for American audiences, are almost inevitably charged with some degree of *tension* and *ambivalence,* as suggested by the title of Thomas Gilmore's study of alcoholism and drinking in twentieth-century literature: *Equivocal Spirits.* A long and varied history of interaction between alcohol and society from the beginnings of civilization (clay tablets from 6000 B.C.E. describe brewing processes[27]) to the new sobriety of the 1980s and 90s (the "Just Say No" campaign, the Betty Ford story, Mothers Against Drunk Driving) has produced a tremendous variety of attitudes toward alcohol and intoxication. On the one hand, drinking and drunkenness connote weakness, waste, sloth, domestic violence, sexual profligacy, mental and physical deterioration, madness, death, and most importantly for American drama, the destruction of the family; on the other hand, drink can suggest vigor, power, masculinity, nourishment, warmth, celebration, community, near magical powers, physical release, sexual pleasure, music, dance, joy, life, and the carnivalesque.[28] For William James (in a Nietzschean mode), "Sobriety diminishes, discriminates, and says no; drunkenness expands, unites, and says yes. It is in fact the great exciter of the *Yes* function in man. . . . It brings him for the moment one with truth."[29] For Benjamin Rush, one of America's first temperance advocates (*An Inquiry into the Effects of Ardent Spirits upon the Human Body and Mind*, 1784), alcohol threatened the development of the new republic. Alcohol related vices on his "Moral and Physical Thermometer" stretched from "Idleness," "Gaming," and Debt" to "Perjury," "Burglary," and "Murder."[30] In American life drink has been both "demon rum" and, in the oft-quoted words of Increase Mather, that "good creature of God."[31]

Twentieth-century Americans who have grown up in the shadow of temperance and prohibition movements that aligned churches against alcohol may not realize the degree to which earlier Americans perceived alcohol as a "positive good," at least until the early 1800s when climbing rates of alcohol consumption and fundamental changes in the social order (the rise of a new middle class, the division of spheres, urbanization and industrialization, immigration) began to construct those forces that would first call for temperance, then abstinence, and finally, prohibition.[32] Many would be surprised, for example, to learn that in 1630 the *Arabella*, along with its load of Puritans, carried ten thousand gallons of wine and three times as much beer as water.[33] In "The Alcohol Problem in America: From Temperance to Alcoholism," Harry Levine argues that prior to the 1900s in America all "liquor was regarded as good and healthy," as "tonic, medicine, stimulant and relaxant" to be "drunk at all hours of the day and night, by men and women of all social classes, and . . . routinely given to children" and that the "'liquor problem'" itself "was not a public issue or fact of consciousness in colonial America."[34] Indeed the integral and largely positive role played by alcohol in early American life (religious, civic, social, occupational) is well documented by social historians, as are, of course, the various campaigns in the last two hundred years to limit or eliminate alcohol's use.[35] This material does not require further review here other than to underscore the obvious lack of a consensus about the proper role of alcohol in American society despite attempts at forging one. One result of this history has been that perhaps in no country in the world are conflicting responses to the use of alcohol so deeply ingrained. It should not be difficult to understand why we have both a high level of per person consumption of alcohol and a high level of abstinence. Clearly this dividedness contributes to the richness of drinking as a stage device; it also no doubt accounts for its thematic return as an issue we find nearly impossible to resolve.[36]

Plays draw upon these potential resonances in various ways. *Country Girl,* for example, represents its protagonist as a victim of drink, too weak to resist its attractions without the help of others:

> *Bernie:* Have you ever left him?
> *Georgie:* Twice left, twice returned. He's a helpless child. (*Wryly, lifting her purse*) Anyone taking a cab to New York?
> *Bernie:* But if he's as helpless as you say—
> *Georgie:* He's not helpless now—he has you.
> *Bernie:* (*earnestly, his voice quivering*) Listen, he has to be watched and handled. You can do that—no one else. I didn't know it before.[37]

Country Girl is part temperance melodrama, part comeback story in which drink clearly stands as a sign of an individual's weakness. *Look Homeward* shifts the spectator's sympathies in another direction. It connects sobriety to the suffocating presence of the mother and her cold economy of money and goods. The father's drunkenness by comparison seems benign, almost positive, linked to his largeness of heart and love of beauty. Both plays draw on long-standing, albeit diametrically opposed, sets of connotations.

All the Way Home turns on these two different attitudes toward drink and drunkenness. Both perceptions are present in the images of drinking that two different brothers represent. Both perceptions also find a voice in Mary, the wife and mother whose crucial insight is that what she thought was a weakness (the view of *Country Girl*) might actually be a strength (the view of *Look Homeward*). The latter position emerges in a speech that comes late in the play as a moment of anagnorisis and peripeteia:

> *Mary:* If he was drunk, . . . just *if* he was, I hope he loved being. Speeding along in the night—singing at the top of his lungs—racing because he loved to go fast—racing to us because he loved us. And for the time, enjoying—reveling in a freedom that was his, that no place or person, that nothing in this world could ever give him or take away from him. Let's hope that's how it was, . . . how he looked death in the face. In his strength.[38]

The distance between this speech and the one just quoted from *Country Girl* reveals the range of perceptions to which this phenomenon is subject and should increase our sense of the openness and potential complexity of this signifier, an openness that allows for the kind of ambivalent response to drink that *All the Way Home* exploits.

Yet another function of alcohol within these plays is its role as an *analog for sexual activity*. The mimesis of drinking can perform this function, because, as a species of appetite, it shares with sexual activity a tripartite rhythm of desire, satisfaction, and satiation, a rhythm easily translated into more explicit moral terms of temptation, sin, and disgust. Jamie in *Misbegotten* aptly conflates both sets of sensations in describing the aftereffects of a night filled with drink and sex:

> *Jamie:* No matter how I tried not to, I'd make it like all the other nights— for you, too. You'd lie awake and watch the dawn come with disgust, with nausea retching your memory, and the wine of passion poets blab about, a sour aftertaste in your mouth of Dago red ink![39]

In addition to sharing these rhythms, drink and sex are frequently paired as moral failures, so that where one is found we often expect to find the other as well. In the group of plays listed near the beginning of the chapter, this combination occurs in several instances: Shannon in *Iguana*, Jamie in *Journey* and *Moon*, and Sherman in *Seven Year Itch*. Indeed texts must usually make a special effort to indicate when this linkage is not in effect (e.g., *Raisin* and *All the Way Home* reassure the spectator of the husband's faithfulness despite his drunkenness).

Alcohol often serves as a release mechanism, in this instance, not of words or emotions, but of sexual inhibitions. Furthermore the act of drinking itself is inherently sensual in its employment of hands, mouth, and lips—in the processes of filling, warming, and loosening. On one level this suggests a kind of infantile satisfaction of oral desire in a rather obvious connection that links breast, bottle, mother, son, and wife, so that Jamie, in a sense, trades in his bottle for Josie's breast in the second half of *Misbegotten*. On another and related level, the mimesis of drinking functions as a convenient substitute for the mimesis of sexual activity. This has led to a certain pornography of the bottle, in part, because drinking allows the representation of an entire process that in sexual terms, at least until recently, could barely be described in detail onstage, let alone shown. The primary medium of theater is, however, showing and, in this regard anyway, a mimesis of thirst, consumption, and drunkenness can be completely explicit. Drink functions as a form of appetite that theater can show in all of its various stages. It also provides a way of dealing with desire without having to tackle the complications of an adultery plot. When, as in

Raisin, a husband's drinking is not connected to infidelity, it makes it easier for both wives and audiences to forgive, forget, and reconstitute the family. Just as the man with the bottle introduces a degree of madness into the predominantly rational context of dramatic realism, so does he bring a diminished, but explicit, mimesis of desire to the relative decorum of a Puritan stage.

My references here have pointedly been to the man with a bottle. In addition to its analogical role, the mimesis of drinking in much of American domestic drama also functions as *a highly gendered phenomenon,* a function of gendered constructs as well as one of their creators. In those plays listed above, the image of the drinker is most frequently a man. Women drinkers in American domestic drama have been relatively absent, "hidden" in the same way female alcoholism has generally been hidden in American culture. Prominent and notable exceptions, of course, come to mind: Blanche in *Streetcar,* Martha in *Woolf,* Mary in *Journey* (morphine may be more exotic, more stigmatized, more potent, but it and the bottle are almost interchangeable).[40] But the more persistent image is of *man* and *bottle,* of Hickey and his bar mates; of Jamie, Edmund, and Tyrone measuring out their drinks over the course of a long New England day; of Stanley and the card players with their beer and whiskey; of Brick and Shannon; of Frank Elgins (*Country Girl*) and Docs (*Little Sheba*). Indeed the image of a man with a bottle has been and continues to be a primary way for American culture to signal a potentially interesting male subject, and male subjectivity (White, middle class, and heterosexual) has, of course, been the conventional focal point of commercial theater in the United States, at least until recent years. This study is clearly interested in examining how theater and the dominant culture constructed and used that male subject, even though we now perceive him not as a generic human being but as one self, one subjectivity, among many.

Ironically or perhaps predictably, when women do drink, particularly in male-authored domestic dramas, the link between drink and sexuality is narrowly and conventionally figured. For women drink almost always connotes the negative half of the madonna/whore paradigm.[41] Male characters in these plays usually perceive women who drink not as fascinating or interesting peers but as disgusting or degraded others. Jamie's words to Edmund seem sadly appropriate here: "Made whores fascinating vampires instead of poor, stupid diseased slobs they really are."[42] The basis of these biases are to be found, at least in part, in the late eighteenth and early nineteenth centuries, in a cultural and social discourse that demonized drink and turned women into angels at roughly the same time. Both moves were funda-

mental to the construction of a new middle class needed to transform
an agrarian society into a modern industrial power. Fundamental to
this process was the development of an ethos of thrift, discipline, and
hard work: all antithetical to chronic drunkenness.[43] The problemati-
zation of drunkenness was one step in the construction of this new
social order, catalyzed also, at least in part, by a very real increase in
the consumption of alcohol: from 1790 to 1830, apparent consumption
of absolute alcohol rose from 5.8 gallons per capita of the drinking-
age population to 7.10, as compared with 2.82 gallons per capita
in 1978.[44]

As social historians often note, another fundamental feature of this
transformation from a home-based, family economy to a wage labor,
factory-based, capitalist economy was the doctrine of separate
spheres: middle- and working-class men, absented from the home for
a major portion of the day by the demands of commercial capitalism,
claimed the "public sphere" as their rightful space, accepting as given
a competitive, acquisitive, individualistic code of behavior; their
wives, for the most part restricted from entering the male workplace,
accepted primary responsibility for mothering, homemaking, and the
promulgation of a moral code suitable to this "private sphere," for
fostering a spiritualized (some would say pseudo-Christian) morality
of home and family that called for entrance into the public sphere
only to protect the claims of motherhood and home, as in the work
of the Women's Christian Temperance Union.[45] These shifts in
American economic and cultural life, particularly among White
middle- and working-class families, receive extensive treatment elsewhere, and although scholars differ in detail and emphasis, they generally accept the broad outlines of this transformation as noted here.[46]

These transformations created conditions that particularly pro-
blematized female drinking and drunkenness. American social discourse cast alcohol in the role of the family's enemy (as in some
instances it clearly was) at the same time as it made the wife/mother
the family's ultimate protector. On a practical level, drinking was
increasingly associated with the "public sphere" in the form of after-
work saloons and was therefore largely off-limits to mothers and
wives. More essentially drunkenness carried strong sexual connotations, and manifest sexuality was inconsistent with emerging notions
of the ideal mother and wife. Drinking made women too present
physically, too available, too vulnerable, even perhaps too energized,
vocal, bacchic and uncontrollable, threatening social and familial roles
at a time when they were being more rigidly defined.[47] Perhaps most
significantly, with the separation of spheres women were cast as specialists in child rearing and that role, as newly redefined, required a

care and diligence that, like work on an assembly line, inebriation would not allow. In *Drinking in America,* Mark Lender summarizes the situation:

> The ideal woman was virtuous and pure; alcoholics were degraded. Women defended the home; alcoholics imperiled it. While mothers strove to raise their children in a morally upright environment, drunkards were constant impediments to the task. Alcohol was considered to be so far from an acceptable standard of behavior for Victorian women that society could explain such conduct only in terms of extreme deviance.[48]

The paradigm, of course, still exists. To this day an image of almost absolute horror in the public mind is that of the crack mother who passes her addiction to the baby in the womb, of the child injured or killed because his mother was high on drugs and did not properly care for him. These images have their precursors in this earlier era of American life. They are prefigured as well in English didactic art, such as Hogarth's well-known *Gin Lane* (1751) in which the central image is of a dazed and drunken mother nodding off as her young child falls headfirst over a stair railing to the earth. Hogarth's illustrations reflected a Puritanical concern, moral and social, over a substantial increase in drinking among poor and working-class people in London during the mideighteenth century, an increase that foreshadowed conditions that would soon develop in the United States.[49]

Because the drunken woman could not play the roles of wife and mother as they were being reconceived, she became almost automatically a member of the only other operative category within that culture, the opposite of the angel, the "whore." The one group of women who regularly drink in American drama are those usually nameless "other women": prostitutes, mistresses, and adulteresses.[50] For women drunkenness and the abject became inseparably linked in the nineteenth century, a linkage that has held through most of the twentieth century, asserting itself with a particular vigor in the reestablishment of domesticity immediately following World War II. Indeed the scarlet letter in American theater could just as well stand for alcoholism as for adultery, the former a metonym for the latter.

O'Neill, as usual, is most representative here from Anna Christie ("Gimme a whiskey—ginger ale on the side") to Mary Tyrone ("Christ, I'd never dreamed before that any women but whores took dope!").[51] Central to the crisis of *Journey,* at least for Jamie, is the inability to conceive of a woman under the influence who is not a prostitute but a mother, indeed, his mother. The situation is representative of mainstream American drama at midcentury: an alcoholic family that cannot accept the alcoholism of its mother/wife; that, by implication, cannot accept the potentially disruptive female sexuality that alcohol or, in this instance, drug use connotes. The coding is quite clear with Josie in *Misbegotten:* when she is "playing the whore" for Jamie, she matches him drink for drink; when she has a change of heart and her virginal/motherly self emerges, the drinking stops. Jamie himself resists Josie's drinking along with her foul mouth: these behaviors disturb and sicken him, because they do not fit with the female image that he would have her play. The connection also occurs in *Ah, Wilderness!* In lines that recall both Anna Christie and Josie, the first words out of the mouth of Belle, the young prostitute, are "drink up your beer, why don't you? It's getting flat."[52] In *The Iceman Cometh,* the only women to enter the bar are the prostitutes Pearl, Margie, and Cora. Wives and mothers have no place here, except in memory. For Cora "gettin' married and settlin' down" means leaving the tavern for a farm.[53]

In *Death of a Salesman,* the nameless woman whom Willy meets in the hotel room urges Willy to have a drink as soon as she enters the scene. Similar connections hold for Martha in *Woolf* and Blanche in *Streetcar.* The latter epitomizes the convention: alcohol, sexuality, and stigmatization merge in an almost inseparable package. Blanche hides her drinking with as much care as she guards the details of her sexual activities. One of her first acts onstage is the surreptitious drinking of a glass of whiskey. Within moments of his first encounter with Blanche, Stanley suspects that she has been drinking his whiskey. The stage directions describe Stanley holding "the bottle to the light to observe its depletion."[54] He then removes his shirt. These initial images of whiskey bottle and discarded shirt, of alcohol and sexuality, prefigure their entire relationship.

Although not an American drama, Caryl Churchill's *Top Girls* (1982) represents a striking recent example of women and the bottle. In the brilliant first scene, women gather from across time and culture (Isabella Bird, Lady Nijo, Dull Gret, Pope Joan, Patient Griselda) to sit down to a table where they will eat and drink in "celebration" of Marlene's promotion. Alcohol plays a major role in this scene from Marlene's first line: "Excellent, yes, table for six. One of them's going to be late but we won't wait. I'd like a bottle of Frascati straight away if you've got one really cold."[55] When Marlene offers Lady Nijo some wine, Nijo's response recapitulates not only a social but also a dramatic convention that Churchill here inverts: "It was always the men who used to get drunk. I'd be the one of the maidens passing the sake."[56] Those who had waited on tables will now sit up to the table; those who had watched men drink will now have wine and brandy, and, as in many American dramas, the wine will act as a lubricant to loosen tongues and release emotional energy. A stage direction toward the end of the scene notes simply: *They are quite drunk*. The scene's final stage directions tell the reader that *Nijo is laughing and crying*, that *Joan gets up and is sick in a corner*, and that *Marlene is drinking Isabella's brandy*.[57] Churchill's women have made the bottle their own. If not initially, by the end of the play our attitude toward this assumption of a traditionally male terrain may be quite mixed. Marlene has moved forward within the system, but the system has not been fundamentally changed. Its inequalities still function. In a similar manner, women and drunkenness in this scene may signal not progress but the failure to imagine a new paradigm. The image of Joan throwing up in the corner at the end of 1.1 does not necessarily inspire confidence. Drinking gives an ironic cast to the celebration, foreshadowing issues taken up later in the play. In the final scene of the play, Marlene drinks whiskey, while her working-class sister Joyce, who has raised Marlene's child in her absence, abstains. The play's concluding image is of Marlene, wrapped in a blanket, drink in hand, speaking to a "daughter" who will probably not be able to survive in the kind of world Marlene has come to accept as a given. This image of a failed mother with drink in hand would make sense to both Hogarth and nineteenth-century advocates of temperance. The image also, of course, supports a major theme of the play: advancement that simply moves women into male roles without a change in the socioeconomic order does not equal progress. Drinking signifies just such an ineffectual change: What does it profit the world if progress simply creates a new group of drunkards?

In *Hollywood Shot by Shot*, Norman Denzin suggests that a new alcoholic heroine has emerged in films such as *Fat City* (1972), *Barfly* (1987), and *Ironweed* (1987): "She will define her own emotionality, her own sexuality, and she will pick and choose the men with whom she forms relationships."[58] It may also be that the degree of social stigmatization is decreasing, although the attention rendered a Betty Ford or Kitty Dukakis may actually underscore the persistence of the prejudice. Furthermore these individuals are usually held up as models for reform, again emphasizing the unnaturalness of the drinking woman as mother, wife, or role model. The character of Murphy Brown on the television series of the same name is, I think, a fair gauge of where the convention stands in the nineties. Brown is a reformed alcoholic, who one rarely, if ever, sees drunk. Her alcoholism is effectively hidden. To some extent she destigmatizes the image of the drinking woman but only so long as the drinking woman no longer drinks, only so long as she is a model of sobriety. Of course in a now famous series of episodes, she also gives birth to a child outside of marriage, apparently destigmatizing the role of the "unwed mother" but also confirming in a sense the connections noted above between alcohol and what had been regarded as nonnormative sexual behavior. One result was, of course, a seriocomic colloquy with Dan Quayle during the 1992 presidential campaign that underscored, if nothing else, the presence of a conservative discourse that felt it could profit from making this image of change, of destigmatization, problematic. The decision of the show to foreground these issues, however innocuously, and of conservatives to pursue them, however ill-advisedly, points to at least the traces of the paradigm described above still moving through the culture, a paradigm that has rigidly pre-scribed representations of women, intoxication, and sexuality.

Traces of this discourse also surfaced in the early 1990s in the complex debate surrounding date or acquaintance rape and its rela-tionship to alcohol use. In particular one line of argument, supported by law in "most states," holds that a woman's sexual consent while intoxicated is meaningless.[59] This assertion, on one level, seeks to create a safe place for female intoxication, a place that is not automati-cally read as "no sexual boundaries here," a potentially liberating space in which women should not have to be continually sober and on guard. It counters conventional representational patterns that link female drinking and the initiation of a sexual encounter. At the same time, this argument, in its own way, reconstitutes the connection between drinking and sexual activity just described and, to some ex-tent, reifies the distinction between two sorts of women: one drunken and sexually endangered; the other sober and more chaste or sexually safe. In its effort to protect women, it maintains the link between women, drinking, and problematic sexuality. The drunken woman must be protected.

In American drama drink is primarily a male activity, and when women enter that domain, they generally surrender their claim to a normative status. These women escape middle-class assimilation, but the cost has been stigmatization and marginalization at best, violence and rape at worst. For men the range of responses to the drinking man is greater: stigmatization and marginalization are a possibility, but so is adoration and even celebration. Particularly significant is the role alcohol plays in letting men explore alternative modes of behav-ior, especially with respect to gender roles. If representations of drink-ing unfairly confine women, they regularly release men, often to emotional states generally off-limits to them because they are stigma-tized as feminine or unmasculine. In other words, alcohol, in at least some of these plays, lets men try on what society conceives of as women's clothing without the danger of stigmatization usually associated with that move; alcohol allows men to experience a kind of gendered otherness. This move is ironic, because society generally perceives male drinking as a way of confirming the drinker's masculinity within American culture, not of escaping its limitations, just as we perceive many of these plays as celebrating gendered norms, not problematizing them by showing their limitations.

In an impressive article on the role of theater in Greek society, Froma Zeitlin argues that tragic theater in Ancient Greece appropriates and to some extent even becomes a kind of female other that male society then uses to better understand itself: in particular Greek "theatre uses the feminine self for the purpose of imagining a fuller model for the masculine self, and 'playing the other' opens that self to those often banned emotions of fear and pity."[60] Alcohol and its theatrical representation perform a similar function with respect to culturally mediated images of male and female selves in contemporary American drama. Earlier I described alcohol's role in extending the range of dramatic realism. Those extensions allow drunken men to behave in ways that narrowly prescribed sex roles regularly prohibit. The male drunk can be passive, messy, weak, dependent, needy, emotional, depressed, morose, irrational, hysterical, sensitive, voluble, self-revelatory: all qualities that are not essentially female but that our culture regularly assigns to the feminine and denies the masculine. The man with a bottle can have his experience of pity and fear, although not perhaps on the grand level of Greek tragedy. The pity may be a morose self-pity. The fear may take the shape of a delirium tremens episode.[61] Western society attributes various characteristics to the feminine as a category, assigns them and this category an inferior status, and then places both outside masculine norms. Alcohol makes these same characteristics available to men (onstage and in life) without, for the most part, threatening male status.[62]

Of course at one end of masculine norms, a distinction exists that ultimately does detect and stigmatize as unmasculine this aspect of male drunkenness. In *The Hair of a Dog*, Richard Stivers argues that in nineteenth-century Ireland, hard drinking served as cultural remission for celibate Irish bachelors who had to accept membership in a pub-based avunculate, because a shortage of land made marriage impossible for many men. Here, however, hard drinking usually excluded many of the behaviors just listed (i.e., a real man knows how to hold his liquor).[63] A similar brand of nonintoxicated hard drinking holds for the stoic heroes of many Western novels and films, as recently described by Jane Tompkins in *West of Everything:* here, the intoxicated town drunk is feminized and ridiculed. Voluble, emotive, needy Jamie of *Moon for the Misbegotten* would merit only scorn in this landscape in which, as Tompkins writes, "Men cannot register their pain because to do so marks them as unmanly."[64] The relatively nonintoxicated, hard-drinking norms of a Stivers's avunculate and Tompkins's wild west resist feminization. They are alternatives to another kind of cultural remission, one more peculiar to American drama at midcentury, one that in plays like *Iceman, Moon, Country Girl, Sheba, Journey, Who's Afraid of Virginia Woolf?*, and *Iguana* allows the drinker an intoxication that steps outside the bounds of sober masculinity. In these and other instances, the intoxicated man can "register" his pain, his fear and pity. Extreme masculine norms, such as those found in Westerns, will still find this move discomforting, accounting, I expect, for some of the scorn accorded the image of a man with a bottle and domestic dramas in general, but the status of drinking itself as a fundamentally masculine activity counters this tendency and creates a space in which men can venture beyond rigidly defined gender roles. The image of a bottle may then signal both the presence of a particular gender system and an admission of its failure: it reifies the norm but also reveals its limitations.

A final function of drinking within these plays concerns issues of *family and class*. Socially and economically, the man with a bottle will, in almost every instance, be a current or nascent member of America's large middle class, a class whose central institution, at least within the world of the drama, is not church or country but family. Consequently how this figure earns a living or voted in the last election or what he thinks and believes about political or philosophical issues is almost always less important than his relationship to his family (parents, spouse, children), the one social/emotional unit that this figure cares about and understands.[65]

James Tyrone's repeated references to money in *Long Day's Journey into Night* indicate the vital role it often plays within these alcohol-soaked plays: what most terrifies the father is not sex or alcohol but waste and poverty. Financial concerns—the loss of a regular income, the mortgaging of the family home, the wasting of an inheritance—are among the most common issues these plays address. Seldom, however, do these matters appear to occupy a central place within the drama—they often seem the mere accoutrements of plot—but like the use of alcohol itself, they often perform a significant role in the total structure of the work as in, for example, the role of inheritances in *Misbegotten, Cat, Look Homeward*, and *Raisin*. Often an underlying fear connected with the image of the man with a bottle is that his drinking will cause the family to lose its position within the middle class, that it will force the family unit into the world of an underclass composed of immigrants and minorities who must depend on charity or public assistance for their survival.

In *The Politics of Domesticity*, Barbara Epstein argues that this was a central issue underlying the temperance movement of the nineteenth century.[66] In that context, German and other immigrant populations, particularly the Irish, were perceived as prone to intemperance and other vices. The fear was that alcohol might drag the middle-class family down to that lower-class level. Epstein gives a telling example of this fear, itself used as a propaganda device, from a temperance speech by Mother Stewart:

> The fore part of this month a woman came to me, saying friends had sent her. . . . (It was the old, old story repeated—Oh, who knoweth how many times!—of wretchedness, woe, misery, privation, neglect, want, pinching poverty, and disgrace for her and her children.). . . *This woman . . . was of an old, respectable Virginia family,* . . . but unfortunately married a man who soon developed an appetite for liquor. He had drifted from one place to another till her family had about lost sight of her. When she came to me she, with her three very bright children, was living in a poor tenement in one of the poorest quarters of the city. *Her neighbors and only associates were of the lowest class of foreigners, and, like herself, cursed by the drink.*[67]

The attack on alcohol was central to the negotiation of status: White, middle-class, Protestant, nativist populations used the temperance movement to distinguish themselves from immigrant, Catholic, non-White (Native American and African American), and working-class populations.[68]

A similar attitude characterizes perceptions of urban populations today, so that a primary stereotype is of an African-American man and his friends either sitting on a porch drinking cheap wine or, more recently, going about the neighborhood selling drugs. Relevant here are the fears of the White middle class that they will in essence become members of a lower or underclass if they, too, are intemperate, so that racial and class prejudices play a primary role both in temperance movements and in the dramatic conventions surrounding the image of a man with a bottle. Significantly, the move of the Younger family in *Raisin* from the city to the suburbs means that Walter must leave behind his drinking buddies and his plan to open a liquor store. This is the price of his entry into suburban American life.

The situation is not, however, quite this simple. The strongest advocate for Walter's temperance is his mother. Recent scholarship on temperance ideology has suggested that the status transactions noted above were not the only forces at play and that the temperance movement was not so monolithic a phenomenon as once thought:

Blocker in his study cites five temperance movements in the last two centuries; McArthur notes that the temperance cause was "fed by a number of streams [in addition to status concerns], including religious perfectionism, economic instability, the emergence of a woman's movement, and the growth of an urban working class."[69] Finally temperance activity itself was not ultimately confined to any one racial or ethnic group. The nineteenth century saw an expansion of temperance involvement that would ultimately include Mama Younger's forebears: African American, as well as Irish and German temperance societies came into being. As John Frick notes, "By the end of the decade [1840s], the anti-liquor ranks included members of all classes, genders, and major ethnic groups, and temperance reform could be classified, for the first time, as a movement of the masses."[70] Depending on one's point of view, this mass movement is either evidence of democratization, the powers of hegemonic assimilation, or both. In any event, antebellum America discovered a widespread interest in issues of alcohol and the family that has continued to fascinate the American public from one decade to the next: the battle for Prohibition, Prohibition itself, its repeal, the beginnings of Alcoholics Anonymous in the 1930s, various campaigns against drugs, co-dependency and the recovery movement, concern over binge drinking on college campuses and date rape, and so on. The man (and more recently woman) with a bottle has pulled at the American psyche for almost two hundred years now and part of that pull has been in terms of class and racial status.

TEMPERANCE MELODRAMA AS PROTOTYPE FOR AMERICAN FAMILY DRAMA

Throughout this chapter I have made reference to the temperance melodramas that flourished almost exactly one hundred years before the group of plays with which this chapter began.[71] *The Drunkard, or The Fallen Saved* by William H. Smith, one of the first American temperance melodramas, opened in Boston in 1844. In 1850 at Barnum's American Museum in New York, it was the first American play to achieve an uninterrupted run of one hundred performances. In his introduction to the play, Richard Moody writes that between 1844 and 1878 there were four hundred fifty performances of *The Drunkard* throughout the United States.[72] This was, however, only one of numerous temperance melodramas performed in England and the United States over the course of the nineteenth century, dramas with titles such as *Fifteen Years of a Drunkard's Life* (London, Douglas Jerrold, 1828); *The Drunkard's Doom* (London, G. D. Pitt, 1832); *The Bottle* (London, T. P. Taylor, 1847, based on George Cruikshank's engravings); *Hot Corn, or Little Katy* (New York, based on newspaper exposé by Solon Robinson, 1853); *Ten Nights in a Bar-Room* (New York, W. W. Pratt, 1858, based on T. S. Arthur's novel); and *The Fruits of the Wine Cup* (John Allen, 1858). Hixon and Hennessee's *Nineteenth-Century American Drama: A Finding Guide* lists over one hundred ten of these plays.[73] These works may seem ridiculous to us now, in part because of the quality of their language and the familiarity of their devices. They were not, however, merely vehicles for coercing men into signing the pledge or enriching the livelihoods of managers and actors, although they often served both of these ends. They were also mechanisms that allowed men and women to address issues of vital concern to their families, particularly the need for the husband to discipline and control his appetites and desires to succeed in a competitive society and so ensure the economic and social viability of a family unit almost wholly dependent upon him for its sustenance and survival.[74] As John Frick notes, "the genre reflected and enunciated, not only the dominant values of the era, but the tensions, cultural ambiguities, and fears which plagued Americans in the decades immediately preceding the Civil War."[75]

Much the same might be said for American domestic drama in the years immediately following World War II. Of course these temperance melodramas were didactic, but this didacticism actually allies them to these more recent plays. Both sets of dramas had to survive as theatrical commodities, but both also hoped to do more. Both present themselves, in the main, as vehicles for the "progressive social ideals of the era."[76] One of *The Drunkard's* partisans claimed it as a "great moral engine, which has been the means of adding thousands to the ranks of reformed men."[77] Williams, O'Neill, or Miller might not use the same rhetoric (Miller might), but all three clearly felt that theater had the power to affect deeply the way people lived, to effect a reformation of the mind and heart.

If it seems that I have made certain twentieth-century dramas sound embarrassingly like the temperance melodramas of the nineteenth century reborn in this century, I would respond by saying that it does seem as if these old and much maligned plays are the prototypes for the postwar American family drama. Indeed I will argue in the following pages that what often appears to be a structural inversion of these earlier plays is actually a reinvestment of their fundamental devices and appeals, that apparently ironic structures are often not nearly as ironic as they may at first seem.

The Bottle and the Prodigal

This study will continue to pursue the image of a man or woman with a bottle, the dramatic functions of drink, and those parallels that make the temperance melodrama the prototypical American play, but I will not use any of these elements as my primary organizational tools for the following chapters. For that I want to return to the hymn of the "ninety and nine" sung by Arthur's mother at the end of *Happy Journey* and its proximity to the parable of the prodigal. I alluded to this larger structure at the beginning of this chapter in discussing a scene between a mother and her son in Wilder's one act. In that scene Arthur's mother makes reference to "speak-easies and night-clubs and places like that" and thus calls up an image of Arthur himself as a man with a bottle. That image, however, resides within a larger set of conventions, within an embracing paradigm that articulates a process of rupture and potential, of departure and return, of leaving home and coming home again.

The action of raising a glass or bottle to the lips and taking a drink performs a final and crucial function within many of these plays: synecdochically, it calls up a complete set of characters, places, and events. Because of their familiarity, these elements will, consciously or not, do much to shape an audience's expectations for a particular performance. Some texts will then satisfy, more or less completely, those expectations: others will alter or frustrate them. Of course the sense that a structure is being played with—altered, frustrated, rearranged, deconstructed, destroyed—actually confirms its presence as a dynamic and viable entity. This structure, that of the prodigal son or (as I will argue) in our tradition, son/husband, is one with a long dramatic lineage. Within the context of this larger paradigm and its various shifts and turns, the following chapters will move.

2

Prodigal Sons, Prodigal Husbands: A Particular Lineage

And not many days after the younger son gathered all together, and took his journey into a far country, and there wasted his substance with riotous living.

—Luke 15:13

Hickey: You've heard the old saying, "Ministers' sons are sons of guns." Well, that was me, and then some. Home was like a jail . . . and so was school, and so was that damned hick town. The only place I liked was the pool rooms, where I could smoke Sweet Caporals, and mop up a couple of beers, thinking I was a hell-on-wheels sport.[1]

LINKS between alcohol and prodigality will probably not surprise contemporary readers, even though the parable itself does not specifically mention drinking. Illustrations of the story from the Middle Ages onward have delighted in depicting scenes of "riotous living" that almost invariably include images of drinking along with feasting, gambling, and sexual play.[2] In nineteenth- and twentieth-century America, prolonged drinking has certainly become one of the most recognizable ways for someone to lose an inheritance or, in more middle-class terms, one's savings, home, and livelihood.[3] Society has also perceived alcohol as a major threat to the integrity of the family so that the rupture of family in the parable parallels the ruptures in family life that alcohol has created. The slide from respectability and prosperity to Skid Row easily mirrors the prodigal's descent: the prodigal in rags among the swine becomes the disheveled drunk who ends up in the gutter or in the backroom of the "last-resort variety" that O'Neill uses as the scene for *Iceman*.[4] Larry Slade's description is memorable: "It's the No Chance Saloon. It's Bedrock Bar, The End of the Line Café, The Bottom of the Sea Rathskeller! . . . No one here has to worry about where they're going next, because there

45

is no further they can go."[5] Part of the lore of recovery programs is that alcoholics must, like the prodigal, "hit bottom" (i.e., feed with the swine) and so come to realize the hopelessness of their situation.[6] Of course these same programs also offer the hope of coming home again, of returning to former roles in the community and, most importantly, the family. So many are the parallels that one might easily suppose that the parable of the prodigal son was a kind of case study of an individual with a chronic drinking problem. Indeed in *I'll Quit Tomorrow*, a popular guide for recovering alcoholics, Vernon Johnson uses the parable as a chapter-long teaching tool (a "far country" becomes Las Vegas), arguing that "all the basic spiritual dynamics of alcoholism are present in the events and relationships" of the story.[7] The main difference is that in Johnson's analogy the fundamental other for today's alcoholic prodigal is not a father or an elder brother but a spouse, in particular, a wife.[8]

In American drama O'Neill's Hickey marks as clearly as any dramatic figure this convergence of the prodigal and drunkard, of son and husband. He is, of course, husband to his long-suffering wife, Evelyn, but he is also the prodigal son who runs away from home for the big city: his inheritance, a loan from the local madam. He did not, however, waste it, at least not all at once and entirely. Instead he used another inheritance, his father's powers of speech, to become a successful salesman. As such he manifests the industry and energy of the parable's elder brother, but the prodigal still lives within him, periodically emerging for a spate of riotous living that leaves him looking like "something lying in the gutter that no alley cat would lower itself to drag in."[9] Hickey makes his adult home with Evelyn, the one love of his life, the all-American girl next door who might as well be *Our Town*'s Emily, a figure so loving and believing that she finally seems more principle or fantasy than person. Hickey never mentions his mother in describing his early years, but certainly she appears in the form of Evelyn, wife/mother to a husband/son who both loves and hates her, who wants to run away from her to the arms of a prostitute and then to run back again, carrying with him the disease of desire, not knowing where to leave it, at home or in Altoona. Hickey the prodigal son effortlessly blends over and into Hickey the prodigal husband.

This phrase, *prodigal husband*, may seem awkward to some, particularly those who find prodigality's essence in the father-son relationship.[10] Yet I will argue here and throughout that American drama needs some term to describe a fairly narrow range of (usually) male behavior that both husbands (who may, of course, also be fathers, usually young fathers) and sons display. I might have used instead the label *domestic reform drama* to refer to plays that feature this behavior. It describes fairly well the set of conventions under examination, but this designation is awkward and even with it a need would still exist for some label, other than *objects of reform*, to describe figures conventionally similar to versions of Wilder's Arthur and O'Neill's Hickey. The word *prodigal*, for male prodigality both cross-and inter-generational, seems, however, most appropriate, because it suggests a movement in and out of the family that both husbands and sons often share, because American literature conventionally confuses and compounds the roles of wife and mother, husband and son, and because the parable itself is flexible enough to allow some variety in who departs from and returns to whom.

Iceman, of course, underscores this vision of a prodigality that encompasses husbands and sons, in a way even more profound than Hickey's story, through the character of Don Parritt. He, too, is a prodigal, one who has left not a father or wife, but a mother, after first collecting an inheritance that he spends in a faraway land, finally ending in a place not far from the bottom of it all. *Iceman* ends with these two American prodigals (husband and son), side-by-side, telling the stories of their journeys, retracing the steps that brought them to Harry's bar, to the end of the line, to a place where they feed among the swine.[11]

THE FIGURE OF THE PRODIGAL: A PARTICULAR LINEAGE

Before describing the fundamental conventions of the prodigal play in American theater, I want to survey at some length its lineage in Western art and literature as a means of identifying particular features that may help explain its function and appeal in American drama. My goal is not just to review earlier appearances of the story for the historical record but to find in those appearances clues for its more recent uses. For instance one of the first applications of the parable occurs in the writings of Augustine who makes several references to it in his *Confessions*, employing it as a metaphor for his own spiritual journey.[12] At an early stage of its dissemination, the parable emerges in an autobiographical context within a reflective, confessional mode. This use mirrors the moment in the parable in which the prodigal son composes his own confession, rehearsing just how to frame the self: "I will arise and go to my father and will say unto him, Father, I have sinned." As a whole, the parable provides a simple structure with which to organize the narrative of a specific life, especially from the perspective of a certain end point: after having passed through a period of crisis, after coming home. At the same time, connecting the narrative structure of the parable with a specific life story (whether Augustine's or Eugene O'Neill's) naturalizes and validates that pattern, makes it seem less like the prefabricated structure that it is and more like a living organism. This twofold process is consistently at work in American drama. The parable provides a way of shaping biographical materials, while the truth claims of biography simultaneously suggest an escape from fiction and convention.[13]

An even more significant source of dissemination has been the role of the parable as a subject for religious art from the Middle Ages to the present, including the work of artists such as Albrecht Dürer (1471–1528), Hieronymus Bosch (ca. 1450–1516), Jacques Callot (ca. 1592–1635), Hans Holbein (1497–1543), Frans Hals (1580/85–1666), Anthony van Dyck (1599–1641), Peter Paul Rubens (1577–1640), and Rembrandt van Ryn (1606–69).[14] Emile Mâle writes that the "story of the Prodigal was very dear to medieval artists" and that it was one of only four parables recreated in the cathedrals.[15] He also comments on the liberties that artists, usually more conservative in their work, took with the text:

> They show the Prodigal Son playing at dice in a tavern, bathing before sitting down at table, being beckoned by the courtesans standing before their doors, crowned with flowers, and then driven away when he had nothing left to give them but his coat.[16]

Of note here is the ability of the story to inspire and absorb imaginative additions, especially in the scenes of riotous living. David Kunzle also discusses various visual representations of the parable in his study of the early comic strip: narrative strips and picture stories ca. 1450 to 1825. For Kunzle a comic strip requires "a sequence of images," a "preponderance of image over text," a "mass medium," and a "topical moral narrative."[17] The same qualities that make the parable an apt subject for the comic strip will also make it immensely adaptable to the stage.

Alan R. Young, in the appendix to his study of English prodigal son plays, indexes over two hundred art works on the parable (many of them with multiple scenes) from the ninth century to the end of the sixteenth: oils, engravings, tapestries, illuminations, etchings, woodcuts, drawings.[18] The story visually provides opportunities for several scenes (twenty-two or more at Chartres Cathedral), although four moments were particularly apt for representation: the departure, riotous living in a far country, feeding with the swine, and the return.[19] A survey of descriptive titles in Young's catalog suggests, not too surprisingly, that scenes of riotous living and of the return were most popular, suggesting areas of appeal to those who would dramatize the story.[20]

In the eighteenth and nineteenth centuries, the parable was a favorite subject for printmakers in England and America, appearing in magazines, children's books, and even on Leeds china plates.[21] In addition to noting the "theatrical quality" of the prints, Edwin Wolf points out that these printmakers chose to portray the prodigal and his fellow characters in "modern" dress.[22] Of course the use of contemporary costumes and settings in theater or the visual arts to depict scenes from distant times is not so unusual, but it underscores the story's adaptability, the ease with which its surface detail lends itself to and even encourages reimagination in terms of the present moment. This contemporizing is the reverse of Brechtian de-familiarization through historification. Here familiarization personalizes the parable, bends it to the current moment, once again naturalizing the foreign or conventional. Furthermore Wolf suggests that this was not a naive practice that we might expect to find prior to the development of historicism but a conscious choice informed by changes in the socioeconomic order:

> [T]he parable was a natural, not for sale to the nobility who had had prodigal sons for generations, but to the rising bourgeoisie, the London bakers and brewers, the mercers and merchants. . . . Their sons were enjoying the advantages of money, as sons of the nouveaux riches have throughout the ages. The Prodigal Son was the hosier Sir Samuel Stockin's son to life. His return to the flourishing business of his father was devoutly to be wished for. As visual prayers, the sets of prints flowered on the walls of English middle-class homes, redolent with the smell of candle wax and roast beef.[23]

According to Wolf these scenes of prodigality took over where Hogarth's *A Rake's Progress* (1734), itself a pessimistic variant of the parable, left off, restoring the happy ending it omitted.[24] The Lukan parable with its optimistic closure lends itself to the ethos of a class that believes that time can be more than a function of deterioration and waste, that it can instead be beneficent. If time creates a space in which one can rise from poverty to wealth through industrious commercial activity, then it can also create a space in which sons can realize the errors of their ways and return to their fathers. For the aristocrat, the wasting of an inheritance has a tragic finality: once assets have been expended, the only prospect of replenishing them is through the death of a wealthy relative. The self-made man can (almost) always make more money.

In his discussion of German ballads based on the return of the transformed son, Tom Cheesman also focuses on the emergence of the parable in European culture and its role in the articulation of a particular worldview.[25] Cheesman's main interest is in a variant of the parable in which a wealthy (not impoverished) son returns to be murdered (not welcomed) by parents who envy his wealth. This "cynical modern transformation" first appears in chapbooks as a factual account in the early seventeenth century.[26] As a motif it has since appeared in ballads, poems, stories, sermons, newspapers, and plays in various countries and languages from the seventeenth century to the present. Dramatic versions include Lillo's *The Fatal Curiosity* (1736) and Camus's *Le Malentendu* (1944). Cheesman argues that the popularity of the parable itself set the stage for this variation. He writes that "in the century or so preceding the invention of the Murdered Son story, the parable of the Prodigal Son had emerged from scriptural obscurity—its role in medieval Christianity was negligible—to become the most frequently cited, recited, and adapted story in Christian teaching."[27] Whether or not the role of the parable in medieval Christianity was "negligible" is arguable, given, for example, its use by Augustine and its role in medieval art, particularly stained glass, from at least the ninth century on. But Cheesman's sense of the parable's proliferation in song, picture, sculpture, drama, and a "plethora of other moral, instructive and catechistic genres of performance and display" does seem apt.[28] Most importantly Cheesman reads the parable itself "as a mythical charter for a patriarchal, religious, political, and social vision" and, in particular, as "an exemplary image of social relations under capitalism."[29] For Cheesman the proliferation of the parable is clearly coincident with and supportive of the advent of early European capitalism in its most benevolent form: its message, "revolt against patriarchal power is sinful, but . . . the conflict can be resolved by the exercise of voluntary subordination by the son, and charity and mercy, by the father."[30] He sees the Murdered Son story as a countervision born from experience in the realities of capitalist life, a vision that recognizes the destructive potential for "family and community life" inherent in "the emerging capitalist mentality and economy."[31] In effect Cheesman takes Wolf's argument and pushes it back further in time. Both authors link the parable to capitalism and the rise of a commercial class; both also offer contrasting narratives (*A Rake's Progress;* the Murdered-Son story) that offer less optimistic dénouements. These studies by Wolf and Cheesman are important in that they point to potential functions of the parable within a social order (as "mythic charter," for example) and toward the possibility that revisions of the narrative might serve additional functions, including a critique of hegemonic values. They also suggest, perhaps unintentionally, the danger of any one reading of the parable's significance. The temptation is to reduce a work of art to a unitary value. In this instance it is to make the parable complicit with capitalism or patriarchy and then dismiss it as retrograde. Insights such as those offered by Wolf and Cheesman about the relationship between the parable and capitalism are central to the concerns of this study (they will be expanded upon in the following pages) but need to be seen as part of a complex whole, not as solutions that in any way preclude further examination or alternative approaches.

Of particular historical importance to the role of the parable in English drama was the influence of the Christian Terence plays of the Low Countries.[32] These sixteenth-century plays comprise some of the earliest adaptations of the Lukan parable to a dramatic form.[33] Latin schoolmasters, following the earlier lead of Hroswitha, used Terentian style and structure to retell biblical narratives.[34] The goal of these Christian humanists was, as might be expected, to teach Latin and morality without contaminating the minds of their students with the paganism of Terence. Clearly the story of the prodigal son with its New Comedy emphasis on the father/son conflict and its potentially didactic emphasis on the repentance/reform of wayward youth was, of all the narratives at their disposal, particularly appropriate for these purposes. Among the earliest and most successful of these Christian Terence dramas was *Acolastus* (i.e., "wastrel" or "prodigal")[35] by William de Volder, also known as Gnapheus or Fullonius: first performed by schoolboys at The Hague in 1528; first printed in Antwerp in 1529; translated into English by John Palsgrave in 1540; a rather literal adaptation of the parable that borrowed from Roman comedy its linguistic style, a five-act structure, and such characters as the parasite, pimp, courtesan, and servant.[36] By 1540 it had gone through twenty editions and, in addition to Palsgrave's translation, had also been rendered in German, Dutch, and French.

Acolastus substitutes proper names for the generic titles (father, younger son, elder son) used in certain earlier dramatic versions and, of course, in the parable itself.[37] This move, like Augustine's application of the parable to his life story, suggests the way in which the parable picks up bits of realistic detail. This version also begins to suggest the story's flexibility: in this instance to the demands of a five-act structure. Along these same lines, Konrad Eisenblicher describes an Italian dramatization of the parable (*Il figliuol prodigo* by Giovan Maria Cecchi) written in 1569–70 that reconstructs the story to allow for unity of time and place (not found in *Acolastus*), sets it in Renaissance Florence, eliminates much of the sermonizing, and finally adds a second plot from Terence in which a servant cheats a miser out of his money.

In England, *Acolastus* and other Christian Terence dramas of the prodigal joined with the native tradition of morality play and interlude (e.g., *The Interlude of Youth,* 1513–29; *Nice Wanton,* 1547–53) to form the basis for the employment of this paradigm during the English Renaissance.[38] Ervin Beck lists almost forty prodigal son plays written between 1500 and 1642. In his study Alan Young lists thirty-five along with thirty more that he excludes but that other scholars cite.[39] Beck notes that Shakespeare uses the paradigm in six different plays, the most obvious instances, of course, *Henry IV, Parts 1 and 2,* the others being *The Two Gentlemen of Verona* (Proteus), *The Taming of the Shrew* (Lucentio), *All's Well That Ends Well* (Bertram), and *The Tempest* (Caliban). Daryl Tippens argues for as many as twenty allusions.[40] Beyond these Shakespearean references, Beck argues that, except for Lyly and Peele, "every important known comic playwright [of the English Renaissance] had a hand in a least one prodigal-son comedy."[41] For him this paradigm represents "one of the earliest, most persistent, and most important strains in drama of the English Renaissance."[42]

In his discussion of prodigal son plays in English Renaissance drama, Beck argues that a strict translation of the parable into dramatic form might include "ten 'segments' of action":

the request (verses 11–12a),
the granting of the request (v. 12b),
the trip to the far country (v. 13a),
the riotous living (vv. 13b–14),
the recourse to work (v. 15a),
the bondage-humiliation-despair (vv. 15b–16),
the recognition-repentance-return (vv. 17–20a),
the generous reception (vv. 20b–21),
the celebration (vv. 22–24), . . .
the elder brother's response (vv. 25–32).[43]

As detailed as this scenario is, it anticipates the tendency toward diminishing the story of the elder brother by compressing the interaction between him and his father into a single unit. As noted above illustrators would often tell the story in four to six key moments. Beck himself admits that the ten segments he lists are too limiting and literal-minded for the construction of a dramatic paradigm and so offers his own five-point rubric for the prodigal son play:

1. The hero rebels against or disappoints a father or father-figure—whether a foster-father, an uncle-guardian, a teacher, or a man who previously had advised his father. This element distinguishes prodigal-son comedy from the "faithful wife" play, in which a young man deserts a faithful sweetheart or wife. . . .

2. The hero's departure from established values is a perverse, radical action; it is a "fall" from some kind of "grace," and not merely a well-intentioned mistake that is easily amended by advice and education. . . .

3. The prodigal son's "fall" is implicitly an initial departure from innocence, a first step towards self-realization. This element rules out plays about middle-aged people, and again, distinguishes prodigal-son comedy from plays about deserted wives. . . .

4. The paradigm assumes that its hero *ought* to return to the good state from which he has fallen. . . .

5. The paradigm is not obscured by a more prominent, even if similar, archetypal story.[44]

This view of prodigality is admirable for its specificity and is perhaps well suited for the study of Renaissance drama. It serves as a good point of departure but is ultimately too narrow for this study. For example I would argue that in American drama it makes sense to identify certain sons who depart from mothers as prodigal figures, as in the example (in miniature) from Wilder's *Happy Journey* that began chapter 1. Also the assumption that the prodigal "*ought* to return" may obscure a significant degree of ambivalence that often attaches itself to narratives of prodigality, particularly in a country with a history of rather fierce individualism and of disruptive departures from various "father-" or "mother-" lands. Furthermore even though Willy tells Linda (in reference to Biff) that not "finding yourself at the age of thirty is a disgrace," it seems to me that self-realization is not limited to youthful protagonists (nor, for that matter is innocence) and that the prolongation of maturation is a conspicuous feature of American drama and its fascination with adult children: Edmund, Jamie, Brick, Walter Lee Younger, Alan Baker, and others. Beck's five-part rubric would eliminate these older and married versions of prodigal-like behavior. This study chooses to include these dramatic figures for the light they might shed on the paradigm and it on them.

In fact Renaissance scholarship recognizes at least two different groups of prodigal son comedies. One set of plays foregrounds the prodigal's spousal relationship in addition to or instead of a filial relationship. Arthur Hobson Quinn in the introduction to his edition of *The Faire Maide of Bristow* (1605, Anonymous) describes this group of plays succinctly: "a rake and a spendthrift . . . deserts his wife for gain or the love of a courtesan, maltreats the wife who remains faithful to him, and after he has sinned sufficiently, is taken into grace again and even rewarded."[45] Muriel C. Bradbrook notes similarly that the "prodigal is generally shown as having to choose between a faithful wife and a wanton mistress, choosing wrongly at first and later being brought to repentance."[46] She cites *How a Man May Choose a Good Wife from a Bad* (1602, Heywood?) as prototypical. The conventions that Quinn and Bradbrook outline are obviously also appropriate to the midtwentieth-century dramas upon which this study focuses.

A second set of plays that some scholars regard as more central to the paradigm emphasizes the father-son (or master-apprentice/ teacher-student) relationship. These works correspond more literally to the structure of the parable itself. For Beck, who emphasizes son-ship in his explication of the paradigm, the most obvious examples of this more narrowly defined group are *Henry IV*, *The London Prodigal* (ca. 1604, Anonymous), and *Eastward Ho!* (1605, Chapman, Jonson, and Marston). Of course both sets of plays overlap whenever the father and the spouse or potential spouse of a prodigal are present, so that the prodigal is subject to at least two sets of perceptions: spousal and parental. Beck concedes that the tradition of the "faithful wife" play merges "with the prodigal-son tradition . . . if the deserted girl is strongly associated with the will of a living or deceased father."[47] This linkage of father and wife is exemplified in American drama by a play like *Cat on a Hot Tin Roof* in which both Maggie and Big Daddy work to bring Brick home. In other American dramas, the father figure disappears altogether, but the wife still possesses the moral authority of one parent or another, usually the mother.

For Beck the "essential concern of prodigal-son comedy . . . is the reforming of the internal desires of the young hero."[48] I would agree with Beck on the centrality of reformation and argue that plays concerning other family members (particularly husbands, potentially daughters and wives), in which the reforming of "internal desire" is a central issue, can benefit from study that approaches them as versions of the prodigal son drama. This emphasis on reform is also what distinguishes prodigals from the libidinous fathers of Plautus and Terence, of *commedia dell'arte* and Molière. The more traditional comic husband/father of Greek or Roman comedy is not a potential object of reformation but an obstacle to be gotten round, usually through cleverness and trickery.[49]

If, however, we do not want to lose completely Beck's distinction between "prodigal son" and "patient wife" plays, then we should consider not two, but three, major types of male prodigals (the question of the female prodigal will be taken up later): 1) the traditional prodigal son, functioning more or less along the lines described by

Beck, but including both father-son and mother-son relationships (e.g., Jamie in *Misbegotten*, although his age would probably disqualify him for Beck's purposes; a younger, more naive version appears in *Ah, Wilderness!*); 2) the prodigal husband (sometimes also a father) traditionally accompanied by the figure of the "patient wife" (e.g., Weston, the husband/father in Shepard's *Curse of the Starving Class*); and 3) the prodigal son/husband, perhaps the most interesting of the three, appearing as both child and spouse (e.g., O'Neill's Hickey with whom this chapter opened; Williams's Brick, son to Big Daddy and husband to Maggie; Hansberry's Walter Lee Younger, son to Mama Younger and husband to Ruth).

In the late seventeenth and eighteenth centuries, the prodigal son, errant husband, and long-suffering wife were among the staples of what we usually refer to as sentimental comedy. This genre is itself difficult to define, and scholars differ over whether or not works like Cibber's *Love's Last Shift* (1696) and *The Careless Husband* (1704), in which a good deal of Restoration-like ribaldry takes place before a fifth act conversion, can be rightly grouped with dramas more chaste and moralistic, such as Steele's *The Conscious Lovers* (1722) or Cumberland's *The West Indian* (1771), in which the appearance of prodigality, as opposed to its enacted presence, is more the norm. The former mixed sentiment and eroticism; the latter, sentiment and didacticism.[50] In both instances the reform of a male prodigal (husband or son; real or apparent) was a central convention of these dramas. Of course the prodigal also appears in dramatic responses to these uses of the paradigm, as in John Vanbrugh's *The Relapse* (1696), a Restoration-like answer to Cibber's *Love's Last Shift*, and Sheridan's *School for Scandal* (1777), a comedic response to the entire tradition of sentimentalized prodigality, not without, of course, a certain sentimentalism all its own.

Prodigality also figures in early instances of domestic tragedy, such as Edward Moore's *The Gamester* (1753) and Gotthold Lessing's *Miss Sara Sampson* (1755), particularly in the form of the son who wastes his inheritance. In Lessing's *Sampson* a servant upbraids his young master in words fit for a prodigal: "What a life you've led! Always together with the lowest gamblers and vagrants—that's what I call them, regardless of their titles. In company like that you squandered a fortune that would have opened your way to the highest posts."[51] In Moore's play the title character has "squander'd away" his fortune upon the "vilest of Passions [gambling], and among the vilest of Wretches."[52] (In visual renderings of the parable gambling was the quickest and most common way for a son to waste an inheritance.)

The Gamester found its successors in domestic melodramas of the nineteenth century like *Trent Ans ou la vie d'un joueur* (Victor Ducange and Prosper Gobaux, 1827), which Frank Rahill describes as "the first of many melodramas" to carry on the "Calvinistic tradition of plays such as *The London Merchant* and *The Gamester*."[53] *Trent Ans* was almost immediately translated and performed in England as *The Hut of the Red Mountain; or, Thirty Years of a Gambler's Life* (Milner, 1827) and in America as *Thirty Years; or, The Gambler's Fate* (Dunlap, 1828). Douglas Jerrold's *Fifteen Years of a Drunkard's Life* (1828), perhaps the first temperance melodrama in England, took its basic structure from this play of gambling and prodigality, in the process cutting the number of years to ruin in half.[54] These gambling plays and the temperance melodramas that followed them, with their downward spirals of loss and waste, as well as their frequent scenes of realization, reformation, and reunion, are the lineal descendants of *Acolastus:* sons, husbands, and young fathers as prodigal figures, wasting inheritances and sinking to the lowest levels of subsistence, finally finding themselves amongst some version of the swine, destitute and in rags; parents, young wives, and children left at home, patiently waiting for the one they love to return, ready to embrace him (occasionally her, as in *Hot Corn*, the story of an alcoholic mother and her daughter[55]) when he has come to himself. According to Frank Rahill, straight revivals of these plays were being performed as recently as the 1940s.[56] This study, of course, suggests that the temperance melodrama was not only being revived in the 1940s but also, in a sense, being rewritten by many of our major playwrights as part of an ongoing tradition of plays in which the prodigal was a central figure.[57]

One feature of the temperance movement that, in turn, helped spawn the temperance melodrama was the confessional testimonial: the autobiographical account of a prodigal life in the tradition of Augustine and of the prodigal son himself. This speech has played a key role in the work of evangelical revivalism, of Alcoholics Anonymous (AA), and their imitators. This interweaving of biography and a prodigal-like narrative manifested itself in the midnineteenth-century "experience" speech, identified in particular with the Washingtonians: a working-class temperance movement of the 1840s in which reformed drunkards reached out to their former partners in drink, persuading them to sign a pledge of total abstinence and then helping them hold to their promise.[58] As described by John Frick, the "experience" speech "presented the spectacle of a lone speaker, a reformed drunkard, on stage narrating the events of his individual odyssey from debauchery to sobriety and relating his personal feelings about the ordeal."[59] As Frick points out, a central narrative feature of these speeches and of most temperance melodramas was their circularity, a quality that, of course, they share as well with the parable: they bring the drunkard home again.

The link between this phenomenon and many American family dramas is our sense of the latter as versions of the "experience" speech, as dramatized biography. Alongside O'Neill's well-known inscription to Carlotta on the completion of *Long Day's Journey into Night* ("this play of old sorrow, written in tears and blood") belongs the story of William H. Smith the author of *The Drunkard*, as well as the first actor to play Edward Middleton, its title role. According to Harry Watkins, a professional actor of the day who himself played the lead in Smith's play on a number of occasions, actor-author Smith "had been a hard drinking man" who had "signed the pledge of total abstinence." The play itself "was written for him; in fact he wrote the greater portion of his own part himself. People looked upon it as a portrait of himself. He was playing his own life."[60] This degree of autobiographical seriousness links Smith's *The Drunkard* to both Augustine and those many American playwrights who have set versions of their lives (particularly their personal, domestic lives) before an audience.

The temperance melodrama provides the most significant link between the prodigal son comedies of the Renaissance and the figure of the prodigal in twentieth-century American domestic drama. It represents both a continuation of the earlier tradition and significant alterations. First of all, as in the contrast between Hogarth's *A Rake's Progress* and the vogue for prodigal son prints in the eighteenth and nineteenth centuries, temperance melodramas make manifest the possibility that the prodigal will not reform but will instead stay on a downward spiral unto death. (This twofold course is also central to the disease concept of alcoholism embraced by AA: the alcoholic will either stop drinking or the disease will kill him.) Even though most temperance melodramas brought the prodigal home, a number followed the more pessimistic course charted in *Fifteen Years of a Drunkard's Life*, Taylor's *The Bottle* (based on Cruikshank's Hogarth-like prints), and Zola's *L'Assommoir*. *Ten Nights in a Bar-room* exercises both scenarios: Morgan reforms, heeding the exhortations of his dying daughter; Slade goes from prosperous miller to death at the hands of his drunken son.

Second, even though the drunkard still moves from prosperity to poverty, the range of classes represented onstage expands to represent more nearly the class range of the audience. Frick and McArthur in their discussions of temperance melodrama note the presence of working-class protagonists, as well as those who are landowners, business owners, middle class, or aristocratic. This class diversification represents a shift from plays about fathers and inheritances to plays about other kinds of economic arrangements that affect families. The paradigm retains the loss of prosperity but begins to employ these relatively different beginning points, a change that reflects differences between the economic order of Renaissance Europe in the early stages of commercial capitalism and nineteenth-century America in the midst of intensive immigration and industrialization.

Related as well is the shift from a focus on prodigal sons to prodigal husbands. As noted above the prodigal husband has a place in Renaissance prodigal plays, just as the prodigal son is still a feature of post–World War II American prodigal plays; but the first group generally emphasizes sonship, while the latter generally emphasizes marital relationships. Temperance melodramas show the balance tipping toward the latter. The most significant relationships in these works are between drunkard husbands and their families composed of long-suffering wives and children. In the parable women are absent, except for the elder son's mention of the harlots on whom the younger son has supposedly wasted his fortune: no wives, no daughters. Property passes from fathers to sons. That structure holds for many of the Renaissance prodigal son comedies, but it gradually gives way in the seventeenth and eighteenth centuries to a co-focus and then primary focus on the prodigal and his wife.

At the beginning of *The Drunkard*, Edward Middleton's father, described as a benevolent patriarch, has died, a death that to some extent signals this shift: the father who would have welcomed home his prodigal son still leaves an inheritance, but a wife and daughter now replace him as those who will wait for the prodigal's return. To a degree the father figure returns in this and other temperance melodramas in the form of an aging, wealthy, and benevolent patriarch, such as Rencelaw in *The Drunkard*, who helps effect the prodigal's return.[61] Like the prodigal's vision of his father when he is in the midst of the swine, Rencelaw intercedes at Middleton's worst moment: he finds him at a "wretched out-house or shed . . . without hat or coat, clothes torn, eyes sunk and haggard, appearance horrible," in a "beastly condition," suffering from a recent attack of the *delirium tremens*, ready to poison himself.[62] Rencelaw, a reformed drunkard, brings the prodigal home. He provides an image of "mature" male experience that has conquered its own prodigality and achieved material success: one image of a father. His words of comfort and admonition stand for a saving vision that gives the prodigal the strength to turn his life around when he has reached the absolute end of his journey, when, in the language of AA, he has "hit bottom."

An important alternative catalyst is also intergenerational, but younger not older: the prodigal's daughter as in Mary Morgan in *Ten Nights in a Bar-Room* who would sing "Come Home, Father" to coax Joe Morgan from the tavern and whose deathbed admonishments eventually brings him permanently home. This shift from prodigal child to prodigal spouse has one major consequence: prodigality does not just affect the prodigal's fortunes; it also affects the fortunes of his wife and children who depend on him for their needs. As the prodigal descends, they are pulled down with him. Their rags mirror his. The Mary in this instance is the wife of Edward Middleton in *The Drunkard:* "A wretched garret—Old table and chair with lamp burning dimly—Mary in miserable apparel, sewing on slop-work; a wretched shawl thrown on her shoulders—Child sleeping on a straw bed on the floor, R., covered in part by a miserable ragged rug— Half a loaf of bread on the table.—The ensemble of the scene indicates want and poverty" (stage directions for act 3, scene 5).[63] The sufferings of wife and children serve as resonators for the sufferings of the prodigal (they almost join him among the swine), even as they complicate the traditional singularity of his journey.

As with the class issues noted above, this shift parallels and interacts with socioeconomic changes, in particular, the emergence in the early nineteenth century of the modern American family marked by a more companionate notion of marriage, a separation of spheres (mentioned in chapter 1) that made women more, not less, dependent on men for their economic survival, and new attitudes toward childhood that emphasized its innocence and uniqueness along with the responsibilities of parents for children's care and nurture.[64] At the same time, according to Mintz and Kellogg, the "ability of a father to transmit his 'status' position to his children declined":

> By the early nineteenth century, families were finding it increasingly difficult to pass on their status by bequeathing land or a family craft to offspring. The practice of partible inheritance, in which the paternal estate was divided into equal portions for all the children, made it difficult for farm or artisan families to pass on farms or family shops over time. An increase in opportunities for nonagricultural work, and the replacement of land as a primary medium of value by more portable forms of capital, further reduced the dependence of grown sons upon their parents.[65]

These economic changes no doubt contributed in some measure to the shift of prodigal activity from fathers, sons, and inheritances to wives, husbands, and incomes.

Relevant to this transition is a distinction Tom Scanlan makes in *Family, Drama, and American Dreams.* Scanlan sees American domestic drama as poised between two models of family life: one is the "family of security," described as "a stable, ordered family life lost (or being lost) to the past" that represents the "urge towards the safety of mutuality"; the other is the "family of freedom," described as "a spontaneous, natural family life to be gained in the future," representing a "contrary urge for independence and selfhood."[66] The first Scanlan locates in both the nuclear family of early American Puritanism and in Jefferson's celebration of the family farm, now most strongly felt in our sense of its absence and a nostalgic longing for its return. Central to this model is the presence of the father within a home/farm that functions as a self-sufficient economic unit, supposedly free from many socioeconomic forces at work in the larger world. *The Waltons* of prime-time television summarized the conventions of this longing, along with other shows such as *Bonanza* and that child of *Bonanza, Little House on the Prairie*—all appropriately located in the American past. Indeed in *Little House*, the counterfamily (weak father, spoiled daughter, demanding mother) lives not on the prairie but in the town, earning its living not from the land but from selling dry goods: town and store corrupt. Mary's longing for a home in *Journey*, although not specifically agrarian, is nevertheless a longing for this family of security, for a place of escape from a world of taverns and hotels, for stasis in place of the continual movement associated with the life of an actor who earns his living "on the road."

O'Neill's Hickey points toward Scanlan's second model, "the family of freedom." His job as a traveling salesman reflects the rise of a "new entrepreneurial culture" in nineteenth- and twentieth-century America:

> As industrialization became the dominant mode of production, the economic basis of the family was removed and a process of dispersion and disorganization began: the modern family pattern emerged. Industrialization demanded mobility and independence. The breadwinner left home each day, and the home followed the job, usually into the city. . . . The wage system meant that young men and, to a lesser extent, young women were less under the control of parents, whose authority had already been weakened by the disappearance of primogeniture. . . . Where previously the Puritan family had separated itself from society, now individuals began to separate themselves from the family.[67]

For Scanlan the key words that describe this type of family are individualism, "self-assertion," freedom from "artificiality," and freedom from "arbitrary authority."[68] As noted in chapter 1, the return of the father from work or the delay of that return if he stopped off at the local tavern became a central element in the rhythm of American family life. Here the television models are shows like *Father Knows Best* or *Leave It to Beaver*, usually set in the present, in which the problems of the day are almost invariably left for the father's nightly return from work. Often implicit in these shows is the notion that Beaver would not have gotten into so much trouble in the first place if Ward had only been around.

Scanlan argues that both models emphasize "self-reliance and self sufficiency" within the context of a democratic society.[69] In the first instance ("security"), the family provides an escape from the economic and "institutional claims of society,"[70] whereas in the second ("freedom"), democracy and capitalism offer individuals, particularly men, a place to exercise their energies apart from the restrictions of the home: one model celebrates family over and against society (the elder brother who stays behind); the other celebrates the individual who goes out into the larger world (city or frontier) to live and prosper (the prodigal as Horatio Alger or the immigrant success story). The former naturally emphasizes the importance of inheritances; the latter values starting from nothing. Like the young boy in *Shane*, the American imagination is caught between the lone gunman/entrepreneur riding across a horizonless plain in control of his destiny and beholden to no one and the peaceful farmer/father who builds his home and works his land for the good of the family unit. As with Willy in *Salesman*, a rift exists between Uncle Bens and their dreams of becoming rich in the Alaskan wilderness (a last frontier) and Lindas with their Brooklyn homes and backyard gardens (a vestige of the family farm):

> *Willy:* . . . Linda, he's got a proposition for me in Alaska.
> *Linda:* But you've got—(*To Ben:*) He's got a beautiful job here.
> *Willy:* But in Alaska, kid, I could—
> *Linda:* You're doing well enough, Willy!
> *Ben,* (*to Linda:*) Enough for what, my dear?
> *Linda,* (*frightened of Ben and angry at him:*) Don't say those things to him! Enough to be happy right here, right now.[71]

Willy's job as a traveling salesman is an accommodation, an attempt at finding some place in-between these extremes, one almost doomed to failure, except, of course, for the rare and elusive example of a Dave Singleman, the mythic salesman who inspired Willy.

This is not to say that a return to the farm or a home-based economy would make all things well again for neither model is totally positive or negative as a system of values. The family of security implies love and mutuality, but the presence of the father (or the mother, as in *Raisin*) can lead to an "arbitrary and unnatural" authoritarianism; it can also lead to isolationism and withdrawal.[72] The family of freedom searches for a way around these problems by minimizing familial ties and obligations, but in the process, the family itself as a place of "warmth, security, and nurture" may be lost.[73] The family of freedom threatened to stop being a family at all. Of course the doctrine of spheres hoped to counteract this tendency, to preserve family in the midst of a commercial society, to use the family to make that society work. Security and mutuality were still to have their place (in the home) and their champion (the wife/mother). Home itself would become a retreat, a private place, a "place for virtues and emotions threatened by the aggressive and competitive spirits of commerce, a place where women and children were secure and where men could escape from the stresses of business and recover their humanity."[74] Temperance melodramas as new versions of the prodigal play testify to the challenges of making this vision a reality.

Scanlan's schema is important to this history of the parable in that this tension between images of "security" and images of "freedom" in American life so readily lends itself to narratives of the prodigal (that figure who trades security for freedom), so that the parable provides one way to rehearse these issues. In the broadest sense of the word, the prodigal is any man who must leave home each day to make a life in a larger world, even if he never touches a drink or another woman: the daily prodigality of the commuter husband is a fixture of American life. Freedom also creates pressures that can lead to prodigal behavior. If individuals in a competitive, capitalistic economy have the freedom to forge their own destinies, to earn their own inheritances, then they must also accept responsibility for their failures. When they do not succeed, they might then turn to the bottle, as with Jamie and his father in *Journey*, Doc in *Sheba*, Frank in *Country Girl*, Walter Lee in *Raisin*, and George in *Woolf*. Even more persistently the figure of the prodigal provides a way for playscripts to voice concerns about the dangers of freedom, about whether or not men can withstand the temptations that they are likely to encounter in the world outside their home. In particular, it asks whether or not the son or husband will be able to resist the allure of women and drink, whether he will make it home after a day at work in the larger world, and whether he will want to return to a place of security and mutuality after a day of competition and freedom.

I am not, however, trying to set up simple lines of causality between social change and dramatic convention. At work in this discussion are at least four elements: 1) dramatic narratives and conventions, 2) social narratives and conventions, 3) the material conditions of families, and 4) the material conditions of playwriting and production. It seems less likely now than ever before that dramatic narratives simply mirror the material conditions of society. Instead we encounter a complex weave of conditions and narratives. In *Domestic Revolutions*, Mintz and Kellogg note, for example, that it was in the writings of Daniel Defoe, Henry Fielding, Samuel Richardson, and Laurence Sterne that readers would learn new ways of marrying and parenting. What does, however, seem clear is that a kind of paradigm shift occurs in the late eighteenth and early nineteenth century that registers in the way American families perceive themselves and function both in society and on the stage and that this alteration foregrounds prodigality as a significant issue but at the same time moves away from the more traditional concern with fathers and sons toward a focus on husbands and wives (in some cases, wife/mothers). The heirs of this change are temperance melodramas and the post–World War II American family dramas that this study describes: plays of the bottle, plays of the prodigal.

A series of prodigal plays exists in Anglo-American drama from at least the sixteenth century to the nineteenth century and, as chapter 3 will show, into the present. Parallel prodigal traditions exist in Germany, Holland, France, Spain, and Italy. These plays have taken a wide variety of dramatic forms: Christian Terence, morality, interlude, droll, puppet play, *auto sacramentale, sacre rappresentazione, commedia erudita, commedia dell'arte,* Elizabethan comedy, domestic tragedy, sentimental comedy, domestic melodrama.[75] They have incorporated allegorical figures from medieval drama and stock characters from Roman comedy.[76] On some occasions playwrights left the story in its own time and setting; on many others they contemporized it. All in all the range of forms is impressive. It speaks to the adaptability of the parable and of its potential to engage a variety of writers, actors, and audiences, certainly not always in the same manner, not necessarily as some universal, ahistorical archetype, but to engage nonetheless, to persist.

Significantly these various manifestations straddle a dividing line between comic and serious representations, for which *Henry IV,* with its alterations of moods, is an excellent example. This ability to move in one direction (the comic), the other (the serious or tragic), or both (tragicomedy) is, as Marvin Herrick points out, inherent in the synthesis that occurred in the Christian Terence dramas, whereby the manner of Roman comedy was wedded to the tone and matter of the Bible.[77] The possibility, as realized, for example, by both the Renaissance and temperance dramatists that the prodigal will not come home and that the happy ending will not take place reinforces this potential for either a comic or pathetic/tragic treatment of the story. The sentimental comedies of the late seventeenth and eighteenth centuries, of course, did much to exploit this paradigm's potential as an evoker of both laughter and tears.

More specifically uses of this structure participate in that movement toward a mixture of styles that Auerbach so brilliantly describes in his *Mimesis* whereby scenes of ordinary middle-class life, particularly domestic life, become subject to serious, problematic, even tragic inquiry. In a chapter entitled, "Madame du Chastel," Auerbach describes a scene from a fifteenth-century French consolatory treatise that features a mother and father who must contemplate the imminent loss of their thirteen-year-old son. For Auerbach the story suggests a fundamental shift in consciousness:

> [T]he place of the action is extremely everyday and domestic, the personages are a married couple, talking over their troubles at night in bed. In the classical conception of the ancients this is no proper setting for a tragic action in the elevated style. Here the tragic, the grave, the problematic appears in the everyday life of the family. And although the people involved belong to the high nobility and are steeped in feudal norms and traditions, the situation in which we find them—in bed at night, not as lovers but as man and wife, grieving under dire stress, and intent upon helping one another—is of a kind that impresses us more as middle-class, or rather as generally human, than as feudal.[78]

Once only the subject of popular farce, the married couple in bed now enters another realm, as the distinction between "the tragic and everyday realism" fades. Similarly the seriousness with which the modern era has taken the parable of the prodigal (another story in which the loss of a child figures prominently) also testifies to the rise of the middle class and the breakdown in the division of styles, to the creation of those middle genres (domestic tragedy and virtuous comedy) that Diderot advocated in the 1700s. If, as Auerbach suggests, the creatural realism of the Christ story formed the basis of a vital medieval realism, then this story, the parable as attributed to Christ—a story that uses the domestic setting as a figure for the relationship between God and man—must also be reckoned with: the image of a family and of a son who goes on a spree is not a comic tale or a fabliau, not a Roman comedy but a narrative of profound significance, theologically and emotionally. It demands to be taken seriously.

The parable as well includes a *creaturalism* that Auerbach finds central to the breakdown of a division that had, particularly in antiquity, relegated the body and lower classes to comedy, spirit and royalty to tragedy. Creaturalism encounters the human body and takes that encounter as something more than an opportunity for scatological jokes. It underscores our "subjection to suffering and transitoriness," as well as our equality "before death, before creatural decay."[79] For Auerbach, the crucifixion of Christ, as portrayed in word and image during the Middle Ages, foregrounds these aspects of existence. The parable finds the prodigal starving, in rags, and in the midst of the swine, a scene bounded on one side by riotous living (Rabelaisian drinking, eating, and sexual play; a pleasuring of the body) and on the other by homecoming (embrace, investiture in new robes, killing of the fatted calf, the banquet table), equally exorbitant in its own way. The body has a central place here. The image of man in the middle of a herd of swine readily lends itself to a comic imagination or at least a pastoral. That this image instead becomes one of pathos and epiphany is a stunning reversal of literary tradition. Equally striking is the seriousness with which nineteenth- and twentieth-century American drama has taken the image of a man with a bottle, of the inebriated prodigal. Drunkenness, with respect to the traditional division of styles, is predictably comic and lower class, but in much of American drama it has instead demanded (like the middle-class domestic interior) serious, problematic consideration.[80]

Again with respect to the biblical imagery that provided in the Middle Ages a counter to the classical division of styles, the man with the bottle recalls, however distantly, the miracles in which Jesus turned water to wine and fed the five thousand. The body and its physical needs merit miraculous intervention. These events, however, only vaguely prefigure the flow of liquor in these plays. In the modern era, drinking and drunkenness indicate a creatural sensibility central to the emergence of the realism Auerbach describes. Drinking foregrounds the body and its processes of ingestion, digestion, and elimination. In extreme instances, thought and articulation disappear, leaving little more than the image of the body as it wavers or collapses into sleep. In the drunken prodigal, we see the body's susceptibility, its vulnerability. Drunkenness, as already noted, is intensely overdetermined as an image, but almost invariably it carries some sense of suffering and mortality: the body suffers the effects of alcohol and in so doing dies, at least, a little. Perhaps one goal of abstinence is to deflect this truth: all will be well once the drinking stops, perhaps because we want to forget our "subjection to suffering and transitoriness," to put away the body and death.

That the image of a man with a bottle could be anything more than a generic device of some slapstick routine, some appendage to the parasite stereotype, or at best an element in the iconography of the grotesque speaks to the force with which the middle class demands its due: "Even our drinking and our drunkenness—once no more than fodder for jokes—is worth serious consideration."[81] The drunken Irishman is a farcical, red-nosed, stage figure, not uncommon in American drama; he is also at the center of O'Neill's late plays. That author in stage directions for *Misbegotten* takes care to differentiate between the drunken behavior of his characters and the comic stereotype: "Tyrone enters, left-front. He does not appear to be drunk—that is, he shows none of the usual symptoms."[82] The ability, however, to make this distinction at all comes from those changes Auerbach describes, from the connection between drinking and the creatural, from the importance of the creatural within the conventions of the modern realism within which O'Neill and so many other American playwrights have worked. The proliferation of the man with a bottle is an icon for the degree to which realism has consumed American drama.

We should not be surprised then to find at the threshold of nineteenth-century theatrical naturalism a play about drinking and prodigality, Zola's *L'Assommoir* (1879, the title is a generic name for a cheap saloon in a working-class neighborhood). Adapted by Zola and Busnach, it ran for three hundred performances in France and five hundred in London as *Drink* translated by Charles Reade. Parisian theaters gave *L'Assommoir* revivals in 1900, 1915, 1921, and 1927.[83] According to Lawson Carter in *Zola and the Theater*, *L'Assommoir* was the most popular of any play with which Zola was connected, and its adaptation "brought naturalism before the public mind more effectively than any other single event."[84] Like many temperance melodramas, it shows the slow decline of a man brought about by drinking. Like the prodigal plays, it offers hope of reformation and regeneration: indeed the husband undergoes a cure and comes home again. But at the celebration, he is tricked into drinking, relapses, and experiences delirium tremens. Significantly with respect to Auerbach and the division of styles, French critics were not ready to accord the play literary status, and they were particularly horrified by the tremens scene, by that intense and sensational eruption of creatural man: "Il boit, et ce n'est plus de l'ivresse, c'est de la folie furieuse. Il pousse des cris inarticulés, it saute, il se roule, il se tord, il bave. . . . Non, on me donnerait 1,000 francs pour voir ce spectacle hideux à l'hôpital, je refuserais, et c'est ça qu'on me donne au théâtre pour m'amuser. . . . Mais il n'y a pas ombre d'art dans tout cela!"[85] ("He drinks and it's no longer drunkenness, it's a furious madness. He howls inarticulately, he jumps, he rolls around, he bites himself, he slobbers. . . . No, they would give me 1000 francs to see this hideous spectacle in the hospital, I would refuse, and that is what they give me at the theatre to entertain me. . . . But there is no element of art in all that.")

In post–World War II American theater, the parallel event is the Living Theatre's production of Jack Gelber's *The Connection* (1959), although here the focus shifts to heroin instead of alcohol (perhaps because the latter has through overuse lost much of its creatural immediacy) and the range of events contracts: now a couple of hours while a few men wait for the arrival of the drug they crave, not the fifteen years of a drunkard's life. The delirium tremens scene is not so much absent as replaced by an equally visceral moment, placed, like the tremens scene, near or at the play's climax. Leach performs "the ritual of fixing and taking the heroin."[86] He "comes to a table at stage center, straps his arm, and plunges the needle into it, only to slump unconscious from an overdose."[87] Richard C. Kostelanetz describes the effect: "the audience has so completely accepted the fiction as actuality that a gasp is usually heard; on several occasions, men (and only men) have fainted—a sign of truly effective theatre."[88] What the French critics decried in the tremens scene is now hailed, at least by some.

This play, with its echoes of both *The Lower Depths* (1902) and O'Neill's *Iceman*, is, like *L'Assommoir*, also part temperance melodrama, part prodigal play. The character of Sister Salvation suggests both narratives. She quotes from the Bible on the effects of strong drink: "Wine is mocker, strong drink is raging: and whosoever is deceived thereby is not wise."[89] The only female character onstage, her goal is to save, to reform, to bring the lost soul home, although in this instance, an end to alienation is imaginary, her presence, ironic. She has come upon the prodigal/drunkard and his friends in the last stages of dissipation, in a place not far from the end of the road, while the jazz musicians provide an accompaniment, just as the musicians entertain the prodigal in illustrations of his story.[90] Although the play makes much of these men's commonality with the audience that has come to watch them and adopts an apparently nonjudgemental attitude toward its subjects, in the end it functions as a negative example, as a warning against leaving home, on the dangers of riotous living in a far country. As one critic wrote, "[Gelber's] purpose is probably to make us *understand* these people and to sympathize with them. The actual effect is precisely the opposite."[91] *The Connection* accuses the middle class of having its own addictive behaviors: "the people who worry so much about the next dollar, the next new coat, the chlorophyll addicts, the aspirin addicts, the vitamin addicts, those people are hooked worse than me."[92] But few audience members probably left the theater equating their aspirin addiction with Leach's overdose. With this and subsequent productions, The Living Theatre would become known for the intense physicality of their performances, for foregrounding their own bodily presences, their creaturalism, and like prodigal sons and daughters, for an ongoing conflict with authority that would take them away from home (to Europe in this case) and then back again. They represent one fairly extreme direction in which a socially conscious, realistic impulse would take American theater, first in works like *The Connection* and *The Brig* (1963), later in works like *Paradise Now* (1968). Eventually the fiction of character would find even less place; Beck and Malina in person, in the flesh, face to face, body to body, would take precedence. In their prime they would have been the ideal company to undertake a contemporary, nonparodied revival of *The Drunkard*.

I would stress, however, that these plays of prodigality and drunkenness *participate in that movement* toward modern realism as opposed to always or necessarily *realizing the end* Auerbach describes. More often than not, uses of the paradigm seem to enjoy exercising other elements—comic, sentimental, Gothic, erotic, didactic—anything other than what we might conventionally perceive, in Auerbach's words, as a "serious representation of contemporary everyday social reality against the background of a constant historical movement."[93] Nonetheless at moments in American drama, particularly in the work of O'Neill, the narrative of the prodigal does aspire to and attain the level of tragic seriousness that Auerbach describes.

This survey of the prodigal lineage and its implications concludes with M. H. Abrams's reference to the parable in his study of the romanticism and modernism, *Natural Supernaturalism*, in a sense ending where this section began in that Abrams also links Augustine and the parable. More importantly he sees the story of the prodigal son as an instance of a narrative structure that predates its appearance in the biblical text, a structure he describes as "one of the most persistent of the ordering designs by which men have tried to come to terms with their nature and destiny."[94] Abrams traces this "design" from pagan and Christian Neoplatonism through Kabbalism and European Hermeticism into the philosophy and literature of the nineteenth and twentieth centuries. At its root is a structure that "holds that the first principle is the One, and that the One is identical with the Good."[95] Multiplicity, separation, and division represent a movement away from and in opposition to this initial unity. They are evil if for no other reason than that differentiation marks separation and distance from primal unity and goodness. Postmodernism and poststructuralism have tended to value fragmentation and multiplicity over and against any fixed reference point.[96] Abrams underscores the presence of a more persistent impulse, one that recognizes the fragmentary nature of our perceptual world but that then tries to put that world back together again; to locate some source or origin from which mind, soul, and matter have arisen; to find unity in diversity; to discover that whole from which the parts have fallen. Concurrently according to Abrams, this movement from the one into the many and back again to the one, from divided to reunited man, often takes the shape of a circle, of a "circuitous journey," the journey of the prodigal out of his home into a far country and back again (unity, unity lost, unity restored):

> Behind many Romantic versions of the internal circuitous quest we can recognize the chief prototype of the circular variant of the ancient Christian *peregrinatio*, that is, the parable of the Prodigal Son interpreted as the type of the journey of all mankind out of and back toward its original home; and in Romantic as in Christian literature, this parable is frequently conflated with the apocalyptic marriage that signalized the restoration of Eden in the Book of Revelation. Accordingly, the yearning for fulfillment is sometimes expressed as *Heimweh*, the homesickness for the father or mother and for the lost sheltered place; or else as the desire for a female figure who turns out to be the beloved we have left behind; or sometimes, disconcertingly, the desire for father, mother, home, and bride all in one.[97]

In Hansberry's *Raisin in the Sun*, Walter Lee describes a series of journeys that take him away from home and then back again. These journeys stand as one example among many of circular progresses in American family drama similar to the pattern Abrams describes:

> *Walter:* Wednesday I borrowed Willy Harris' car and I went for a drive . . . just me and myself and I drove and drove . . . Way out . . . way past South Chicago, and I parked the car and I sat and looked at the steel mills all day long. I just sat in the car and looked at them big black chimneys for hours. Then I drove back and I went to the Green Hat. (*Pause*) And Thursday—Thursday I borrowed the car again and I got in it and I pointed it the other way and I drove the other way—for hours—way, way up to Wisconsin, and I looked at the farms. I just drove and looked at the farms. Then I drove back and I went to the Green Hat. (*Pause*) And today— today I didn't get the car. Today I just walked. All over the Southside. And I looked at the Negroes and they looked at me, and finally I sat down on the curb at Thirty-ninth and South Parkway and I just sat there and watched the Negroes go by. And then I went to the Green Hat.[98]

Walter's journeys, of course, reveal a sense of limitation as an African-American man tries to enter American life. But they are also typical of prodigal narratives, of a tension between home and the world beyond home: a world of highways and taverns. Furthermore these trips away from home reflect the tension and disunity within the Younger family triggered by questions of how money should be spent: either for a tavern (a symbol of family disunity) or for a home (a symbol of family unity). An even more profound disunity arises over how money should be earned, specifically, over whether or not Walter should accept money that would disgrace the family. Walter's final decision to turn down the neighborhood association's offer reunites him with wife, mother, and sister, a reunion that the move to their new home reinforces. The family travels from the many to the one, from a negative state of fragmentation to a positive state of unification. This pattern repeats itself over and again in plays of the prodigal in which the happiest of ends—realized or potential—is always that which brings the wayfarer home again and makes the family whole. The absence of this wholeness is what figures so prominently in the final moments of O'Neill's *Journey*.

Abrams study also emphasizes the variety of images available to express this movement, usually circular, from the one to the many and back again. From his perspective the switch from waiting father and prodigal son to waiting wife/mother and prodigal husband is not particularly surprising in that it reflects a tendency, often evident in biblical typology, but evident as well in other forms of literature, whereby elements that "signify the same thing are interchangeable with each other."[99] As an example of this, Abrams cites a remarkable passage from Augustine's *Confession* in which "the goal of the composite journey is at once a country and a city and a home, both a place and a person, both male and female, and a father who is also the mother, the bridegroom, and the spouse":[100]

> Let me *enter into my chamber* and sing my songs of love to Thee, groaning with inexpressible groaning in my pilgrimage, and remembering Jerusalem with my heart stretching upwards in longing for it: Jerusalem my Fatherland, Jerusalem which is my mother: and remembering Thee its Ruler, its Light, its Father and Tutor and Spouse . . . the sum of all ineffable good because Thou alone art the one supreme and true Good. So that I shall not turn away but shall come to the peace of that Jerusalem, my dear mother, where are the first-fruits of my spirit . . . and there Thou shalt collect from my present scatteredness and deformity all that I am, and Thou shalt re-form me and confirm me into eternity.[101]

I do not offer this as an explanation of the general shift from fathers and prodigal sons to mothers and sons or wives and husbands that this study explores, but Abrams's example illustrates the openness of a structure reflected in the image of the prodigal son to various substitutions similar to those found in American drama.

Abrams also identifies a significant variation on the image of the circuitous voyage: a variation that turns the circle into a spiral so that each revolution marks some degree of evolutionary progress, however slight. Walter Lee's return to the center of the family with his decision finally to reject the neighborhood association's money suggests this variant, an upward spiral, a return with a difference, not to the same place, but to a better one, signified by the family's move from an inner city apartment into the suburbs.

Critics frequently employ the word *understanding* to describe this upward movement: a word that often denotes, in addition to forgiveness, a new integration of fragmentary knowledge and experience, the discovery of some unity in a sea of difference; it is a word that might apply to the perception of a spectator, as well as to that of a character. We often assign value to plays of prodigality according to whether or not they represent this process. Even if the prodigal does not technically return home, a sense of some new *understanding* will often mark the completion of the journey from the many to the one, if not for the character, then at least for the spectator.

A final value of Abram's study is, as with these other historical instances, the insight it provides as to the kinds of energies the parable relies on and evokes. Abrams's study underscores the parable's place within a certain structure, whether we think of it as a universal pattern or as a historical tradition, as archetype or convention. Most importantly he calls attention to the way in which the tension between unity and disunity inherent in that structure energizes the parable. Although he notes that traditionally "the one" has been celebrated over "the many," uses of the parable need not necessarily follow this course. For visual artists scenes of dissipation (of multiplicity) were nearly as popular as scenes of the return (of unity).

Of course not only in our plays but also in our public discourse does America seek some mediation between fragmentation or differentiation, on the one hand, and homogeneity or unity, on the other, that is, between differences so profound that they leave no common ground for building a community and hegemonic entities (cultural and economic) that obliterate all sorts of individuation and that lead to the extinction of distinct forms and ways of life. The family has been in many ways central to this tension, both metaphorically and literally. On one extreme it is perceived as the one unifying structure that still makes sense in an increasingly structureless world, even as we recognize its historicity and argue over its defining characteristics (nuclear, blended, extended, single parented, gay and lesbian parented; the intensity of the arguments surrounding these definitions underscore its ongoing importance to all concerned); on the other extreme, particularly in the form inherited from the early nineteenth century (breadwinner, housewife, obedient child), perceived as a frightening monolith that threatens individual identity, especially for those women whose lives (even once they also become wage earners) are directed toward serving the needs of that whole but also threatening the identity needs of men and even children.[102] The family then is a matrix, perhaps the matrix, for this struggle between unity and multiplicity that Abrams describes, although "the one" is not so now clearly identified as being synonymous with "the good." The story of the prodigal provided American drama in the years following World War II with a vocabulary with which to explore this tension. The specific terms of that vocabulary are the subject of the following chapters.

3

Prodigal Sons, Prodigal Husbands: Rupture and Potential

Tom: There is a fifth character in the play who doesn't appear except in this larger-than-life-size photograph over the mantel. This is our father who left us a long time ago. He was a telephone man who fell in love with long distances.[1]

Cora: You like being out on the road, don't you? You like to pretend you're still a young cowboy.
Rubin: It wasn't a bad life.[2]

Lottie: Something inside of him just got up and went for a walk, and never came back.[3]

Lee: So, Mom took off for Alaska, huh?[4]

First Characteristic of the Prodigal: Rupture

PRODIGALITY in American family drama relies on two related sets of conventions encompassed by the terms *rupture* and *potential*. *Rupture* suggests brokenness, pain, and violence. More specifically and intimately, it sometimes serves to describe the breaking of the hymen in intercourse, a moment in the consummation of a relationship. The same word, however, might also describe a relationship's fragmentation, a kind of deconsummation that the prodigal's departure initiates. Similar associations attach themselves to the breach/rupture of birth and the breach/rupture between parent and child that occurs when the prodigal leaves home. In all these senses, *rupture* suggests violent actions of breaking and pushing, of pulling apart and knocking down—of doors, of walls, of human tissue—experienced on a visceral level. Rupture refers to the separation of people (parents and children, husbands and wives, lovers with histories) joined at the bowels, people

73

attached to one another by ties of blood, birth, intercourse, or sexual-ity. Lighter attachments—acquaintances, friendships—generally fall outside the paradigm.

These ties and the concept of family itself may, of course, on occa-sion be more metaphorical than literal in nature. Alternative forms of family are more than possible. The key issue with respect to the paradigm of the prodigal is whether or not the ruptured relationship has the strength of that between people we perceive as members of a family. To take one idiosyncratic example, Shannon in Williams's *Night of the Iguana* is not directly connected to an earthly family, yet we still see him as a prodigal, because the play relies on religious imagery that consistently figures spiritual issues in familial terms. Indeed this is a central metaphor of Christian theology and a primary function of the parable itself: the concretization of religious experience by way of the family. To some extent Shannon is the prodigal behind the parable: his flight from God is the condition that biblical language renders in the story of a father and a son. Drink and sex connect Shannon and other rogue priests à la Graham Greene to the sons and husbands of American drama.

Shannon's presence as a spiritual son, as an embodiment of the figure for whom the son of the parable stands, also reminds us that the parable addresses more than domestic issues: it embraces two planes of perception. The first is a domestic drama, a story of two sons, a father, the wasting of an inheritance, and a coming home; the second is a spiritual drama, a story of sin and repentance, of separa-tion from and return to God. But in the dramatic adaptations of the paradigm that this study examines, the domestic scene has become not so much a means to an end as an end in and of itself. Vehicle has become tenor, a transformation partially marked by the shift from generic titles (father, younger son, elder son) to proper nouns (Tyrone, Willy, Big Daddy, Jamie, Biff, Brick): the latter are an index of speci-ficity; of the presence of the particular and the local, as opposed to the universal; and of a move away from allegory toward dramatic realism.

This dichotomy is not, however, quite as clearly drawn as these comments would seem to make it. The midcentury family dramas listed in chapter 1 are more than elaborate case histories. As with the parable, we draw abstractions from particulars, especially when they are embodied in a profoundly familiar social unit. We do not, of course, read these plays as allegories, but we do perceive them in terms of two different frames of reality (the family specific and the family in general), and in this way they resemble the workings of the parable. Furthermore dramatic uses of this paradigm often retain some of the spiritual/theological resonances of the parable, especially resident in references to separation and reunion, so that, to some extent, these family narratives are spiritualized, even when specific references to God or religion are absent. Second more than any other parable this story has achieved a certain primacy in its own right, so that one might read it as a narrative almost without a secondary level of meaning, as simply a moving and exemplary story of a father's patience and love: a story that reassures us that sons will come to themselves, that fathers will forgive. In other words, more than any parable, this one—in part, because of its domestic setting—has captured the imagination and emotions of readers apart from its figural functions, especially middle-class readers who come to the tale with a strong investment in family cohesiveness.

Returning to the concept of *rupture* itself, the mimesis of drinking (the drinking of Shannon and the more literal fathers and sons of these midcentury plays) conventionally stands for this breach or rupture in relationships, representing in miniature a kind of riotous living in faraway lands, even though this riotousness might take a son or husband no farther than the nearest tavern, the liquor cabinet across the room, or in the case of Wilder's Arthur with whom this study began, the front seat of the family car and his mother's explicit fears of future dissipation. Hickey and Evelyn, Frank and Georgie (*Country Girl*), Doc and Lola (*Sheba*), Brick and Maggie or Big Daddy (*Cat*), W.O. and Eliza (*Look Homeward*), Walter Lee and Mama Younger (*Raisin*), Jay and Mary (*All the Way Home*) all provide examples of ruptured relationships (parent/child; husband/wife) marked by the presence of a bottle. Drinking may or may not cause that rupture. If temperance melodramas conventionally saw it as a cause, many of these midcentury dramas just as conventionally perceive it as an effect, a sign of some deeper emotional problem. In any event in these American dramas the mimesis of drinking, a process that can be both social and communal, often signifies division and strife.

All the Way Home plays with this sense of rupture more self-consciously than many of these plays, using drink as a starting point and then moving beyond it to other concerns. Jay, the husband, is a reformed alcoholic, but even in his reformed state, his wife senses a gap or gulf between them, evident in differences over parenting and religion. I quote at some length from this work, because its examples are almost primers in the positions that undergird prodigals and their opposites, positions that, of course, parallel cultural narratives that America's middle class has more or less firmly embraced for the past two hundred years:

> *Jay:* It's kind of hard for a fellow to know where he stands around here. You tell him [his son, Rufus] to stay away from the older boys, and I tell

him to win 'em over. You say the surprise is up in the sky some place, I
say it's right here on earth. . . .
Mary: He's just a *child.*
Jay: All that about priests and *heaven*—! Sets my teeth on edge.
Mary: Oh Jay, sometimes I pray—
Jay: That's your privilege.
Mary: Now I can't say what I was going to say.
Jay: I'm listening.
Mary: But you're keeping your distance. As you always do when these
things come up. There's a space of about a hundred miles between us.[5]

The space between Jay and Mary is precisely that space of rupture or
potential rupture, the space that marks the paradigm of the prodigal.
Indeed a major focus of this paradigm is the monitoring of that space,
watching it shrink or grow, a process facilitated by the technology of
the box set with its carefully delineated walls and doors. A few
speeches later in this scene, after Jay has gone into another room (a
small departure), Mary stands in the center of her world ("in the
middle of the kitchen," lemonade pitcher in hand) and prays, while
her husband "bangs his pipe," symbol of masculinity, into an ashtray
in the other room:

> *Mary:* Oh Lord, in Thy mercy, Who can do all things, close this gulf
> between us. Make us one in *Thee* as we are in earthly wedlock. For Jesus'
> sake, Amen.[6]

One could not ask for a more concise image of American domestic
drama (midnineteenth or midtwentieth century) than this, of a woman
named Mary (mother/wife/saint/god) asking Jesus from the center of
her kitchen to bring her man back to her, even though he is only in
the next room.

Later in the play, Jay of course does go on his journey. Ironically,
however, his movement is back and forth between two homes, from
wife to parents and part way back, but the text makes it clear that
Jay loves the journey itself, loves this space in between, loves driving
alone on the road at night, loves freedom and distance as much as
Mary fears it. His journey suggests another set of images that reflect
both a vision of America itself (as a dream of space and escape, prodigal son of England and Europe) and a vision of the American male
(from Natty Bumppo and Daniel Boone to Sam Shepard and Chuck
Yeager).[7] Toward the end of the play, Mary summarizes and romanti-
cizes this male ethos as succinctly as she earlier did an image of
the American wife/mother. The rupture of death now dwarfs Jay's
relatively benign prodigality. Death forces Mary to examine those

forces that threaten to pull men away from home, forces marked more than anything else by the pull of desire, partially concealed here, but evident nonetheless. American drama celebrates the prodigal impulse as much if not more than it condemns it. The following is an excellent example of that celebration:

> He'd be gone for a night, or a day, or even two, and I'd know he hadn't touched a drop. And it wasn't any of the other things that come to a woman's mind. . . . Those are easy enemies. It was Market Square. And talking to country people about country secrets that go way on back. . . . And any one who'd sing his sad old songs with him. Or all night lunch rooms. What's an all night lunch room for, he'd say, except to sit all night. And drink coffee so strong it would burn your ribs. And it was locomotives, I suppose, and railroad people, and going fast, and even Charlie Chaplin. What's wrong with Charlie, he'd ask me. . . . He's so nasty, I'd say, so vulgar, with his nasty little cane, hooking up skirts. And Jay would laugh and go off to see Charlie Chaplin and *not come home*.[8]

This speech underscores the way in which plays often connect alcohol with a whole set of elements that the wife/mother perceives as threatening to her home. Beyond this it moves in contradictory directions. On the one hand, it reassures the spectator that, regardless of his faults, Jay was sexually faithful to his wife, and then it promptly transports Jay to the middle of a sensually rich environment: the songs, the night, the secrets of the country people, locomotives and railroads, and Charlie's cane. But ultimately it will not tell the spectator where Jay did go after the movies. *Iceman*, of course, does:

> *Hickey:* What I'd want was some tramp I could be myself with without being ashamed—someone I could tell a dirty joke to and she'd laugh.[9]

Someone, for example, who could enjoy a Charlie Chaplin movie. Jay is Hickey sanitized; the sense of rupture, ultimately dissolved by affection and grief:

> *Mary:* Why couldn't I let him have those things, whatever they were, if they meant something to him. Why can't I let him have them now. The dear. He always worked his way back.[10]

Evelyn, of course, could say the same for Hickey, Jay's darker brother. Arthur also worked his way back in *Happy Journey*, so, in their different ways do Jamie in *Misbegotten*, Edmund in *Journey*, Frank (*Country Girl*), Doc (*Sheba*), Richard (*Itch*), Brick (*Cat*), W.O. (*Look Homeward*), Walter Lee (*Raisin*), even George and Martha in

Woolf. American dramas like to bring their prodigals home again and again.

The convention of rupture is primarily spatial. It describes the central fact of prodigal space: the recognition of radical separation within the family unit. As Mary notes, the presence of a bottle often signals this separation, but other scenic elements conventionally appear, particularly as the bottle takes the shape of a tavern placed in opposition to the home. John Henry Raleigh in his study of O'Neill notes that this playwright's "greatest plays . . . take place, respectively, in a decayed bar and in a middle-class home":

> These two habitations were the polar places of existence in O'Neill's world: the bar signifying drink and song, artificial conviviality, penitential outpourings, the racial and cultural melting pot, the masculine world, and the world of down-and-outers. . . . The house, on the other hand, was the place where memory, etched into the walls, the furniture, the books, was almost tangible, the place where the family was thrown back on itself and each member on himself or herself with an explosive power.[11]

Although Raleigh writes eloquently of these two "polar places of existence" in O'Neill, this scenic dichotomy is characteristic not only of O'Neill's oeuvre but of American domestic drama in general. Earlier in the same paragraph, Raleigh describes what for him is the essential O'Neill image: "the grieving woman and the lonely self of mankind," the two figures that inhabit home and tavern.[12] This image is the visual equivalent of rupture, of radical separation that this chapter describes: Mary waiting in her hotel room for Tyrone to be dumped at her door, while still on their honeymoon; Josie waiting all dressed up for a drunken Jamie to return from the inn; Evelyn waiting for Hickey's return after yet another periodical; Richard Miller's mother worrying and waiting for her son's first drunken homecoming in *Ah, Wilderness!* But for all of these quintessential O'Neill images we might also substitute Linda Loman darning her old stockings while Willy offers a pair of new ones to the woman in the hotel room, Willy's own joy at Biff's return from his wanderings, Big Daddy and Maggie hoping that Brick will sober up, Mary waiting for Jay to come home from the Charlie Chaplin film, as well as the wives and mothers of America's temperance melodramas wondering when, if ever, their drunkard husbands and sons will return to them from the local tavern or inn. The convention, of course, has deep roots in literature and mythology. Who can hear the phrase "grieving woman and the lonely self of mankind" and not think of Penelope and Ulysses. But most noteworthy is not this image's mere presence in American drama so much as its weedlike proliferation, a proliferation that crowds out so many alternative scenes and concerns.

These conventions of rupture suggest a certain landscape, a prodigal space: the dramatic world in which male prodigals move, a world created by both scenic designers and the words of the text, a world both seen and imagined. We might easily diagram the conventions of this space, just as artists have sketched the story of the prodigal from the Middle Ages to the present. For American domestic drama, such a diagram would begin with a place called *home:* smoke curling from the chimney, tree and garden at its side (to remind us of our agrarian origins) with a church nearby and a cemetery for children lost in infancy or at birth. If we fold back the walls of this home, as dramatic realism with its facility for the representation of interior spaces is wont to do, we find within a parent or spouse waiting for a son or husband (much less frequently daughter or wife) to come home. The presence of those who wait is so constant there, they become part of the furnishings. The door from the domestic interior to the outside world marks, literally and metaphorically, the point at which separation is made manifest. With few exceptions dramatic convention traditionally encourages men to cross this threshold, just as it generally discourages women.

Opposite an image of home, this diagram would locate a tavern, inn, or bar (*nonhome*), typically located in the city (classically in New York or San Francisco or New Orleans), with a hotel room conveniently attached for quick, impersonal sex. Here a folded-back exterior wall would reveal something like the setting for O'Neill's *Iceman:* a kind of "home" that has as its most distinguishing characteristic its status as the place that is *not* home and *not* work, being instead a fraternal, sometimes vaguely homoerotic, or in any event homosocial, alternative to the complications and responsibilities of family life and the work ethic. These *nonhomes* provide for nourishment, companionship, and sexual release by reassigning domestic functions, usually using several people to do what had been the wife or mother's job alone. At one extreme *nonhome* also includes the encounter with the swine: scenes of deprivation and poverty, of famine and rags. It takes the prodigal back to a place among the animals, to a fundamental earthiness that we often do not want to acknowledge. Harry's bar in *Iceman* incorporates this element without the change of scene that the parable requires. The place of the prodigal's riotous living also becomes the end-of-the-line. Its occupants laze about like pigs in the mud. The image of famine is inherent in their corporate shortage of funds, concretized in their worn clothes and in the "desiccated" ruins of "dust-laden bread and mummified ham or cheese" that adorns their tables.[13]

Between these two nodes (*home* and *non-home*), we find movement and open space, usually drawn as highway and automobile, as in Willy's car in *Salesman* or Jay's in *All the Way Home;* in our western mythos, as trail and horse;[14] in O'Neill's early plays and in Edmund's famous fourth act monologue from *Journey,* as ship and sea; and in Mary's monologue (*All the Way Home*), train tracks and locomotives. All ultimately move on a circular course with the spectator's perception of them dependent on the attitudes of individual characters and on whether they are carrying the prodigal away or bringing him back. These texts celebrate the open road as a male domain in opposition to the stasis of home. Work, in general, takes the husband/son out of the home and onto this road unless the work is home-based, once the norm but, as already noted, in the nineteenth and twentieth centuries increasingly a rarity. Occupations that stress this tension between home/stasis and work/movement include being a travel guide (*Iguana*), touring as an actor (*Journey*), riding in rodeos (*Fool for Love*), shipping on a freighter or sailing ship (*Long Voyage Home, Beyond the Horizon, Journey*) and, preeminently, working as a traveling salesman, a calling almost invariably linked to prodigality (*Iceman, Salesman, Dark at the Top of the Stairs*). This rough sketch, of course, simplifies conventions surrounding the concept of rupture, but it represents the basic spatial elements with which this paradigm plays.

Within this space rupture signals a departure from authority figures and social norms. The prodigal leaves behind parents or a spouse as well as the routines of daily life to explore other places, other ways of living and doing business. Tom Cheesman in his discussion of the parable and related ballad traditions sees the space of this rupture in terms of an oedipal revolt: "The son wishes his father were dead, and acts as if he were dead in order to create an independent existence and an autonomous identity (in relation to paternity, kinship and community) for himself."[15] Cheesman also observes that in conventional versions of the story this revolt fails and that the father, "standing for the authority of all father-figures," plays the role of the "benevolent patriarch" who "generously restores" the son to his former position.[16] This return, as noted earlier, makes the parable fundamentally conservative, an affirmation of the social order. The structure takes son or husband away from the family but also conventionally brings him back, more aware than the elder brother will ever be of the importance of home and certainly more tightly bound to the family structure than before he left. This study emphasizes the persistence of that return, the desire to bring prodigals home (whether to parents or spouses) again and again in exercises of forgiveness and understanding that reaffirm the family unit. It argues that even though specific plays may severely attenuate these processes they still persist. The following section—on potential—describes this persistence and the extremes to which it will go, but the conservatism of this moment of return cannot entirely obliterate the radicalness of the departure, a moment that Cheesman describes as a murder.

Just as male drunkenness may question as well as celebrate constructions of male identity, so might uses of this paradigm call into question some of the roles it seems to perpetuate by the very intensity of the ruptures they depict, ruptures so intense that final images of consolation cannot erase them. In other words just as these plays may confirm the power of fathers and particular versions of the family, they may also question them, however tentatively. Between fathers and sons, they reveal a level of animosity not previously seen. Between husbands and wives, they underscore the inability of a married relationship to satisfy its participants. The tension here may be comparable to that which Northrop Frye describes between comedies emphasizing the figure who stands in the way of lovers, "the blocking characters" (here comparable to rupture) and those emphasizing the romantic union of the lovers, "scenes of discovery and reconciliation" (here comparable to potential).[17] In like manner some family dramas will emphasize rupture, others potential, most some combination of the two. *Iceman, Journey, Moon for the Misbegotten, Streetcar, Cat on a Hot Tin Roof* and even *The Drunkard* all communicate images of profoundly fragmented families: Hickey has killed his wife; Parritt has sold his mother; Mary Tyrone wanders the upstairs while her men sink into a drunken haze; James Tyrone sleeps with a prostitute atop his mother's coffin; Stanley rapes Blanche, while his wife carries his child; Brick withdraws into an alcoholic cocoon; and Edward Middleton, in delirium, sprawls on the ground. Despite various efforts at recuperation described in the following section, these images persist, just as, for example, images of Lear's madness persist after his sanity has been restored or images of Denmark's disarray after Fortinbras's final speech: closure does not banish memory. My argument is that American domestic drama traditionally wants to find a way to end with some version of "Home, Sweet Home," but that this music cannot quite drown out what has gone before. Although we try to fix the family, something is not quite working in the way it should: even though the prodigal son comes home, life in that household will never quite be the same.[18]

If the prodigal son suggests oedipal revolt, the prodigal husband suggests a revolt, often quasi-romantic, against the kind of White, middle-class families that arose in the nineteenth and twentieth centuries. In many instances the prodigal finds this kind of family no more acceptable than do many of its contemporary critics. He rebels against its stasis, its strictures, its economic responsibilities. He does not want to be married to an angel with little angel children. He wants a life much more fluid and sensual. In *The Hearts of Men: American Dreams and the Flight from Commitment*, Barbara Ehreneich discovers, particularly in the mass media, various versions of this male discontent with the traditional American family in the years immediately following World War II. She makes a number of relevant points: 1) that in the 1950s and 1960s "adult masculinity was indistinguishable from the breadwinner role"; 2) that the adult male who failed to perform that role faced a number of sanctions from charges of immaturity and infantilism to "the taint of homosexuality," with fear of the latter being used to keep "heterosexual men in line as husbands and breadwinners"; 3) that in the face of these expectations and despite these threats a male revolt occurs in the postwar years, including among its manifestations a critique of conformity and other-directedness (Reisman's *The Lonely Crowd*), the Beat movement (further discussed below), the Human Potential and Counterculture movements of the late sixties, and perhaps most importantly, *Playboy* and the *Playboy* philosophy ("when the articles railed against the responsibilities of marriage, there were the nude torsos to reassure" men "that the alternative was still within the bounds of heterosexuality"); 4) that although this revolt "has roots in a narcissistic consumer culture, it is equally rooted in the tradition of liberal humanism, that inspires feminism" and "can be seen as a blow against a system of social control that operates to make men unquestioning and obedient employees"; 5) that this revolt parallels a revolt waged by women, the feminist movement, but that men, at least economically, have been more successful in achieving its ends than have women; and finally 6) that "male culture seems to have abandoned the breadwinner role without overcoming the sexist attitudes that role has perpetuated: on the one hand, the expectation of female nurturance and submissive service as a right; on the other hand, a misogynist contempt for women as 'parasites' and entrappers of men."[19]

Ehreneich's study suggests that in various guises the dynamics of what I term rupture and she calls male revolt were fundamental features of White, middle-class, postwar American life. Whether the latter explains the proliferation of prodigals in American drama or merely represents parallel manifestations of these narrative conventions, I cannot say. But Ehreneich's work does provide a sociological and mass media context for the figure of the prodigal in American domestic drama. The prodigal and the playboy have much in common: particularly freedom (or its illusion) *and* consumerism. Ehreneich notes that in the late fifties *Playboy* magazine "fattened" itself "on advertisements for imported liquor, stereo sets, men's colognes, luxury cars and fine clothes": the accoutrements of a prodigal lifestyle.[20]

Finally although prodigality and rupture often involves wayward, weak, foolish behavior, this same sort of behavior also often plays a central role in narratives of adventure and self-discovery with their passages into adulthood or some higher level of awareness. Nancy Corson Carter discusses this double perception:

> The language of the parable . . . emphasizes the sexual aspect of prodigality—the prodigal is described as one who "squandered his property in loose living"; his elder brother accuses him to their father as one "who has devoured your living with harlots." Yet this is only one perspective. . . . The prodigal has many qualities we admire: his "drivenforthness" includes the initiative of a rugged individualist, the risk-taking and sensual drive of a romantic, the joie-de-vivre of a "good buddy."[21]

Although these remarks speak to the image of the prodigal son, they also apply to an almost hidden admiration for the prodigal husband as someone brave enough to break the bonds of an imposed bourgeois domesticity. Scenes of rupture articulate various degrees of discontent with the families we inherit both as children and as spouses. Even though scenes of homecoming tend to displace this desire to depart, it still persists.

Second Characteristic of the Prodigal: Potential

In addition to conventions of rupture, the prodigal requires a second element to be fully recognizable. This element is *potential*, in particular, the potential for reform, for coming home again, which, of course, is also in force whenever we sense that it has been sacrificed or endangered. In terms of rupture, this is the potential for reunion, for an end to separation, and for making whole what has been fragmented, often signified by an embrace: filial, erotic, or both. In Arthur's instance (*Happy Journey*), this means a chance to cry and make up over a handful of hot dogs, to return to his mother's side from his exile in the front seat of the car. In Hickey's case the text pushes this potential to the point of absurdity, as if a few days after having killed the fatted calf, the younger son has pawned his ring and robe to return to the whores, to return to the swine, to come home again, and then repeat this process again and again and again. Evelyn and Hickey seem caught in a ruthless cycle of potentiality. With regard to a second prodigal in *Iceman*, Don Parritt, we may agree with John Raleigh that he is a moral leper, that he "can never be forgiven and pardoned, even temporarily,"[22] but in his and Hickey's instance, the text seems to be deliberately playing with the limits of forgiveness (as perceived by the character himself, by other characters, and by the spectator), exploring the terrors of a potential for reform and the nature of the unpardonable. When Peter asked Jesus how often he should forgive one who sins against him, the well-known answer was "seventy times seven." *Iceman* wants to know about "seventy times seven" plus one, about the potential for reform, for coming home, at that point in a prodigal's career. As if to escape the convention, Hickey tries to eliminate potentiality by killing Evelyn. This attempt works on two levels; first by eliminating the source of forgiveness, and second by engaging in an action that is apparently unpardonable. Hickey and Parritt both seem to have crossed into a land from which they cannot go home. They are, however, still within the paradigm, but in an area marked more by the absence of potentiality than by its presence, an absence near the center of the play, near the center of a national drama that is afraid that time and Manifest Destiny have run out, that the rupture between self and home, whatever form it takes, will finally be too great for even an ever-optimistic country to cross.

To better understand how central these two characters are to the paradigm of the prodigal, I want to explore further the function of potential in prodigal drama in terms of the central event of the narrative, homecoming, and its principal variant, homecoming denied. To begin with *potentiality* means that the prodigal must not do what both Parritt and Hickey have apparently done: commit the unpardonable sin. In Matthew, Jesus describes this sin as "blasphemy against the Spirit,"[23] which, appropriately enough, some theologies perceive not as literal blasphemy but as prolonged resistance to the ministrations of the Holy Spirit, a hardening of the heart over a period of time to the voice that calls the sinner home. In American domestic drama, however, middle-class norms, not theology, decide what is and is not pardonable. In this context, a *potential for reform* conventionally and effectively means that the prodigal must not have committed any crime or sin that an American audience could not readily forgive. His sins must not have been so great as to prevent him from beginning again the life he once left behind, usually without the complications of the law and jail. In the parable, the youngest son fears this will not be the case, but a major point of the story—the one to which the eldest brother most objects—is that life can return to something like normal. This requires either an enormous fund of grace or a certain limit on the kinds of transgressions allowed. The latter, as has been the point of this paragraph, is the course American drama most frequently follows.

Although texts obviously enjoy playing with an audience's levels of tolerance, the standard is that the need to forgive should not extend beyond what might be called the three w's of American drama, particularly in the immediate post–World War II era: *whiskey, womanizing,* and *waste.* So persistent is the connection between these moral misdemeanors and prodigal behavior that whenever we encounter one or more of these elements within a domestic drama, we might well expect that prodigality will have some part, large or small, within the structure of that work. Any one of these three elements can serve as a trigger for the entire paradigm, that is, be the part that suggests and stands for the whole. *Death of a Salesman* (1949), *Dark at the Top of the Stairs* (1957), and *Come Blow Your Horn* (1961), for example, all have prodigals, even though these plays substitute one form of potentially pardonable male desire (the man with a woman) for another (the man with a bottle). *Salesman,* for example, has, like O'Neill's *Journey,* three prodigals. The first is Willy, the husband and father whose prodigality is underscored by his job as an itinerant salesman; he is the philandering, but relatively sober, husband of a long-suffering wife. His opposite in *Journey* is Tyrone, whose prodigality is underscored by his career as an itinerant actor; he is the alcoholic but sexually faithful husband of a long-suffering wife. The second prodigal is Biff, the son who goes on a long journey. He is relatively sober and chaste, but his father perceives him as a prodigal, because he has wasted his natural gifts and talents. His rough equivalent is Edmund, also a veteran of long journeys to far-off countries, who is also perceived by the father as having wasted his talents, now being wasted away by disease. The third, of course, is Happy, the son who might, like Jamie, play the role of the responsible brother that stays at home but instead wastes time, money, and energy on relatively empty pleasures. Happy and Biff, as do Jamie and Edmund, split between themselves the qualities of the prodigal son, sharing them as well with prodigal fathers.[24] One of the ways in which we identify these figures as prodigals is their participation in actions that conventionally cause a sense of rupture within the family but that can also be readily forgiven, especially if, within the terms of the convention, the prodigal experiences a sincere change of heart.

Whiskey, womanizing, and waste denote a fairly narrow range of male behavior, relatively acceptable and forgivable, more limiting than they may at first seem. For example in its most conventional incarnation, this paradigm scrupulously avoids almost any form of sexual activity more unusual than a one night stand with a usually nameless woman. For a son or a husband to participate in a relatively mechanical, emotionally uncommitted sexual act is conventionally forgivable, but he must not, as a rule, corrupt children, virgins, or young men. *Salesman* plays with this convention in having Happy tell Biff that he has just bedded a young woman about to be married, breaking a code that the father no doubt respects. Williams plays with it in *Cat* by introducing the possibility that the other woman is a man and then offering an image of a father willing to welcome his son home regardless of his sexual orientation. Axelrod's *Itch* offers yet another variation (fantasy), one that turns on making the "other woman" into the "girl next door." The interest here is in rather timidly raising the age of the man and lowering the age of the woman/child in directions ultimately obvious. None of these variants would work as they do, however, were it not for the clear distinctions made by figures like Jamie Tyrone, one who, like American drama in general, knows the difference between the girl next door (Josie) and the "blonde pig": the woman without a name or, in this instance, even a physical presence, who is, in this instance, painfully dehumanized as well.

Conventionally prodigals are also not allowed to fall in love with this "other" nameless woman, perhaps because this tends to humanizes her and therefore complicates the spectator's feelings of allegiance. Once the prodigal perceives a particular woman as more than an object for the quick satisfaction of desire, the entire paradigm becomes confused, although not necessarily to its detriment. Such is the case in August Wilson's *Fences* (1985), an excellent example of the persistence of the prodigal in American drama. It plays with the paradigm by giving the husband something more than a sexual interest in the other woman who takes him away from his home. The result is a more interesting protagonist, but this also means that the second woman must both live and conveniently die offstage in order to finally return the play to a focus on the relationship between the prodigal husband and his ultimately forgiving wife. Adultery and prodigality overlap only when the spouse's liaisons are relatively loveless and rather mechanical in their repetition.

A *potential for reform*, for *coming home again*, usually means that with these certain carefully defined weaknesses (womanizing, whiskey, waste) the conventional prodigal will be what Fiedler in *Love and Death in the American Novel* calls a "Good Bad Boy": someone flawed, but finally solid; weak perhaps, but not a criminal.[25] He may waste his own fortune, but within the main line of the convention, he will rarely appropriate another's. *The Drunkard* clearly demonstrates this principle, even though it predates post–World War II American drama by a hundred years: the villain Cribbs tempts the drunkard Middleton to forge a check, but he refuses. As a drunkard Middleton sinks quite low in life but not so low as to steal another man's money. The fear that the prodigal will turn criminal is primary. In this instance, however, it is not realized. This absence of crime and sedition applies as well to prodigals such as Doc in *Sheba*, Frank in *Country Girl*, Jamie in *Journey* and *Misbegotten*, Jay in *All the Way Home*, and to almost every protagonist within the plays mentioned thus far, even to most of the denizens of Harry's bar, whose worst offenses have been participation in the almost normative, institutional graft of urban life.

Prodigals are almost by definition good members of the middle class who have not yet quite found perfection: a successful hardware salesman, actors with at least the potential to be near the top of their profession, a chiropractor who might have been a doctor, an athlete/announcer, a small businessman and craftsman/artist, a lawyer, a member of the clergy. Plays of prodigality are then about, among other things, the perfectibility of the American male. Even if the prodigal does not take advantage of the potential for reform, his character will still stand as a model for good citizenship, precisely because it admits no more than a few carefully prescribed faults within a dramatic figure who does not fundamentally challenge the established socioeconomic structure: spending one's money on women and liquor is not, after all, a renunciation of commercial capitalism, even if it represents a temporary vacation from its rigors. Relevant in this context are Paul Goodman's comments with regard to the protagonists of Jack Kerouac's celebration of American prodigality, *On the Road:*

> One is stunned by how conventional and law-fearing these lonely middle-class fellows are. They dutifully get legal marriages and divorces. The hint of a "gang-bang" makes them impotent. They never masturbate or perform homosexual acts. . . . To disobey a cop is "all hell." Their idea of crime is the petty shoplifting of ten-year-olds stealing cigarettes or of teen-agers joyriding in other people's cars. . . . Their behavior is a conformity *plus royaliste que le roi.*[26]

This description brings us back to Hickey and Parritt and the question of their potentiality. Prior to killing his wife, Hickey would have fit within the set of characters described in the preceding paragraphs. Prior to killing his mother (by sending her to jail), Parritt's wasting of his money on prostitutes would have put him in the foregoing group as well. But in the dramatic present in which *Iceman* operates, the potential for Hickey or Parritt to go home again seems to reside only in the past, although the audience may not realize this until the climax of their parallel confessions.

In this Hickey and Parritt introduce a major variant that nevertheless resides within the paradigm's core: the prodigal who cannot go home, a dark version of the type for whom prodigality is the first step on a descent into hell, the first step in "a rake's progress." I mentioned above Middleton's refusal to commit a crime and his subsequent reformation in *The Drunkard*. There exists, however, a second kind of temperance melodrama in which the drunkard/prodigal never reforms, a version that chronicles instead one long, sickening slide into crime, murder, and usually madness or death.[27] In these works such as Taylor's *The Bottle* (1847) or Jerrold's *Fifteen Years of a Drunkard's Life* (1828), the crime that damns the drunkard is the murder of a wife/mother, the same crime that damns Hickey and Parritt. Indeed America's archetypal villain, Simon Legree, also describes a descent from prodigal son, potentially reformable, to villain bound for hell. His story, like those of Hickey and Parritt, is also one of *rupture, potential,* and *potential lost:*

> *Legree:* In early childhood a fair-haired woman has led me, at the sound of Sabbath bells, to worship and to pray. . . . Boisterous, unruly and tyrannical, I despised all her counsel, and would have none of her reproof, at an early age, broke from her to seek my fortune on the sea [*rupture*]. I never came home but once after that; and then my mother, with the yearning of a heart that must love something, and had nothing else to love, clung to me, and sought with passionate prayers and entreaties to win me from a life of sin. . . . My heart inly relented [*potential*]; there was a conflict, but sin got the victory. . . . I drank and swore, was wilder and more brutal that ever. And one night, when my mother, in the last agony of her despair, knelt at my feet, I spurned her from me, threw her senseless on the floor [*metaphorical, if not literal, murder; potential lost*], and with brutal curses fled to my ship.[28]

Legree goes to his ship; Parritt flies from the East Coast to the West; Hickey walks to Harry's bar. All three are prodigals apparently cut off from the possibility of ever going home.

Grace, however, by which I mean "unmerited favor" combined with aesthetic invention, can amaze. A final twist can return the son or husband to his home, even if he has violated the normal boundaries of reformation. Robert Turner in describing the influence of Renaissance prodigal husband plays (e.g., *How a Man May Choose a Good Wife from a Bad*, 1602; *The Fair Maid of Bristowe*, 1603–4; *The Dutch*

Courtesan, 1603) on *All's Well That Ends Well* discusses the ways in which these works often force a husband to undergo a scene of purgation to justify his moral regeneration. To this end in "almost all the plays the hero is accused of murder, he is tried and found guilty, and just as he gives up his life, the murdered victim appears very much alive to prove the falsity of the case."[29] Here a potential for reform grows out of a distinction between "appearance and reality," along with the effect of that distinction on the prodigal's character. The question at hand is whether Hickey and Parritt might not in some way participate in an American version of this Renaissance convention that in one way or another resurrects the dead, especially whether or not we perceive them as experiencing significant regenerative change through traumatic suffering and whether or not potentiality in some form arises from its absence. The answer, I think, is *yes* or, at least, *perhaps*. For Parritt the peace of death is a sort of homecoming, a return to the mother as the great unconsciousness, a return based on choice born of suffering. For Hickey the return to illusion ("You know I must have been insane, don't you Governor?"[30]) is also a kind of final homecoming, a return to the house of illusions that believed in a continual *potential for reform*. By affirming his love, Hickey implicitly denies his responsibility for Evelyn's death and, in a sense, brings her back to life. His, even more than Parritt's dénouement, is a contemporary, albeit ironic, version of the Renaissance convention, mixing *rupture*, *potential*, *potential lost*, and *potential regained*, as Hickey exhausts the parable, exhausts the homecoming, exhausts all but the last remains of love and forgiveness, and maybe even that.

As in these instances, potentiality, and this is one of its primary strengths as a dramatic device, allows for scenes of recognition and reversal, scenes central to the genres of tragedy, comedy, melodrama, and the well-made play. Key moments in these narratives of prodigality are often those in which the prodigal undergoes a process of recognition or realization and then decides in one fashion or another to attempt the return home. Just as rupture signals a departure from the status quo, potentiality involves a return to it, an acceptance of authority, of social institution, and hegemonic culture. As noted above Cheesman, Beck, and Lieblein all underscore the relative or at least potential conservatism of the parable in their discussions of its uses by various artists.[31] In visual renderings of the parable, equally popular as the scenes of riotous living were those featuring the prodigal's return, that is, scenes of the father's embrace. In parent-child dramas, this moment confirms the wisdom of the adult world and the folly of the child, forever putting one in the other's debt, confirming the power of the father and maintaining the childhood of the son. In spousal dramas a husband's return conventionally signals the value of marriage and family as opposed to alternative social arrangements or an individualism that might more successfully meet the needs of either the husband or the wife. Muted but relatively straightforward versions of this dénouement occur in plays like *The Country Girl, Dark at the Top of the Stairs, The Seven Year Itch,* and *A Raisin in the Sun.* Considerably more problematic reunions take place in *A Streetcar Named Desire, Cat on a Hot Tin Roof* and *Who's Afraid of Virginia Woolf?* As noted above, more optimistic versions of the homecoming read the return as the end of an upward spiral. The prodigal comes home a person changed for the better; a new level of understanding is reached. Beck uses the word "integration" to describe this change, referring to the "resolution of internal contradictions."[32]

At this point similarities between the potentiality of the paradigm and Victor Turner's discussion of the potentiality inherent in rites of passage deserve at least a brief comment.[33] In *From Ritual to Theatre,* Turner describes three phases in a rite of passage (*separation, transition,* and *incorporation*) based on the work of Arnold van Gennep in the early twentieth century. A number of parallels exist between these phases and the parable. Rites of *separation,* for example, often involve "reversals or inversion of things," such as, in the case of the parable, a son taking his inheritance before his time and then departing from home.[34] Separation also inaugurates a different sense of time (sacred, as opposed to secular) and changes in status. Although the prodigal's change in status is self-evident, it may seem a stretch to think of "riotous living" or extreme impoverishment as sacred, but this has more to do with Puritanical notions of the sacred than correspondences between the parable and initiation rites. Certainly in collecting his inheritance and going to a new land, the prodigal departs from a daily secular routine, from a daily rhythm of life and work, entering a radically different temporal mode. In the parable the son leaves behind the father's time for a time of his own, just as in *Iceman,* Hickey leaves work and family time to embark on one of his "periodicals."

The *transition* phase of the initiation rite corresponds to the prodigal's sojourn in the far country, including the trip to the swine. According to Turner it comprises a passage "through a period and area of ambiguity, a sort of social limbo which has few (though sometimes these are most crucial) of the attributes of either the preceding or subsequent profane social statuses or cultural states."[35] With respect to initiation rites, the far country of the parable is a marginal or liminal space: a threshold (i.e., "limen") between one category of experience (the prodigal's life before he leaves home) and another (the prodigal's life after he returns home). Rites of passage often have geographical coordinates as well, although, as with versions of the prodigal described above, they may involve as little as a step forward or as much as "a long, exacting pilgrimage and the crossing of many national frontiers."[36] Liminal periods also foster communitas. Its analog is found in illustrations that show the prodigal and his "friends," male and female, seated around a table, eating, drinking, and listening to music. Together they experience a certain communitas, even if it lasts only as long as the prodigal's spending money. *Iceman* is again exemplary, particularly in terms of the breakdown in communal feeling once the occupants of Harry's bar try to leave that liminal space and return to the society that exists beyond the doors of the tavern.

The movement into the animal world, into the realm of the swine, also parallels aspects of liminal phases in which initiands "are stripped of names and clothing, smeared with the common earth rendered indistinguishable from animals."[37] Disorder and antistructure (whether of the banquet, of drinking, of sexuality, of a bacchanalia, of feeding with the swine even) characterizes this stage in general as opposed to the structure and order of pre- and postliminal states. That disorder, of course, also finds itself in the drunkenness with which this study began. Many liminal or quasi-liminal rites involve drinking and intoxication, such as charivaris, fiestas, and Saturnalias. Transition also often features the ritual death of an old self and the birth of a new one, just as the prodigal's father proclaims on his son's return that one who was dead is now alive again.

Finally the prodigal's return, the father's embrace, and the killing of the fatted calf correspond to rites of *incorporation:* "the return of the subjects to their new, relatively stable, well-defined positions in the total society."[38] As with many versions of the prodigal narrative, Turner notes that this "usually represents an enhanced status, a stage further along life's culturally prefabricated road."[39] With respect to this chapter, *separation* and *transition* correspond most obviously to the notion of *rupture; incorporation* to *potential.* Turner, however, stresses that transitional or liminal phases (far countries, "riotous livings," places among the animals) are not just places of rupture and letting off steam but also places of learning, of trying on new or different behaviors. Temporally he refers to them as an "interval, however brief, . . . when the past is momentarily negated, suspended, or abrogated, and the future has not yet begun, an instant of pure *potentiality.*"[40] Although this chapter has stressed the role of *potentiality* in homecomings, Turner's models reminds us that it also plays a role in all departures.

As rite of passage, the narrative of the prodigal has served as an

initiation myth for commercial capitalism in the sixteenth and seventeenth centuries and for the modern American family from the late
eighteenth century to the present. As initiation myth the parable helps
to maintain the status quo while allowing for periods of play and
variation. At the same time, the popularity of the prodigal narrative
also relates to another phenomenon that Turner describes in the same
essay: the creation in industrial societies of a distinction between *work*
and *leisure* time, a discrimination foreign to preindustrial, tribal, and
agrarian societies that primarily differentiate *not* between work and
play but between "sacred *work* and profane *work*."[41] With this change
leisure time activities take on many of the characteristics of liminality
but are different enough to merit the label liminoid: resembling the
liminal "without being identical" with it.[42] Liminoid phenomena
(e.g., literature, drama, sport) tend to emphasize commodification,
the individual, play (as opposed to sacred work), and, most significantly, *choice* (as opposed to obligation). Turner specifically cites bars
and pubs as permanent liminoid settings. From this perspective the
popularity of the parable confirms not just its role as an initiation rite
for entry into capitalist life but also as a microcosm for the changes
industrialism has wrought (i.e., the prodigal as an embodiment of
consumerism, of leisure culture, of a liminoid existence). But even
here sharp distinctions do not come easily: certainly it seems as if the
prodigal *chooses* to leave home and the husband *chooses* to visit the
tavern. Neither are under the kind of obligation felt by initiands in
tribal societies, yet the prodigal's departure has about it a certain
inevitability, just as within the construct of American masculinity
drink, drunkenness, and the trip to the local tavern come close to
being obligatory rites of passage.[43] Whether strictly liminal or liminoid, narratives of prodigality clearly resonate with the structure
of initiation rites, with processes of separation, transition, and
incorporation.

A SET OF PRODIGALS

Based on these conventions surrounding notions of *rupture* and
potential, here then is a set of prodigals drawn from plays written
during this immediate postwar period. This set builds upon and adds
to the list of plays at the beginning of chapter 1, including, for example, some works in which male prodigality appears without a heavy
reliance on the image of a man with a bottle. The plays and characters
listed below differ from one another in many ways, but they also
constitute a cluster of works (illustrative and obviously noncompre-

hensive) in which the prodigal assumes a substantial, often predominant, role. These examples have been and will continue to be my primary sources in endeavoring to understand the shape and function of this phenomenon:

Hickey (son/husband), Don Parritt (son), *The Iceman Cometh*, 1946 (also, Jimmy Tomorrow, Harry Hope, and others),

Stanley Kowalski (husband), *A Streetcar Named Desire*, 1947,

Jamie Tyrone (son), *A Moon for the Misbegotten*, 1947,

Willy (husband), Biff (son), and Happy (son) Loman, *Death of a Salesman*, 1949,

Frank Elgin (husband), *The Country Girl*, 1950,

Doc (husband), *Come Back, Little Sheba*, 1950,

Richard Sherman (husband), *The Seven Year Itch*, 1952,

Brick Pollitt (son/husband), *Cat on a Hot Tin Roof*, 1955,

James (husband), Jamie (son), and Edmund (son) Tyrone, *Long Day's Journey into Night*, 1956 (secondarily both Mary and James's fathers function as prodigal figures in the past),

W.O. (husband) and Ben (son) Gant, *Look Homeward, Angel*, 1957 (Eugene Gant's departure at the end of the play with an inheritance from father, metaphorical, and his older brother, literal, is that of a newborn prodigal for a far-off land),

Rubin Flood (husband), *The Dark at the Top of the Stairs*, 1957,

Walter Lee Younger (son/husband), *A Raisin in the Sun*, 1959,

Jay Follet (son/husband) and his brother, Ralph (son/husband), *All the Way Home*, 1960,

Shannon (metaphorically son and spouse), *The Night of the Iguana*, 1961,

Alan (son) and Buddy (son) Baker, *Come Blow Your Horn*, 1961,

George (husband) and Martha (daughter/wife), *Who's Afraid of Virginia Woolf?*, 1962.[44]

Each of these characters creates or contributes to a rupture in a relationship between the prodigal and a spouse or parent. Each has, in one way or another, gone into a far country. Each has also had, at one point or another, the chance to come home.

The final selection on this list does, however, require some comment on the ability or general inability of American drama, at least until recently, to imagine a female prodigal without seeing at the same time and more profoundly the image of a fallen woman or a failed wife/mother. In the language of this chapter, *potential* belongs more readily to male than female dramatic figures, at least in terms of postwar New York–produced domestic drama. Blanche Dubois, for example, has many of the characteristics of the prodigal (drinking, sexual activity, the wasting of an inheritance), but the text denies her the possibility of return, of redemption. Indeed Stanley's ability to return to Stella, however tentatively, and Blanche's unacceptability to Mitch once he learns of her past clarifies the meaning of *potentiality*. Stanley can be forgiven or at least reintegrated into the family on some level; Blanche cannot. The example of *Streetcar* is harsh and horrible, a negative exemplar: female prodigals, some anyway, are not *reformed*, they are *raped*. Within the economy of this play, once used, the woman, unlike the man, is no longer redeemable.[45] Williams's playscript uses echoes of the parable to tell a story of violence and deep pain, of sadness and loss.[46]

Mary Tyrone, on the other hand, can come home again, if she is able. (As with male prodigals, chemical dependency is more readily forgivable than sexual irregularities.) Indeed the attitude of the Tyrone men toward her parallels that of other mothers and wives toward alcoholic men in that they perceive her as caught in a struggle between weakness and will power:

> *Edmund:* Mama! Please Listen! I want to ask you something! You—You're only just started. You can still stop. You've got the will power! We'll all help you. I'll do anything! Won't you, Mama?[47]

Yet her prodigal behavior is primarily a function of Tyrone's initial prodigality, of being forced into a life on the road that denied her a home. That denial along with, ironically, her husband's miserliness, contributed, more than any other factor, to her addiction. Even though she has in a sense joined the ranks of the three men in her life, we and they tend finally to regard her as more of a victim of prodigality than a prodigal herself—a failed or exhausted wife/mother. To a degree this relationship is communicated by the similarities and the differences between morphine and whiskey: in her weakness/addiction/intoxication, Mary is like the men, but she is also clearly different.

Albee's Martha perhaps comes the closest of these three characters to being a female prodigal within a work that enjoys playing with illusions (in this context, a synonym for dramatic conventions) both about and within the American family. She has, for example, a series of speeches that would in almost any other American play be given not to the wife but to the prodigal husband. George plays the role conventionally reserved for the long-suffering wife:

> *Martha:* [referring to George] . . . who has made the hideous, the hurting, the insulting mistake of loving me and must be punished for it. George and Martha: sad, sad, sad.
> *Nick (Puzzled):* Sad.

Martha: . . . who tolerates, which is intolerable; who is kind, which is cruel; who understands, which is beyond comprehension. . . .
Nick: George and Martha: sad, sad, sad.
Martha: Some day . . . hah! some night . . . some stupid, liquor-ridden night . . . I will go too far . . . and I'll either break the man's back . . . or push him off for good . . . which is what I deserve.[48]

Martha's relationship with her father also suggests tension between the role of the good daughter and a prodigal daughter. Nevertheless she is also the wife who must live through her husband's career, a woman who must create a child because she cannot perceive of herself as complete without one. Like Blanche she reveals the tension between the role of the prodigal and the difficulty much of American drama has had imagining a woman inhabiting this role. The marginality of the female prodigal is, of course, underscored by an understanding of her as a variant of a male form, by the presence of this apologia itself, a sort of footnote to the official list. Finally even more ironic in this context is the suggestion that Blanche (Williams's own suggestion) and Martha are not actually women at all but men in drag. What interests me about this proposition is not so much its validity in terms of authorial intention but the way in which it "solves" the problem of anomalous (i.e., prodigal) female behavior ("Those aren't really women; they're men in disguise"), a solution that is in itself a reflection of how difficult, although not necessarily impossible, it has been for American domestic drama to grant female characters access to these conventions of *rupture* and *potential*.[49] Whether or not the figure of the prodigal daughter provides a positive space for the representation of women is an open question, one that will resurface later. Unfortunately that position has been regularly closed off: the effect is a diminishment of the entire set of conventions this study explores, a stunning foreclosure of potential.

DRAMATIC FUNCTIONS OF THE PRODIGAL

The prodigal is a popular dramatic figure, therefore it seems appropriate to introduce its dramatic functions in terms of a three-part rubric once prescribed for the creation of another popular form, the "top forty" record. The requirements are or at least were in the fifties and the sixties: "Keep it *simple;* keep it *sad;* keep it *sexy.*" If this seems cynical or condescending, I would note that these same three elements describe *Romeo and Juliet* almost perfectly and that few majors works of dramatic literature function without at least two of these three elements. The story of the prodigal may well be the dramatic equivalent of country and western music, but it would be well to remember that the traditions from which the country/western has arisen are long, varied, and vital: traditions that reach through folk music and ballads back to the Middle Ages and beyond.

One of the greatest strengths of the parable in its various forms is its profound *simplicity*, a story of loss and recovery, of separation and wholeness, of departures and returns, of death and rebirth: "for this my son was dead, and is alive again; he was lost, and is found." This simplicity is evident in the limited number of scenes it takes to tell this story, as earlier noted in reference to its appearances in stained glass, painting, and printmaking. These visual representations are proto-dramatic in nature, telling in time and space a story with a clear beginning (receiving the money and leaving), middle (brothel and pig sty), and end (return and feasting), a story with almost classical scenes of recognition and reversal. Few narrative structures are so elegant. When combined with the spectator's familiarity with the story, the result is a structure extremely open to processes of revision and variation. Even more importantly this simple narrative, in part because of its simplicity, allows for the exploration of a wide number of elements, issues, and themes, many of them in pairs: youth and age, authority and rebellion, wealth and poverty, earthiness and spirituality, famine and feasting, suffering and exaltation, rags and robes, the everyday and the foreign, and finally the faithful son and the errant one.

The loss of a family member (child or spouse) forms the basis of this structure's emotional appeal ("keep it *sad*"), expressed first in grief at the departure (a grief similar to that encountered at the death of a child) and secondly, in joy at the prodigal's return (a joy that celebrates a victory, however temporary, over a symbolic death). In particular, the loss or potential loss of a child lies near the heart of the parable. In the original, this child is the prodigal. As the prodigal ages and becomes a husband and father, another child often emerges (the prodigal's child), compensating for the emotional power lost by the prodigal's aging. This child often serves as a foil or even double for the prodigal: mirroring the processes of *rupture* and *potential* mentioned above. Mary Morgan's death in *Ten Nights in a Bar-Room* represents both elements: her death, a result of a child's attempt to bring her father home from the tavern, underscores the radical rupture that prodigal behavior can effect; this death also leads to the prodigal's reformation (her dying wish) and so marks the radical potential for homecomings. The metaphorical death of the prodigal among the swine manifests itself here in the real death of a daughter. In a similar manner, *Raisin in the Sun* also uses a child to bring the prodigal home, to mark rupture and potential. Mama Younger forces her son to perform his act of self-negation (selling out to the neighborhood association) in the sight of his young son, making manifest the loss inherent in that gesture and the nature of the rupture it would create. Seeing himself through his son's eyes saves him, just as Mary Morgan's supplications save her father.

Children readily provide clear-cut, emotionally laden images of rupture and potential: the latter most potently in the imminent birth of a child, as in the pregnancy of a character such as Ruth Younger for whom the child is the future, one threatened in this instance by economic hardships, racism, and the father's potential prodigality; the former in the death of a child, particularly at or near birth, as found in the experience of Mama Younger and numerous other women in American drama. The deaths of children, often very young children is, as was noted earlier, as central to American family drama as the bottle.[50] In *Country Girl*, the death of a child figures in the husband's alcoholism. In *Come Back, Little Sheba*, another childless, alcohol-threatened marriage looks back on the loss of a child: "I wish the baby had lived, Doc. I don't think that woman knew her business."[51] O'Neill's *Journey* looks back toward the death of a child named Eugene. *All the Way Home* looks forward to the birth of a child, a foil for the death of the homeward bound father; *Cat* contrasts an overabundance of unsentimental children ("no-neck monsters") with the absence of a child in Brick and Maggie's life: Brick's "homecoming" promises a birth. This study, of course, began with a *Happy Journey to Trenton and Camden*, but the reason for that journey was not so happy: the death of a newborn baby, a death that Wilder revisits in act 3 of *Our Town* and in *The Long Christmas Dinner*.

No American drama, with the possible exception of *Buried Child*, makes richer use of this convention than *Who's Afraid of Virginia Woolf?* in which an imagined child, like the imagined children of American drama, represents all hope and potential, all rupture and loss: awaited like the prodigal son of the parable, but never welcomed home. Here, too, the sweetness and pathos of the child image makes the violence and anger of George and Martha's relationship more bearable. Even though we never see the child, few American plays value children more.

Christopher Durang's *Marriage of Bette and Boo* (1985) epitomizes the convention, while turning it into a *reductio ad absurdem*. In this autobiographical play narrated by its author (the family's son, on occasion performed by Durang himself), the long-suffering wife of an alcoholic husband ("Do you remember when you used to smell your father's breath to see if he'd been drinking?") has one stillbirth after another. Durang turns these stillbirths into a comic bit: "Doctor: The baby's dead. (*Drops it on the floor.*)" The author even gives precise directions on how to construct the baby prop ("a believably shaped 'bundle'" that will make "a thud when dropped") so that it evokes both laughter and pathos: "For all the oddness of my representing the babies' deaths the way I have, it does still communicate that Bette has lost a child." The words of the husband speak not just to the mother but to a tradition: "Bette, let's not have any more. (*Mournfully:*) I've had enough babies. They get you up in the middle of the night, dead. They dirty their cribs, dead. They need constant attention, dead. No more babies."[52] The speaker's wish will not, however, be granted. American drama will not readily surrender such a potent, even if nearly exhausted, emotional device. From Little Eva and Mary Morgan to Christopher Knowles as "wonder-child," image of innocence and futurity in Robert Wilson's *A Letter for Queen Victoria* (1975) and Gavin Cato in Anna Deavere Smith's *Fires in the Mirror* (1992), we return to the child again and again as a fundamental figure of hope, loss, and innocence.[53]

Also of special note in discussing the emotional effects of these plays is the presence of tears or a broken voice, a sign that tears are being held back. Perhaps nowhere in American drama are these characteristics more prominent than in these stories of prodigality: *Iceman, Journey, Misbegotten, Salesman, Raisin,* and others. For many audiences these indicators of overpowering emotion are especially significant whenever they manifest themselves in a man, where they are valued as signs of true feeling and, when appropriate, of deep repentance, in part because the shedding of tears does not conform to everyday standards of masculinity. They signal, by convention, a unique moment in male experience. The use of tears is, in a sense, another solution to the problem that Robert Turner examines in terms of how to convince the spectator that the prodigal has truly reformed. The words that we often use to indicate reformation or moral regeneration—we say that someone has had a "change of heart"—themselves suggest why tears, those outward manifestations of the heart, should be so important.

This leads to a wider set of assumptions about the relationship between feeling, goodness, and knowledge that underlie many of these plays; namely, that goodness and truth in their most profound manifestations are not known, but felt and that this is the proper order of things.[54] Sadness then, and its corollary, joy (both often expressed in tears), are not just emotional adornments. They are ways of knowing and living, something we should not be surprised to find in a drama that has at its center the tension between love and hate within the most intimate of all social units. We might well employ the term *sentimental* to describe works that reveal these characteristics. Indeed we would be slightly disappointed if one could not say this about a narrative that has formed the basis for so many songs about "cheatin' hearts" and "lonely nights." The term, however, is as much if not more confused than most literary labels that receive heavy use. Therefore I will try to avoid its use until I have an opportunity later in this work to clarify more precisely the set of characteristics that for me it describes.

The third element that this narrative offers to any play that would employ it are its scenes of appetite and sexuality ("keep it *sexy*"), scenes that are in contrast to these gentler emotions of sadness or joy and an affirmation of a felt goodness, that offer instead images of lust, drunkenness, waste, and degradation. Painters frequently depict the moment of the prodigal's homecoming, a moment of intense joy and affirmation, but equally, if not more, popular are two other scenes: drinking with the "harlots" and feeding with the swine, two encounters, albeit in different forms, with appetite and desire. Vicariously the spectator can, like the prodigal, have it both ways: he can indulge in "riotous living" and then come home to the joys of forgiveness and the comforts of a daily routine. Indeed American males play out a variation of this narrative every weekend as they take to the mountains, deserts, or beaches to ride motorcycles, off-road vehicles, horses, or surfboards—appropriately costumed, of course—to then return in three-piece suits for work on Monday morning, hoping someone will notice their tan.

A major strength of this simple structure is the way in which it brings together within a minimum number of images this mixture of sex and forgiveness, sensuality and sadness. Each play will, of course, shift these elements in different ways, but since the late seventeenth century and the attempt to soften and moralize Restoration comedy, the general tendency, evident in one way or another in almost all of the works under discussion, is toward a kind of soft or sweet eroticism, that is enhanced by the substitution in American drama of the wife/mother for the father (see chapter 5). We should not be surprised to find such a conflation in a drama of families that so persistently confuses the functions of wife and mother, husband and son.

I began this study by marking the recurrence of a simple action—the mimesis of drinking—in several plays from the end of World War II to the early sixties. This discussion led to an exploration of several functions that this action performs, in particular, its synecdochic connection to the figure of the prodigal. I now want to add a second major dramatic figure. Of course the prodigal of the parable requires a whole cast of others: the harlots whom the elder son mentions; the friends with whom we suppose the younger son wastes his fortune; the landowner who employs him; even the servants whom the father employs. Although given scant attention in the parable itself, each of these subsidiary characters plays a role in creating the story's milieu. But obviously the parable focuses on the roles of two others in particular: the father and the elder brother. The presence of each of these characters is so strong within the narrative that some biblical scholars suggest that a second story (that of the father and the elder son) had been grafted onto the first (that of the father and the younger).[55] Whether or not this hypothesis is valid, it underscores an obvious structural division between two different actions within the parable: one concerns a son's relationship to his father; the other concerns an elder brother's relationship to both a younger brother and a father. In chapter 5 I examine the role of the one who welcomes home and forgives. In the next chapter, I explore what happens when the man with a bottle has a brother.

4

The Brother

And he said, A certain man had two sons.

—Luke 15:11

Linda: It was so nice to see them shaving together, one behind the other, in the bathroom. And going out together. You notice? The whole house smells of shaving lotion.[1]

NEAR the beginning of *Death of a Salesman,* Linda Loman describes her two sons standing together before a mirror, doubling one another in their movements, reflected and reflecting, a complex image of interconnection and, at the same time, distinction, two brothers shadowed in turn by other Miller brother pairs scattered throughout his oeuvre. Other sets of American brothers meet in a way more appropriate to the beginning point of this study: they come together over a glass of whiskey or bottle of liquor, which, however, is not too unlike Linda's mirror in its potential for the revelation of both continuity and discontinuity between two related selves. In act 1 of *Come Blow Your Horn,* Alan mixes a drink for his younger brother Buddy who has just run away from home and does not yet know Scotch from Bourbon. Their relationship is similar to that of Ben and Eugene Gant in *Look Homeward, Angel:* the elder is wise in the ways of women and drink; the younger is just ready to begin. In *All the Way Home,* an older pair of brothers meets over a bottle: one, a former alcoholic, is an image of strength and will who has vowed to kill himself if he ever gets drunk again; the other, a practicing prodigal, is an image of weakness who can only vow that he will think about taking his brother's vow the next time he gets drunk. They are two different shapes, reflected in whiskey. In Williams's *Cat* yet another pair of brothers—one, a teetotaler; the other, an alcoholic—meet over a drink. For Gooper, the sober elder brother, closest of all these figures to the Lukan elder, this meeting signals his defeat, his realization that the younger brother

101

will in one way or another, drunk or sober, make it home, that excellent management skills are no match for a father's love. To one extent or another, all of these pairs are also reflected in one more meeting of two brothers over a bottle, that of Edmund and Jamie in act 4 of *Long Day's Journey into Night*, perhaps the most memorable brother scene in American drama.

Here then are six pairs for examination. In each case, the elder brother, when ages are known, is listed first, the younger, second:

Biff and Happy, *Death of a Salesman*, 1949,
Gooper and Brick, *Cat on a Hot Tin Roof*, 1955,
Jamie and Edmund, *Long Day's Journey into Night*, 1956 (written 1939–1941),
Ben and Eugene, *Look Homeward, Angel*, 1957,
Ralph and Jay, *All the Way Home*, 1960,
Alan and Buddy, *Come Blow Your Horn*, 1961.

Each of these pairs stand with Happy and Biff before the bathroom mirror: doubled, reflected, mirrored and mirroring; clearly bound to one another; just as clearly separated; two selves merging into one and then dividing again. Each of these brother pairs also sits with Jamie and Edmund drinking into the night while a father listens or a mother waits nearby, trying with Jamie and Edmund to sort love from hate, caught between a desire to embrace and an almost simultaneous desire to push away.[2]

In examining the uses of the two brothers in plays of prodigality, I will concentrate on two related sets of conventions that reflect the dynamics of Biff and Happy at the mirror and Jamie and Edmund at the table. In the first instance, *conventions of separation* exist without which we would not be able to tell one brother from the other; in the second *conventions of mentorship*, through which we understand more clearly those ties that bind two brothers together, make them one. Having explored the basic shape and function of these conventions grounded in notions of doubleness (*separation*) and singularity (*mentorship*), I will then focus on their use for the purposes of representing a divided self.

Separation

Every dramatist begins his work within a sea of nondifferentiation in which the characters, especially those of the same sex and similar ages, are initially identical, what we might call virtual twins. One of the most fundamental operations performed by any dramatic text is to somehow delineate one of these twins from another. The recurrent anecdote of the supporting actor who loses a job, because he looks too much like the leading man provides a practical example of this problem. Most audience members have also had the experience at one time or another of seeing a play or film in which physical similarities or poor costume and make-up choices created unnecessary confusion about who was who. Some plays—*Comedy of Errors* and its Plautine progenitor are the obvious examples—exploit this confusion of identity for comic effects, which, of course, depend almost entirely on the audience never being confused at all. This simple problem (how to tell character A from character B) lies at the source of processes involved in the representation of character. Any dramatic text must find some way to enable spectators to tell one dramatic figure, one twin, from another. To do so it must employ, consciously or not, some convention that will make it possible for the audience to keep the identities of twins separate.

Of course one way to solve this problem is to make one twin male and the other female. Clothing can, however, quickly re-confuse the issue, as in, for example, *Twelfth Night,* although not usually for long. Plays with brother pairs, however, must usually find other ways of separating one self from another, even though in some instances a gendered distinction is made by suggesting that one brother is more like the father or the mother than the other, more "masculine" or "feminine." In *Love and Death in the American Novel,* Leslie Fiedler describes another solution based not on gender but on coloring, as in Cooper's juxtaposition of a fair Alice's innocence and a dark Cora's sensuality in *Last of the Mohicans.*[3] Movie melodramas often use this same device to separate heroes from villains (white hats/black hats) or to more clearly define co-leads, as in the pairings of a Robert Redford and a Paul Newman (*Butch Cassidy and the Sundance Kid*) or, interracially, Nick Nolte and Eddie Murphy (*48 Hours*), Danny Glover and Mel Gibson (*Lethal Weapon*). Fiedler focuses on the metaphorical and ideological significance these shadings hold, but they also serve a more mundane purpose. They give the reader or spectator a way to begin distinguishing one dramatic or literary figure from another. We take these conventions for granted, but without some form of them representation would be almost impossible. Differences such as these (gender or color) give spectators the chance to assemble the incomplete puzzle that characterization inevitably is. They are like those straightedged border pieces that provide, for most of us anyway, a clear place from which to begin putting together the puzzle.

Brother stories also use many other simple differences in physical appearance to separate one figure from another: the mark of Cain (a sign itself of separation), Joseph's coat of many colors (an eventual cause of separation), Esau's hirsute exterior, young David's "ruddy" and "beautiful countenance."[4] Miller's *The Price* (1968), a more recent play of two brothers, contrasts the police uniform of one brother with the camel's hair coat and "well-barbered" look of the other, a successful surgeon.[5] Shepard's *True West* (1980) begins with the sharp physical contrast between a younger brother ("light blue sports shirt, light tan cardigan sweater, clean blue jeans, white tennis shoes") and an older one ("filthy white t-shirt, tattered brown overcoat covered with dust, . . . 'Gene Vincent' hairdo, two days' growth of beard, bad teeth").[6] (Of course as the play progresses, it blurs these distinctions and challenges the stability of identity.) The Broadway production of Williams's *Cat* simplifies the process by casting a Paul Newman in one role and a Pat Hingle in the other. O'Neill's *Journey* works somewhat more subtly than these other examples but still makes a clear physical distinction between Edmund, "taller, thin and wiry," and Jamie, "broad-shouldered" and "deep-chested."[7]

There exists, however, external differences with a more fundamental process of differentiation, a long-standing convention for separating one brother, one twin, from another that the example of Esau, just mentioned above, also recalls: "The *first* came forth red, all his body like a hairy mantle; so they called his name Esau. *Afterward* his brother came forth."[8] We know these brothers, Jacob and Esau, through two different ways of separating one twin from another: by appearance but also by temporality, by a distinction, of only a few moments in this case, between the elder and the younger. Age is one of the oldest conventions for separating individuals often nearly identical in other respects, a device as present in American domestic drama as in the book of Genesis.

In the parable age differences take the place of proper nouns. We know the two sons in its English translation not as a Jamie and an Edmund but as the elder brother and the younger. Over time we have come to associate certain characteristics with each of these designations. In his study of the parable, J. Duncan Derrett summarizes these qualities from a biblical perspective. According to him the basic tendency throughout the Hebrew Bible is to celebrate the youngest child, often at the expense of the older brother or brothers. He notes, for example, that all of the patriarchs after Abraham were younger brothers. His list includes Abel, Moses, Jacob, Joseph, Saul, David, Solomon, Gideon, and Judas Maccabaeus. We might add to his list the example of Ishmael and Isaac, sons of Abraham by Sarah and Hagar: one, elder and cast out; the other, younger and favored. Derrett argues that the Bible usually portrays elder brothers as "worldly, niggardly, orthodox," and "hypocritical," while younger sons are usually "idealistic" and "rebellious, but fit for repentance."[9] He also suggests that in a biblical context to be younger is to be "inferior and weaker," therefore, requiring patronage.[10] For these reasons when a younger brothers achieves fame, it is a sure sign of his status as a chosen one.[11] Derrett points out that this is consistent with the Jew's own image of themselves as God's chosen: the weak, but favored sons of Jacob and Joseph. Later the church would see "the younger brothers of Jewish history as 'types' of Jesus."[12] In a possibly anti-Semitic reversal of this imagery, Jill Robbins notes that in Augustine's *Confessions* he, as have other exegetes, perceived the elder brother as "a figure for the Jew, specifically the Jew in relation to the gospel."[13] Keppler in his *Literature of the Second Self* recalls that in medieval legends Jesus himself played the role of a younger brother to an elder in the form of Judas Iscariot. It is also possible to conceive of Jesus as a younger brother to John the Baptist: the younger, the "Lamb of God"; the elder, not worthy to loose the sandals of the other. Even more strikingly, Keppler cites a Gnostic tradition that saw Jesus as a younger brother to an elder referred to as Satanaël:

> . . . the gloomy and awful figure of Antichrist, the former Lucifer whose morning-star splendor has been dimmed by the fires of Hell, the essence of active evil that came into being with the birth of the God of Mercy as His antithetical Twin, the mystery of iniquity that stands at the left hand of the sun of justice.[14]

Although the sources for this Gnostic tradition are, by Keppler's own admission, incomplete,[15] one can easily see in the Christ story similarities to the structure of the parable: a son leaves home and symbolically becomes a prodigal by taking upon himself the sins of the world, eventually returning to an awaiting father. Opposite this story is that of Satan, a proud and eternally displaced figure, one who suggests in various ways the biblical tradition of the despised elder brother.

Bruno Bettelheim's *The Uses of Enchantment* and other studies of folk and fairy tales place these age-based distinctions within an even larger context. Bettelheim also identifies the youngest child as a weakling, the "dummy" or "Simpleton" who nevertheless prevails in the end, even though his older brother or brothers might possess more innate talent and conspire against him. From Derrett's biblical perspective, stories of David, his brothers, and Goliath or of Joseph and his brothers would illustrate this pattern. One of Bettelheim's central examples is the story of "The Three Feathers" in which a king who is growing old and weak sends his three sons on a series of quests. The two almost identical older brothers work together and in opposition to a lone youngest son. Nevertheless the youngest succeeds, because he dares to extend his search to the underworld, which, in Bettelheim's psychoanalytic reading, represents the unconscious. The elder brothers fail, despite their strength and cleverness, because they content themselves with whatever can easily be found on the earth's surface. According to Bettelheim they represent the functioning of a "much depleted ego, . . . cut-off from the potential source of its strength and richness, the id."[16] When Bettelheim turns specifically to tales of two brothers, for which hundreds of versions exist from as early as 1250 B.C.E., his descriptions of their narrative conventions coincide with many of Derrett's observations: one brother (obviously the eldest), is often "cautious and reasonable," with a "tendency to remain safely home, tied to the parents," while the other is frequently more adventurous, "striving for independence and self-assertion," often choosing to leave home and "live in accordance with his desires."[17]

The *Motif-Index of Folk-Literature* provides a third treatment of classic age-based distinctions between brothers. An entire section (L0-L99) records examples of the "Victorious youngest child" within the larger category of a "Reversal of Fortune."[18] The index refers to numerous stories of victorious younger sons from a wide range of literatures: Irish, Icelandic, Spanish, Jewish, Indian, Hawaiian, Tahitian, North American Indian, African, and others. Cross-references give a rough indication of the conventional framework within which these motifs work in terms of the roles played by older and younger brothers. They reinforce both Derrett's and Bettelheim's observations. All three sources reveal a remarkably persistent way of separating a pair of individuals, of telling one twin from another based on their relative ages. At the same time, they indicate at least one reason for the convention's popularity. The youngest child is the classic underdog, almost by definition the smallest, least experienced, most vulnerable member of the family group. And most of us, as Bettelheim suggests, whether or not we are youngest children ourselves, can find reassurance in the victory of one who feels "abused and rejected" or "stupid and inadequate."[19]

We need, however, to turn from motif-indexes and fairy tales to the presence of these conventions of separation in American drama. Before making that turn, however, I would emphasize again the fluidity and flexibility of these structures. For example some works distinguish between brothers solely on the basis of who stays home and who leaves without emphasizing their relative ages at all. One method uses time to help establish identity; another, space. Of the latter

Miller's *The Price* is an obvious example with its clear distinction between the son who stayed to help his father through the depression and the other who went off to pursue his own career. In other instances age differences are clear, but instead of the younger leaving, the elder goes, as in O'Neill's *Beyond the Horizon* (1920) or Miller's *Salesman*. Indeed, *Horizon* seems to say to the spectator/reader, "Look at what happens when elder brothers, who should stay home, sail for foreign lands and younger brothers, who should take ship, try to run the family farm." In each of these dramas, the process of staying or leaving, with or without reference to age, is fundamental to each brother's identity.

Even subject to revision and reformulation is the persistent tendency to make the younger brother the hero and the elder brother something more or less of a villain. Like the distinction between he who leaves and he who stays, moral contrasts may operate without reference to relative ages or in opposition to conventional expectations. For example Shakespeare and others after him often establish brothers' identities primarily in terms of moral values. We would expect, based on the conventions discussed thus far, for the good brother and the younger brother to be the same person, as with Oliver, who specifically compares himself with the Lukan prodigal, and his elder brother Orlando in *As You Like It*, but we also find in the same play a good elder brother, the Duke Senior, and an evil younger brother, Frederick. *Lear* and *Hamlet* also reverse the usual alignment between a brother's moral identity and his age, as do various other plays, such as Schiller's neo-Shakespearean drama, *Die Räuber*. Among the American dramas under consideration in this chapter, *Salesman* represents the elder son, Biff, as the favored of the father, a favoritism that the spectator is likely to share given the way in which each son is presented. An effect of this reversal may be to create a degree of emotional confusion for the audience member normally prepared to love the cute younger brother at the expense of a more negatively stereotyped elder brother. Here the younger brother is not so appealing, and the elder is the one who has just returned from a journey to a far country. All the conventions for separating one brother from another (age, favor, proximity to home) are present, but they are not all located where we expect them to be. The result is a text that uses conventional formulas to draw the spectator into a brother relationship, but that then disturbs those formulas, confusing conventional expectations and creating a degree of uneasiness in a way perhaps more felt than understood.

Given an awareness of this variety and flexibility in the application of these conventions, I would like to turn to two specific examples of

brother pairs—Brick/Gooper from *Cat*, Edmund/Jamie from *Journey*—to emphasize the vitality of the conventions described by Derrett, Bettelheim, and others. Williams's brothers, with their separate
identities, conventionally established, seem like direct descendants of
the biblical pair. Brick is, of course, the younger son. He fits Derrett's
description as the more "idealistic" and "rebellious" of the pair. His
broken leg and compulsive drinking make him seem more vulnerable
than his sober, respectable, self-sufficient elder brother. He is an excellent example of the weak but favored younger son: a prodigal whose
father, mother, and wife all want to come home. After Bettelheim he
is the son who is willing to go on a journey, in this case into his past,
one that will bring him into contact with aspects of the self that
others, such as Gooper, are either unaware of or deny. His courage
and honesty give him a moral superiority, especially when compared
to Gooper's hypocrisy and greed.

Gooper differs from Brick according to conventional age-based
characteristics. After Derrett he is "worldly, niggardly, orthodox" and
"hypocritical." His occupation as a corporate lawyer is apt. Although
he has moved to the city, he has maintained an interest in the family
business, as does the elder son in the parable, and he keenly desires
to take over its operation when the father dies. He is in many ways
the brother who has never left home. Also like the eldest son of the
parable, he feels that his father has slighted and neglected him. Like
the elder sons of "The Three Feathers," his focus is on superficial
values with little interest in what lies beneath that surface in himself
or others. Williams's *Cat* even moves toward a kind of happy ending,
whether we find it in Williams's own version, which shows Brick
working through, however tentatively, to some truth about himself
and others or in the Broadway/Hollywood versions, which offer varying degrees of reconciliation with Big Daddy and Maggie.

Our sense of *Long Day's Journey into Night* as autobiography often
stands in the way of perceiving its conventionality. We might agree
with Jamie when he tells his father that he and Edmund are "not like
the usual brothers,"[20] that they stand outside the kinds of conventionality that Derrett, Bettelheim, and the folktale index describe. In fact
at first Jamie and Edmund do not seem to provide us with the sharp,
clear contrasts of the parable and fairy tales, of Brick and Gooper,
or, to cite a more recent example, Shepard's Lee and Austin (*True
West*). Jamie and Edmund are, however, more like Brick, Gooper,
and other brother pairs than they at first seem. Of course their shared
prodigality creates a feeling of similarity or sameness between them
that I would not discount. In the next section of this chapter, I will

focus on it, but for now I want to examine how Jamie and Edmund differ according to the conventions just described.

Edmund, of course, is the younger brother. He, too, fits Derrett's rubric of "idealistic" and "rebellious, but fit for repentance." Edmund's illness also makes him the weaker of the two, at least physically. Furthermore, he has about him a degree of naïveté, at least in his past, and this quality links him to the younger brother as the *simpleton* or *fool*. Jamie refers to him as "The Kid," the brother who must be wised-up by a more experienced elder. Like the prodigal Edmund, too, has moved away from home, passed through personal crisis, and has now come back to the father. Indeed one way to read the first half of act 4 is as a scene of reconciliation between a father and his prodigal son. His journey has also been, as in Bettelheim's reference to fairy tales, a quest in which he seems to have gained some knowledge of the self that his elder brother still lacks.

More problematic is the character of Jamie. In the context of the parable or Derrett's list of characteristics, we do not expect the older brother himself to be an almost perfect prodigal son: drinking, whoring, wasting money, angering the father. Instead we might imagine his opposite, someone ready to scorn the younger brother and his foolhardy behavior. In this instance, however, the elder has been a source for that behavior, a mentor of prodigality. But if we look beyond this prodigality for a moment, Jamie resembles more closely the traditional elder brother of the parable. He has not, for example, left home, and like the Lukan brother, he continues to work with the father in the family business, in this case, the theater. Also he perceives himself, as do others, as both the stronger and the cleverer of the two. At the same time, he resents Edmund's success as a writer and is jealous of the favor accorded the younger by his parents. Jamie shares with the conventional elder brother a certain malevolence cloaked by hypocrisy. Jamie's act 4 speech of confession offsets this impression but also conforms to a tradition of last act conversions. Therefore except for the prodigal tendencies of the elder brother, Edmund and Jamie match the Lukan brothers and those of many fairy tales almost as closely as do Brick and Gooper. Both works rely on conventional devices to help the audience distinguish one virtual twin from another.

Thus far the focus has been on a fundamental process of characterization: a text must find some way to help an audience tell one character from another. From these relatively simple and perhaps overly obvious mechanisms of differentiation, I would now like to turn to an opposing movement. To do this I return to Jamie. His prodigality functions as a dynamic variant on the structures of the parable. His drinking and its connection to Edmund runs counter to the pull of their differences, just as it runs counter to one set of expectations for brother pairs. It creates a tension between their sameness and their differences, between a tendency to pull together and push apart, between continuity and discontinuity, wholeness and fragmentation.

MENTORSHIP

Jamie: Made getting drunk romantic. Made whores fascinating vampires instead of poor, stupid, diseased slobs they really are. Made fun of work as sucker's game. Never wanted you to succeed and make me look even worse by comparison. Wanted you to fail. Always jealous of you. Mama's baby, Papa's pet![21]

Drinking can and often does set one brother off from another, but it can also connect and unite. For Edmund and Jamie, drinking represents conventions of mentorship and identity that run counter to those of difference and division described in the preceding paragraphs. Mentorship itself is a form of identity, one that distinguishes teacher from pupil, but more profoundly, it represent a counterforce to those elements that conventionally separate one brother from another. It tends instead to erase differences; it reminds the spectator of the ties that bind; and it underscores a shared identity, exploiting an aspect of the elder brother/younger brother pair that the parable does not explore. To demonstrate these conventions of mentorship, I will use two plays that may at first seem an unlikely pair: O'Neill's *Journey* and Simon's *Come Blow Your Horn*. Biff and Happy from *Salesman*, as well as Ben and Eugene Gant from *Look Homeward*, are also relevant, but these two works, so different and yet so similar, offer the richest examples for the purposes of illustration.

Come Blow Your Horn was Simon's first commercial success: a family drama that begins with the younger brother's decision to leave home, quit the family business, and move in with his older brother in the city. Buddy's older brother, Alan, and Jamie have several traits in common: both are bachelors who relate to most women as sexual objects; both have acrimonious relationships with their fathers, but have not left the family business, be it wax fruit or melodrama; both spend freely, even prodigally, whatever money they have; in each case, their fathers use the same word to describe them (*bum*). The differences between these two eldest brothers are primarily of degree and complexity: Jamie is an older, wearier, more corrupt and more complex version of Alan. Both brothers resemble prodigal sons who have never quite been able to make the break with home.

But what most interests me about these two eldest sons is their role
as mentors for younger brothers whom they educate in the ways of
the world. In Simon's play Buddy is even more typical than Alan of
the younger brother as a "Simpleton" or "dummy," someone almost
totally inexperienced in the ways of the world. For Alan, the older
brother, the first two steps in this process are to get his brother a
drink and then a girl. In a relatively short period of time, Buddy
learns to do both things for himself, thus becoming a prodigal or, in
his father's words, a "bum" in his own right. In Simon's play we see
this process; in O'Neill's, which deals with brothers a dozen years
older, we hear about it as a series of events in the past. Both older
brothers initiate their youngers into a world of sexual, even prodigal
experience that alters their lives.

In both plays this loss of innocence is treated with some ambivalence. Just as both fathers used the same word to describe their prodigal sons, *bum*, so do both older brothers use the same word to describe
their creations as mentors. Of Buddy, Alan says, "I've created an Ivy
League Frankenstein";[22] of Edmund, Jamie proclaims, "Hell, you're
more than my brother. I made you! You're my Frankenstein."[23] What
Frankenstein represents in both contexts is continuity between two
individuals, between the maker and his creation, between a mentor
and his protégé: a process that dissolves distinctions until, appropriately, two different entities share the same name. Of course no one
is likely to confuse the monster and the scientist/doctor, but the conventions of mentorship stand for those forces that make it more, not
less, difficult to tell one from the other. Mentorship asserts a tendency
to remake the world in one's own image, a tendency opposite the
modes of differentiation just described, a tendency toward sameness
and wholeness, toward a single, shared identity. If some distinctions
work to dispel the confusions of twinship by separation, others work
to dispel them by swallowing them up, to make not twins but a single
whole being. Finally the allusion to *Frankenstein* also suggests that
mentorship has a darker side to it, that it creates a monster.

As I said near the beginning of this chapter, the predominant characteristic of brother pairs is movement back and forth between two
extremes. Jamie and Alan both demonstrate this motion in renouncing
their roles as mentors, therefore articulating a break with their brothers. Alan makes this move in a scene with Buddy toward the end of
Horn in which he criticizes his younger brother for his prodigal lifestyle, a lifestyle that Buddy learned from him. In doing so Alan becomes "cautious" and "reasonable," leaving Buddy to the more
traditional role of the prodigal younger brother, who will, no doubt
eventually come home. Jamie, like Alan, also warns his younger

brother away from any further emulation of his behavior, tells him not to assume his older brother's identity, to stay away from him in general: "Make up your mind you've got to tie a can to me—get me out of your life—think of me as dead—tell people, 'I had a brother, but he's dead.'"[24]

In a sense both elder brothers undergo reformations. Alan's is perhaps the more obvious one. In practical terms this means that he must become a successful (i.e., productive, profit-making) partner in the family business and, equally important, that he must settle down, marry a good woman, and begin raising a family, thus ending the play of free-floating desire and his life as a bum. *Horn*'s ending affirms family, financial security, and the middle class, while offering young men in return a brief period of social and sexual freedom, a kind of sanctioned prodigality, seen as an inevitable, but transitory stage of growing up. Its genre, the light Broadway comedy, demands this sort of dénouement. O'Neill's genre, middle-class domestic tragedy, demands almost the opposite. Nevertheless Jamie also finds his woman of substance to redeem him, only in this case the process takes longer. The Fat Pearl episode introduces the possibility of humanizing the almost mechanical relationship between the prostitute and her customer. Jamie relates to Pearl not as an object for pleasuring himself but as an individual with feelings and concerns of her own. She is an ironic equivalent to Alan's Connie. Of course *Moon for the Misbegotten* expands this possibility into an entire play: Fat Pearl becomes Josie who becomes Jamie's woman of substance, as pure, if not more so, than Connie. In the end Josie saves Jamie, just as surely as Connie saves Alan.

Jamie and Alan both represent the kind of elder brother who draws the younger to him, while also portraying another kind of brother, one who stands apart and separate: in the first role, the elder brother embraces the younger; in the latter, he pushes him away. Death, of course, would end this process of approach and avoidance, but while both brothers live, it will almost inevitably continue. Jamie's final scene with Edmund rests on this movement back and forth, indeed, is powered by it. Jamie himself alludes to this principle in his revised version of a line from the New Testament: "Greater love hath no man than this, that he saveth his brother from himself."[25]

Jamie's revision of the gospel should call to mind his guilt/responsibility—in his mother's perception and most probably his own—in the death of one brother already, for the death of Eugene (the brother who died in infancy, when Jamie exposed him to mumps), a figure whom we cannot help but in some way merge with Edmund. The mentor then has blood on his hands: he infects others with diseases (literal or figurative) that kill. He is a benevolent and a malevolent figure, one who tries to help the younger, but whose most valid piece of advice is "don't trust me; don't trust the mentor; he is trying to kill you." In this we find the irony that brother pairs conventionally represent images of both ultimate love and ultimate enmity or hate. On the one hand, we hear, "He ain't heavy, he's my brother," and on the other, we see images of civil war, of Eteocles and Polyneices fighting one another, of Atreus and Thyestes and other antagonistic brother pairs from mythology, folk tales, literature, and history, of so many battles pitting brother against brother, tearing asunder what should be inseparable.

Of course, Jamie's mentorship of Edmund stands as a supreme example of this split image. At one point Jamie defends himself to his father by invoking the benevolent, caring image of an older, wiser brother looking after the younger, scorning the false mentorship of most older brothers for a tutelage both practical and compassionate:

> *Edmund:* All right. I did put Edmund wise to things, but not until I saw he'd started to raise hell, and knew he'd laugh at me if I tried the good advice, older brother stuff. All I did was make a pal of him and be absolutely frank so he'd learn from my mistakes that—(*He shrugs his shoulders—cynically.*) . . . You know how much the Kid means to me, and how close we've always been. . . . I'd do anything for him.[26]

Later, of course, Jamie reveals that his mentorship itself—that which was supposed to signal brotherly love—was actually a weapon by which he hoped to destroy his brother's life, infecting him with a sort of fatal disease just as he had infected the infant Eugene. Love and hate potentially inhabit the same process: a potential that O'Neill's text exploits both in Jamie's protestations of innocence and in his professions of guilt, finding animosity in mentorship and mentorship (sacrificial mentorship) in animosity. The process is one of almost continual subversion, of an alternation between the desire to embrace and the desire to push away, more sharply expressed here than in any of the other works considered in this chapter, even though each of these pairs participates to some degree in the tension that O'Neill's text makes explicit.

Although Jamie uses his role as a mentor/model to destroy, we do not generally perceive mentorship or modeling itself as the source of difficulty. In general I think we perceive sameness or identity between brothers as essentially safe, banal even, while in radical differences we find sources of danger and violence. We have, however, already noted that sameness—as in the likeness of twins—represents a source of chaos and confusion, so that a primary task of any dramatic structure is the establishment of meaningful differences. Also relevant here is René Girard's argument in *Violence and the Sacred* that identity, especially identity that has its source in mentorship or modeling, is a profound source of violence, that the same motion that pulls two brothers together also ensures that they will turn against one another, and that the perception of significant differences may not be violence's cause but its remedy.

Brothers and doubles are both central to Girard's work, so it seems appropriate to mention here, however briefly, his reading of these relationships in literature. For him if a younger brother models himself after his older brother/mentor, then he will naturally want whatever the mentor/model wants. The key element in what he calls "mimetic desire" is not the object of desire—it will vary—but the process of mentorship or modeling itself that determines the object.[27] Conflict arises naturally from this process in that it produces multiple longings for singular objects, so it is that siblings will ignore a toy for weeks, then fight violently for it when one or another wants it, then forget about it again as soon as one or the other loses interest. One can, I think, hear in Jamie's pleas with Edmund to dissolve their relationship, the clear desire to be left alone with the mother and the father, to have Edmund no longer as a copy of his desire, to be left with what he wants most and cannot share, what the elder son of the parable thought he had at last achieved, until that is, the prodigal came home: "Mama's baby, Papa's pet!" Indeed the obvious message is that if Edmund does not leave him alone with the object or objects of his desire, Jamie will do his best to complete a murder that he has been working on for a long time.

According to Girard a primary mechanism for escaping the violence that mimetic desire creates is the creation of difference, in particular, a strategic difference between those brothers who would live together in unanimity and some other individual or group who must become a scapegoat: the recipient of the violence that mimetic desire has created. In this light much of *Journey* is spent in efforts to create tiny communities of unanimity—between two brothers or a husband and a wife or a parent and a child—by identifying a suitable scapegoat: a doctor, a father, a brother, a wife, a mother. We can read *Journey* as documenting the crisis that arises when a community fails to find a suitable other on which to cast the blame. For example Edmund and Jamie create a small community by scapegoating the father. The first references of the play establish this opposition, as Mary and Tyrone (onstage) hear the boys laughing (offstage):

(A burst of laughter comes from the dining room. She [Mary] *turns her head, smiling.)*
[*Mary:*] What's the joke, I wonder?
Tyrone: (Grumpily.) It's on me. I'll bet that much. It's always on the Old Man.
Mary: (Teasingly.) Yes, it's terrible the way we all pick on you, isn't it? You're so abused![28]

Act 4 reverses the situation. The two brothers are onstage, and the father is listening offstage. Alignments, however, have now changed, particularly after the long scene between Edmund and Tyrone that precedes Jamie's entrance, a scene that has established at least a temporary unanimity between father and son, a scene in which at least one prodigal has come home. When Jamie tries to reestablish the father as their scapegoat, the change in alignments is clear:

Jamie: What a bastard to have for a father! Christ, if you put him in a book, no one would believe it!
Edmund: (Defensively.) Oh, Papa's all right, if you try to understand him— and keep your sense of humor.[29]

Out of this failure of consensus comes Jamie's own attack on Edmund for his responsibility in taking the mother away from his older brother. Certainly Jamie's animosity has origins beyond this moment, but our awareness of it must wait until a system for directing anger and blame onto the father has collapsed.

But violence for Girard is a reciprocal process, therefore we should expect some response from Edmund, who instead seems almost benign. Where then is the violence against Jamie? The answer might be that the violence is not in the play so much as it is the play, that the text of *Journey* itself, among other things, not only documents the failure of an accord between brothers but also participates in that failure. In a sense it proclaims an alignment with the father against the elder brother.[30] Even more fundamentally it may represent a way of possessing the objects of desire, particularly the presence of the mother and a success that bests the father, beyond the power of mother, father, or brother ever to interfere.

These functions of *separation* and *mentorship* represent the central tension of brother pairs in American drama: the tension between a desire to embrace, to become, in essence, one being and a desire to push away, to become two distinct, often antithetical beings. This brings us back to those initial images of Happy and Biff before the mirror or of Jamie and Edmund sharing a bottle of whiskey, images of distinct but strongly linked dramatic figures: two who are one; one who is two. The remainder of this chapter will explore the potential function of these conventions and images for the representation of forces at work upon and within the self. It will explore one of the oldest roles of the tale of two brothers: its ability to represent in concrete terms an image of a fragmented or divided personality.[31]

MENTORSHIP AND THE DIVIDED SELF

We might logically expect to observe this function (the representation of a divided self) in plays that clearly separate brother pairs in ways similar to those outlined in the first half of this chapter (appearance, age, proximity to home, and so forth), but the convention of a brother as mentor also serves this end. In an analysis of the Jamie/Edmund scene from the final act of *Journey*, Travis Bogard offers their relationship with its Frankenstein imagery as a paradigm that both reflects and illuminates much of O'Neill's work, particularly those plays employing brothers pairs or other doubles: *Beyond the Horizon, Desire under the Elms, The Great God Brown, Mourning Becomes Electra, Days Without End, Hughie*, and others.

> The image shifts, dazzles, puzzles, but the provocative possibility is that O'Neill believed that his brother had done as he claimed, and that part of him *was* Jamie, and, therefore, that Jamie was more than his brother, was somehow an image of himself, an image that was a hostile double, bent on his destruction, a form of *doppelgänger*.[32]

Bogard goes on to suggest that much of O'Neill's work as a playwright may have been a process of sifting identities, of trying to understand what part of himself was Jamie's creation and what part his own: a search born out of the problems that mentorship creates for an individual trying to understand the origins of his behavior. In other words brothers may face the same problems as the spectator who encounters a stage full of twins: the inability to distinguish one self from another.

This process suggests the image of a divided self to the extent that a dramatic figure, in this case Edmund, has internalized some aspect or aspects of another individual, in this case Jamie. The problem is then, as Bogard suggests, one of discerning and perhaps eliminating the presence or presences of that internalized other, a process that assumes the existence of an original or essential self that this other has in some way infected or polluted. We might, however, invert this perception and see the mentor not as agent but as agency, not as the source of energy but as a reflector of energy originating elsewhere. In this respect Jamie may function as a mirror upon which his bother projects some aspect of himself: anger, violence, self-hatred, sexual appetite, incestuous desire. In doing so texts make these forces subject to processes of dramatic representation within the conventions of dramatic realism. For Otto Rank the double, of which the mentor is a type, provides not only a sense of control over these elements but also the possibility of shifting guilt from one self to another:

> The most prominent symptom of the forms which the double takes is a powerful consciousness of guilt which forces the hero no longer to accept the responsibility for certain actions of his ego, but to place it upon another ego, a double, who is either personified by the devil himself or is created by making a diabolical pact.[33]

From this perspective it seems only appropriate that the description of Jamie at his first entrance links him to the figure of Mephistopheles.[34]

The mentor may then be a device for articulating forces at work on a particular individual, whether we perceive those forces as truly external to the self or as fragments of the self externalized and embodied in a second human being. In the examples of mentorship just discussed, Alan and Jamie both represent forces (internal or external) affecting these younger brothers. Initially, these elder brothers objectify, more than any other element, the pull of desire. This function corresponds to their roles as mentors of prodigality, as elder brothers who initiate younger brothers into a world of sexual experience and desire represented by women and drink. As already noted later in each play they each adopt a voice more consonant with the restrictive voice of authority—especially in Alan's case—a voice that advocates discipline and control, usually associated with the father.[35] The irony here is that the same figure, the elder brother, functions both as a voice of appetite or desire and as a voice of discipline and control. Buddy accuses Alan of acting like his father, and after Jamie finishes his warnings to Edmund in the final act of *Journey*, his father immediately confirms the connection between Jamie's words and his own: "I heard the last part of his talk. It's what I've warned you. I hope you'll heed the warning, now it comes from his own mouth."[36] When a text specifically assigns either of these tendencies to an elder brother, then the drama has at its disposal a powerful device for the representation of internal conflict. The paradox here is that while we usually think of mentorship in terms of continuity and solidarity, dramas may actually employ it as an analytical tool, as a way of portraying fragmentary, contradictory aspects of the self. In this dual role, mentorship participates in the tension between synthesis and division that has been this chapter's focus.[37]

SEPARATION AND THE DIVIDED SELF

Those dramatic functions that allow for the representation of a divided self are not, of course, confined to mentor relationships. This chapter began with the potential confusions of twinship and the need to create conventions that would clearly separate one brother, one virtual twin from another in the spectator's mind, some way to separate Happy from Biff as they stand before the mirror or Jamie from Edmund as they sit across from each other at the table with a whiskey bottle between them. Ironically the same quality—virtual twinship—that mandates the development of processes which will clearly separate one brother figure from another also turns brother pairs into engines for the expression of differences fundamental to the human personality. On a scale of similarity, brother pairs range from Siamese, identical, and fraternal twins, on one end of the scale, to step- , adopted, and surrogate brothers on the other. In between these extremes lies the largest class: brothers born at different times but to the same biological parents, raised in the same home. This set describes all of the brother pairs listed at the beginning of this chapter from Biff and Happy Loman to Alan and Buddy Baker. Obviously from a scientific point of view, the environmental and hereditary bundles of each individual within any of these pairs are far from identical, but this is relatively unimportant, because popular perception, not science, is what matters here and, according to popular perception, two individuals with so many elements in common (family, race, nation, religion, and so forth) should themselves be alike. Therefore when two brothers are different, as is so often the case, we tend to perceive these differences as functions not of heredity and environment, because these causes have been minimized, but of some deeper level of difference fundamental to the nature of the human self, as differences not caused but immanent.

A synopsis written for a rather bad play summarizes the mechanics of this phenomenon fairly well:

> Three doctors decide to take twin boys and separate them. . . . One, Bob, is placed in a home of wealth, refinement, surrounded by the best people. His brother Eddie is placed in the slums. He is a piano player in a dive. He has no advantages whatsoever, but through his own efforts is trying to better himself. Bob, with everything in life, is a cad, a rotter.

Therefore environment plays no part in his life. Eddie with nothing is a
fine upright honest boy—but his environment doesn't affect him, as he
is far above it. It can't be heredity because Bob and Eddie are exact twins!
   What is it, then? When our play ends we find our three doctors arguing,
although thirty years has elapsed.[38]

Of course the convention that separates these two brothers is that of
moral differences: the good brother and the bad brother, the "upright
honest boy" and the "cad." The doctors, however, cannot explain
these differences, because they have created a situation that nullifies
causes specific to an individual life, which is, of course, only an exag-
geration of what normal brother pairs tend to do anyway. Brothers
are therefore apt means for the representation of characteristics that
we tend to perceive as fundamental to human nature, precisely because they seem to lack idiosyncratic causes of dissimilarity. They
often leave us then with strongly contrasted and usually dualistic ways
of perceiving the self.[39] This phenomenon contributes to a perception
of each brother not as a discrete individual with a specific history (a
norm of dramatic realism) but as a fragment of a single consciousness
or the embodiment of a choice or choices that a single consciousness
must face (a norm of dramatic expressionism and allegory). So it is
that brother pairs make available to realistic drama certain quasi-
expressionistic devices.
   If one perceives life as an endless struggle between good and evil,
then the two brothers might serve as embodiments of opposing moral
forces. Of course instead of good and evil, a spectator might instead
perceive them as representing some other set of terms, generally contrasting, from one of several available narratives of fragmentation.
Christian allegory, for example, might think of Jamie as a representation of man's carnal nature, as the flesh attempting to corrupt the
spirituality of Edmund. O'Neill himself approaches this sort of allegorical treatment in the conflict between John and Loving in an earlier
work, *Days Without End* (1933). Jungian analysis might see Jamie as
a Shadow figure; Freudian as a manifestation of the id or oedipal
desire. I am not particularly concerned about which system of partiali-
zation (moral, philosophical, religious, psychological) the spectator or
critic employs, although we will almost always employ one or the
other. The significant point for the moment is the presence of a structure that encourages the diagrammatic representation of contradictory
energies or impulses within the psyche. The tale of two brothers is,
almost by definition, the tale of a divided self.
   This representation of a fragmented or divided self through conventions of separation, as opposed to the representation of this same

condition through conventions of mentorship, is evident in most of the brother pairs within these plays of prodigality. It even appears in plays of mentorship (*Journey* and *Horn*), for when the mentor reverses himself to become an advocate of restraint and not release, then images of separation take over and with them the sense of an internal dialogue between opposing aspects of the self. The only mentor play within this group that does not move in this direction is *Look Homeward* in which the elder brother/mentor (Ben Gant) dies and is idealized by the younger. More obvious examples of this representation of fragmentation through contrast are those plays that do not emphasize mentorship in the first place such as Williams's *Cat* and Mosel's *All the Way Home*. Brick and Gooper obviously represent contradictory elements of the psyche. We might, for example, see Brick, using Fiedler's terms, as the Good Bad Boy and Gooper as his opposite the Bad Good Boy. The first appears to be the essence of appetite or desire as he downs one drink after another but is actually almost pure conscience or ego-ideal in search of relief from a terrible guilt; the latter appears to epitomize control and propriety but is actually a mass of greed and desire. Each in turn has a wife that doubles for and contrasts with the other. Even the presence or absence of children contributes to this process of doubling and opposition: the "no-neck monsters" are appropriate images of desire run wild, born of "that monster of fertility," Mae; the absence of children, in this sense, is more positive than negative.[40] The two families are in a sense a single family divided, fragmented by various forces and pressures at war within and upon the self. For Jay and Ralph in *All the Way Home*, the central image of division is their encounter, alone onstage, over a bottle of whiskey: one, desperately thirsty, unable to stop drinking until the bottle is empty; the other, able to drink the bottle dry without seeming to taste the liquor at all, so strong is his determination never to be drunk again. One is an image of weakness and flaccidity; the other is an image of strength and will. Each marks the presence of what seems absent in the other but is only hiding. The bottle itself joins them into a single image in space; their individual and contradictory perceptions of it, however, fragment that image into two opposing, yet nevertheless complementary, entities.

Even more pronounced is the example of Happy and Biff in *Salesman*. As noted already, we see them through Linda's eyes shaving before the bathroom mirror, two parts of a whole, but also together in their bedroom at the beginning of the play and, of course, at their father's grave at its end. In the opening scene, we find one image of division in their perception of women; at their father's grave, we find another in their perception of Willy. As with Brick and Gooper, Jay and Ralph, the nature of the divided self is clarified by bringing two brothers into the same space, by focusing their attention on the same object (an inheritance, a bottle of whiskey, a woman, a grave) and then allowing contrasting perceptions of that object to suggest the fragmented nature of the self's response. Miller uses a similar technique in *All My Sons* (1947), although in this case, one half of that perception takes the form of a letter from a son now dead. In *The Price* two brothers meet in a room filled with objects from their past: one brother is the prodigal who left to pursue his own life, who now wants in some way to come home again; the other is the brother who stayed behind to labor for his father. Perhaps (along with Shepard's *True West*) the best recent example of the representation of a divided self through differentiated brothers, Miller's play is structured around an image of two individuals, together in the present, surrounded by objects from the past, engaged in the process of seeing that past as they stand side-by-side, revealing in the irreconcilable differences of their perceptions the fragmentations and divisions of the self. Miller's production note for *The Price* comes close to being a summation of the conventions here described on the use of contrasted brothers to represent contradictory aspects of a single self:

> A fine balance of sympathy should be maintained in the playing of the roles of Victor and Walter. . . .
> As the world now operates, the qualities of both brothers are necessary to it; surely their respective psychologies and moral values conflict at the heart of the social dilemma. The production must therefore withhold judgment in favor of presenting both men in all their humanity and from their own viewpoints. Actually, each has merely proved to the other what the other has known but dared not face.[41]

In other words each brother represents to the other a neglected aspect of the self, social and psychological, made explicit, concretized by differences in their perceptions of objects and events.

Whether through conventions of mentorship or conventions of separation, these uses of brothers to represent a fragmented or divided self often conflict with other dramatic conventions also at work within playscripts. They conflict, first of all, with the pretenses of dramatic realism (the dramatic style that these works most consistently draw upon) by confounding one image of character—as a specific individual with a concrete past—with another—as an atemporal fragment of some psychic whole. Secondly these conventions conflict with an even more fundamental convention of dramatic representation, that which asks the spectator to build an image of a whole character in time and space around the physical presence of an actor using numerous synecdochic bits and pieces of information. This latter convention, of course, extends well beyond the boundaries of dramatic realism and consistently works to frustrate the mimesis of a fragmented or divided self. The central tendency of the dramatic process is to make whole characters out of thousands of separate parts, not to perceive fragments of a self where dramatic convention has trained us to see a complete human being.[42]

Brother pairs, however, actually seem to enjoy this tension between fragmentation and wholeness. They, more than almost any other dramatic device, alert spectators to the possibility that in them we might expect to find two or more parts of a whole. Brothers broadcast (in some instances more clearly than in others) a double message: "We are different; we are the same. We are two complete selves; we are fragments of the self at work within a single psyche."

5

He (Or She) Who Waits

And he arose, and came to his father. But when he was yet a great way off, his father saw him, and had compassion, and ran, and fell on his neck, and kissed him.

—Luke 15:20

Eunice: You can't beat on a woman an' then call 'er back! She won't come! And her goin' t' have a baby! . . .
Stanley (humbly): Eunice, I want my girl to come down with me!
Eunice: Hah! (*She slams her door.*)
Stanley (with heaven-splitting violence):
STELL-LAHHHHH!
(*The low-tone clarinet moans. The door upstairs opens again. . . .*)[1]

Stella: . . . when men are drinking and playing poker anything can happen. It's always a powder-keg. . . . He was as good as a lamb when I came back and he's really very, very ashamed of himself.[2]

In some part of the American imagination, Stanley and the prodigal of the parable commingle, as do those who forgive them: the prodigal's father and Stanley's Stella. The dynamic of each pair depends on a state of rupture created by son or husband: one has taken his inheritance and gone to a city in a faraway land; another lives there, in New Orleans, the type of city that the Lukan father might well fear. Stanley has gone even farther: he has brought a kind of riotous living into the home, has made it a place of men and drinking, of "seven-card stud" and, finally, violence. More importantly for the purposes of this chapter, each narrative contemplates the prodigal's return and his forgiveness by a father or wife/mother. In Luke the father's welcome stops short the prodigal's speech of repentance; in *Streetcar*, Stanley stands in the street, separated from his wife by the walls of a home and in calling her name asks to come home. Their embrace makes clear a link, potential, if not implicit, between Eros

123

and forgiveness: as Stanley kneels and "presses his face to her [Stella's] belly, curving a little with maternity" he is boy and man; her pregnancy reminds the spectator that she, eyes "blind with tenderness," is mother and wife.[3] The explicit sexuality of this moment is not a perversion of or deviation from the paradigm of the prodigal's return, but a metaphor for it, an extension of what it always implies: an end, if even for a moment, to fragmentation and division, a return to a certain unity, the discovery of one where there were two. This unbroken circularity after all is the meaning of the ring that the Lukan father gives to his son.

This chapter focuses on a final set of dramatic figures essential to the paradigm of the prodigal, on those who resemble the father of the parable, figures like Wilder's Ma Kirby and Williams's Stella. Without characters such as these, the paradigm is unrecognizable: the prodigal must have someone to leave behind, someone to come home to. Here again is the list of prodigal figures from chapter 3 and opposite them the names of those from whom they are separated or to whom they might return.[4]

Prodigals	He (or She) Who Waits
Iceman	
Hickey	Evelyn
Parritt	Rosa and Larry
Streetcar	
Stanley	Stella
Misbegotten	
Jamie	Josie
Salesman	
Willy	Linda and Biff
Biff	Willy[5]
Country Girl	
Frank	Georgie
Sheba	
Doc	Lola
Seven Year Itch	
Richard	Helen[6]
Cat	
Brick	Big Daddy and Maggie[7]

Journey
  Tyrone   Mary
  Jamie and Edmund   Tyrone

Look Homeward
  W. O. Gant   Eliza

Dark at the Top of the Stairs
  Rubin   Cora

Raisin
  Walter Lee   Mama and Ruth

All the Way Home
  Jay   Mary
  Ralph (Jay's brother)   Sally (his wife)

Iguana
  Shannon   Hannah Jelkes[8]

Woolf
  George   Martha
  Martha   George

We lack a simple term such as "prodigal" for these characters and so must invent one for the purposes of this chapter. In many instances the designation "patient," "faithful," or "salvific" wife would work, connecting these characters with earlier dramatic and literary figures that stretch back through Renaissance literature to "Patient Griselda" and others before her. Even though in American drama the substitution of a wife/mother for the father figure is the significant adaptation of the parable, these terms would eliminate male characters and women other than wives who perform similar functions. More recent labels are, of course, also possible. Family therapists and recovery programs in the 1980s coined the term *co-dependent* to describe male and female behavior similar to that described in the following pages, but I want to save the discussion of the relationship between this term and these plays for later in this study.

For the purposes of this chapter, I propose to refer to the dramatic characters in the second column, as "grace" figures, "fixed" figures, or "functional others." I suggest the first phrase, because these characters seem most marked by the expectation that they will practice acts of patience and forgiveness, that they will play the role of the "angel in the house." The prodigal son may not expect nor perhaps deserve this forgiveness, but the conventions of the story demand these acts of benevolence, as in Cheesman's description of the prodigal's father as a "benevolent patriarch" who "generously restores" the son to his former position.[9] The problem with the phrase *grace figure* (and I do not underestimate it) is that it brings with it a halo effect, a positive connotation that may suggest approval of or nostalgia for the type. This is not, however, my intent. The exercise of "grace" in these plays may not signal strength and goodness, but weakness, vulnerability, and oppression, particularly if it only moves in one direction, as it often does in American domestic drama, from women to men. Even within the paradigm, texts might celebrate the presence of this "grace" or condemn it. The former, of course, is the persistent tendency, but the latter is also possible, as a discussion of Shange's *for colored girls* in chapter 6 will show. The term is meant to denote a function that both male and female characters perform within these plays: the dispensation of unmerited favor, often coupled with a high degree of other-directedness. Because I employ it in this rather technical sense, as a critical term to designate that character who stands in rough equivalence to the father in the parable, I will mark it off in the discussion that follows with quotation marks. Those marks signal the presence of a character that we may well perceive as a male construct, lacking his or her own subjectivity, existing primarily as an object of fantasy, a form of wish fulfillment. To use a softer, more neutral term would be to misrepresent the nature of the role as found both in the parable, in which the father represents God's grace toward sinners, and in these plays, in which parents and spouses often represent a longing for understanding and forgiveness, usually on the behalf of the male protagonist. If the term seems vaguely theological, it reminds us of the strong links between the ethos of these plays and Christianity, particularly Protestant evangelicalism in which the notion of grace as "unmerited favor" is a central precept. I use it then in a sense similar to that employed by Wendy Kaminer in her discussion of the recovery movement, which I believe is another form that the paradigm of the prodigal has taken in the nineteenth and twentieth centuries (see chapter 6): "The ideology of recovery is the ideology of salvation by grace. More than they resemble group therapy, twelve-step groups are like revival meetings, carrying on the pietistic tradition."[10]

I will also on occasion use the phrase "fixed" figure to describe these characters. They are fixed in that they usually remain in one spot, at home, while the prodigal, either literally or metaphorically, takes to the open road. Their fixedness is their primary attribute; they are fixed in space and fixed in their role by the expectations of the dominant culture. In other instances I will use the term "functional other" to emphasize the extent to which these characters often seem located outside the realm of the playscript's subjectivity (therefore, "othered") even as they serve (therefore, "functional") the needs of that subjectivity, often centered in the figure of prodigal. Despite its relative clumsiness, this label will underscore an absence (of subjectivity) that has often made many of these roles painful for women to play and that would no doubt move some to suggest that these often thankless parts be played by men in drag, by the men who created them, thus foregrounding their status as male constructs.[11]

The purest incarnations of this group of characters—as in the prodigal's father or Hickey's Evelyn—stand opposite the prodigal with arms outstretched and love in their hearts, waiting for the least sign that the lost one is ready to come home. The archetypal "grace" figure, male or female, conventionally performs three major functions, all of them dependent on the actions of another. First he or she *waits*. Patience is, as Mary Hyde suggests in her discussion of these conventions in Elizabethan literature, the "conventional foil" of prodigality in that our notion of this phenomenon generally includes a positive sense of duration:[12] given enough time, the prodigal, usually male, will come to himself and will come home. In addition to this, waiting also implies stasis. The role of the prodigal is to wander; the role of the father/mother/wife is to stay at home and wait for the return, to be Donne's "fixed foot" that makes the circle just, that enables prodigals to end their journeys where they began. Second this "fixed" figure *listens:* the emphasis is not on creating discourse but on receiving it, on being its receptacle, a huge ear, as empty as the house in which s/he waits. This listening may, however, be terminated in order to move into a third and final phase of action, that is, the *response* to the prodigal's return, the actual process of opening doors, of killing fatted calves and getting robes, one of *forgiveness* and *embracings* (chaste and intimate), of happy ends and tears all around. Later in this chapter, I will further discuss these three conventional actions— *waiting, listening, responding*—using O'Neill's *A Moon for the Misbegotten* as my central example, but first I want to further examine some of the variations this figure encompasses in terms of idealization and gender.

IDEALIZATION

In many male-authored American domestic dramas, women possess as their distinguishing characteristic an undeniable moral and spiritual superiority.[13] Ma Kirby, with whom this study began, certainly perceives herself in this way. Indeed she threatens to turn into a self-righteous parody of the convention. She, not the husband, is the conscience of the family, the arbiter of morality and the final authority on matters of character. But this fussy goodness describes only one facet of her character. We glimpse another in her response to Arthur's repentance, in her quickness to reunite and forgive. The playscript invites us to see this goodness most fully embodied in the final moments of the play in which she personifies love itself outfacing and, at least momentarily, overcoming death, in those moments in which, alone with her daughter who has lost a child at birth, she brings solace and comfort. Ma Kirby's character in fact represents a basic convention for the presentation of goodness: it must veil itself in some way. A foreword to the acting edition of *Happy Journey* delineates the problems faced in making this process work:

> [T]he director should constantly keep in mind that Ma Kirby's humor, strength and humanity constitute the unifying element throughout. This aspect should rise above the merely humorous characteristic details of the play.
>
> Many productions have fallen into two regrettable extremes. On the one hand actors exaggerated the humorous characters and situations in the direction of farce; and on the other hand, have treated Ma Kirby's sentiment and religion with sentimentality and preachy solemnity. The atmosphere, comedy, and characterization of this play are most effective when they are handled with great simplicity and evenness.[14]

Evenness is the key word here in that it denotes the balancing act going on between the revelation of "grace" ("strength and humanity") and its obfuscation via the "merely humorous." Texts must continually find ways to do this, so that they can maintain the distinction, possibly false, between "sentiment" and "sentimentality" or, perhaps more accurately, between blatant sentimentality and its more subtle forms. By their nature these strategies create an impression of inherent goodness continually rising to the surface, as does the decision of the prodigal to reform, return, and begin a new life.

This tension between the revelation or presence of goodness and its ambiguation or absence provides a way in which to begin to describe various "functional others." For example Evelyn (*Iceman*), Linda (*Salesman*), and Mama Younger (*Raisin*) are all relatively idealized, orthodox character types. Their lineage stretches back through Mary Middleton of *The Drunkard* to Lady Easy of *The Careless Husband* (Cibber, 1704) and Cordelia of *Lear* (ca. 1605), to the cult of the Virgin Mary and Dante's Beatrice. I am not asserting that Evelyn, Linda, and Mama Younger are all Cordelias or that they are all as successful as Beatrice in redeeming their men or even that their influence is necessarily benevolent, only that their role is clearly that of the good, patient, ultimately forgiving, and potentially redemptive mother/woman/wife. Hannah Jelkes (*Iguana*), although not literally wife or mother to Shannon, exemplifies the type.

Other "grace" figures resemble more closely Ma Kirby in that we perceive their goodness through certain disguises or watch it slowly assert itself during the course of the play. This group includes Josie in *Misbegotten*, Lola in *Sheba*, Maggie in *Cat*, Mary in *All the Way Home*. Ironically the disguise might be that of either too much goodness, of an oppressive or particularly narrow moral vision (Mary Follet and Ma Kirby), or it might take the shape of some moral failure, that of the "fallen" or sexually compromised woman. Josie and Maggie are examples of the latter device: in one instance a virgin after all; in the other excused by extenuating circumstances. In either case (excessive goodness or moral weakness), the final perception of the disguised "grace" figure is of a solid, undeniable, near angelic goodness. In *Country Girl* a director thinks that Georgie is sabotaging her husband's attempts at reform to maintain power in the marriage. Finally he realizes he is seeing no more than a disguise that Georgie's husband has constructed, one similar to those that texts use to momentarily hide the presence of human goodness. He sees that beneath the disguise lives the woman who saves her man, who is home when the prodigal returns, is indeed home itself. He has seen Georgie perform this function for Frank and imagines her filling the same role for him: "You could be a home for me."[15] This last statement, no doubt meant and perceived as a compliment in the 1950s, stands today as an example of the way in which this convention turns flesh, blood, and mind into wood, brick, and concrete.

The absence of "grace," not its presence, defines a third set of dramatic figures: failed or exhausted parents and spouses. These characters demonstrate the power of this convention to the degree in which they are perceived (reflectively or by others) as not being able to embody a certain standard of behavior. O'Neill's late plays offer two obvious examples, Mary Tyrone and Rosa Parritt: one exhausted; the other, failed. Mary represents the accumulated weariness of American wives and mothers confronted by prodigal husbands and prodigal sons, the great weariness and fatigue of the Linda Lomans and the Georgie Elgins and the Cora Floods. She has spent too many nights in cheap hotels, been too long without a home of her own, too often seen her husband and one or more of her sons carried home drunk from the bar. Nora in *A Touch of the Poet* was able in her peasant toughness to keep going; Hickey's Evelyn could somehow endlessly, almost mechanically, forgive and forgive and forgive. But Mary finally comes to a point after which she can no longer emulate her namesake, after which the best escape is a drug-induced withdrawal to a time

before men and drunkenness had entered her life. She is present at
the end of *Journey*, but it is the presence not of Mary the mother or
Mary the wife but Mary the convent school girl, a presence that marks
the absence of the one who should, according to dramatic convention,
redeem her men:

> *Jamie:* . . . this time Mama had me fooled. I really believed she had it
> licked. She thinks I always believe the worst, but this time I believed the
> best. (*His voice flutters.*) I suppose I can't forgive her—yet. It meant so
> much. I'd begun to hope, if she'd beaten the game, I could, too.[16]

Instead of giving forgiveness, Mary needs it, an inversion of the convention almost impossible for O'Neill's men to accept. Earlier I mentioned Evelyn as an example of an idealized figure, but like Mary
forgiveness has exhausted her, an exhaustion for which her murder
at Hickey's hands is the clearest sign. Both *Iceman* and *Journey* move
toward the realization that these conventional figures—Evelyn and
Mary—only have a presence as long-suffering wives within a narrative
of the past. In the dramatic present, they are unavailable for duty.[17]

A third conspicuous example of a missing or absent "grace" figure
is Parritt's mother, Rosa. The image of an anarchist in jail is apt for
a character that seems to break away from these conventions, but for
all her struggling only emphasizes their presence more profoundly.
On the one hand, Rosa has tried to escape the bourgeois morality of
family life. She has refused confinement within the world of domesticity; she has entered the larger world of political and social causes. As
a leader of men and women, she has rejected the role of any one man's
wife or lover and, from Parritt's perspective, much of the traditional
nurturing and compassion that we associate with the mother. Her
son is, as a member of Hickey's "lodge," a fellow prodigal who has
wasted his money on whores (betraying his mother with one), collected a Judaslike inheritance, and now journeyed to a far country to
finally find himself feeding with the swine. Eventually he will come
to himself and do what he must do. Unlike the father in the parable,
Rosa cannot be expected ever to welcome her repentant son home.
Justice, not grace, is her theme. So it is that Parritt imagines her
response when she will hear of his death:

> *Parritt:* It [his own death] ought to comfort Mother a little, too. It'll give
> her the chance to play the great incorruptible Mother of the Revolution,
> whose only child is the Proletariat. She'll be able to say: "Justice is done!
> So may all traitors die!" She'll be able to say: "I am glad he's dead! Long
> live the Revolution!"[18]

On the other hand, the reference to Rosa as the "Mother of the Revolution" reveals the degree to which the conventions she has been trying to escape have co-opted her. Her role in the movement is as its mother. In this sense Rosa has not moved out of the home and into the world so much as redrawn the former's boundaries so that it now includes more of the latter: a strategy central to the social reform movements women created in the nineteenth century, movements from which Rosa's activism directly descends.[19] Rosa's role as a force for benevolence is, however, personal, as well as metaphorical. Despite her own enjoyment of sexual freedom, she still places herself in opposition to her son's visits to the prostitutes, recreating the conventional mother/whore dichotomy. Even more particularly Parritt shows us Rosa as a function of Larry's prodigality in an image that foregrounds not justice but forgiveness, an image that suddenly calls to mind Hickey's Evelyn:

> *Parritt:* Do you know, Larry, you're the one of them all she cared most about? Anyone else who left the Movement would have been dead to her, but she couldn't forget you. She'd always make excuses for you. . . . She'd blame it on booze getting you. She'd kid herself that you'd give up booze and come back to the Movement—tomorrow! . . . I suppose what she really meant was, come back to her. She was always getting the Movement mixed up with herself.[20]

Rosa plays the role of a failed or nonfunctioning "grace" figure: literally absent from the stage, imprisoned on the West Coast, murdered by her son, unable to perform for him the role of the Lukan father. In another sense she is a disguised "grace" figure: the one about whom there is nothing "soft or sentimental,"[21] yet who cannot throw away Larry's letters; one who, in her son's perception anyway, would still bring at least one prodigal home. Ironically she, like many "fixed" figures, is literally imprisoned, confined to a specific cite, that is, she to her jail cell, they to their homes. She shares their stasis with them.

Nevertheless Rosa is finally as functionally absent as Evelyn and Mary. This means that Hickey and Parritt must find replacements for Evelyn and Rosa. The latter turns to Larry Slade (his father, metaphorically, if not literally) in an effort to work out his salvation, to find some release from self-hatred and guilt, a release that finally happens when Slade agrees with Parritt's decision to end his life. Hickey finally forces the inhabitants of Harry's bar to fill this same function, unwilling though they are. In Hickey's case, the corollary to being forgiven is the sharing of the illusion that the "real" Hickey was not responsible for the death of Evelyn nor for the words of hatred he spoke, that he must have been insane, just as Evelyn always believed that the "real" Hickey was not responsible for his drinking and infidelity.

In general one is struck by the absence of women, idealized or not, in these two plays: Rosa is imprisoned; Evelyn is dead; Mary is drugged. Harry's former wife Bessie is also gone and we even learn that his loving memories of her are an illusion. He actually thinks of her as a "nagging bitch," while her brother calls her a "God-damned bitch."[22] Jimmy Tomorrow's former wife, Marjorie, is, of course, also absent: her husband cannot even remember the color of her hair. He admits that he was glad when he found her in bed with another man, because the incident gave him an excuse to leave her permanently for the nearest tavern. The prostitutes—Maggie, Cora, and Pearl—are, of course, present, but as Bette Mandl points out, they are "external to the central movement of the play."[23]

Given these significant absences, the presence of Josie in *Misbegotten* is remarkable. Suddenly where no women were, now one is available to wait, to listen, to forgive, and to take the places of Mary, Bessie, Marjorie, Evelyn, and Rosa. Indeed within Josie we find not one, but several women, a discovery appropriate to a character of her physical dimensions. She is, for example, woman as laborer, as one who works alongside the father in the fields, "able to do the manual labor of two ordinary men."[24] Indeed her efforts seem vital to the economic survival of the farm itself. This Josie claims freedom from domesticity and the sexual double standard. She would not "marry the best man on earth and be tied down to him alone."[25] Instead she seems, at least initially, to enjoy a proud, bull-like promiscuity that mocks the guilt-laden image of the fallen woman.[26] In this role she almost functions as a female version of the prodigal son. At the same time, however, her faithfulness to her father and her industry as a worker also suggest qualities of the elder brother. She stays at home; her brothers, like the prodigal, depart—brother Mike with a small "inheritance" stolen by Josie from their father's "little green bag."[27] In either case Josie's status in these instances is closer to son than daughter.

To these personae we might add a number of others. For example we see Josie in the past, as a young child with her "hair brushed and a ribbon in it,"[28] being used by Hogan to soften James Tyrone's heart when the rent is overdue, stepping almost directly from the scenario of a nineteenth-century melodrama or, at least, a convivial and self-conscious reenactment of one. In the opening scene of the play, immediately after emphasizing her bull-like qualities, a different image suggests another role, this one, maternal. Josie recalls her role as a mother to a younger brother: "Well, that's the last of you, Mike, and good riddance. It was the little boy you used to be that I had to mother, and not you, I stole the money for."[29] Although she makes it clear that these maternal feelings are in the past, her actions in helping her brother escape suggest that these feelings and this role still retain some force in the present. Later in the first act, we perceive Josie in yet another role, that of a young girl obviously infatuated with James Tyrone. In act 2 she plays the seductress who tries to entrap and blackmail her victim whom she suspects of betraying her father. This is in addition to what Jamie calls her "brazen-trollop act,"[30] her rough speech and pretense of sexual availability, a role that despite the bull-like freedom mentioned above still conventionally carries with it the sense of a devalued (because sexually used) woman, good enough for Jamie perhaps, because he is a drunkard used to whores, but not suitable for any "decent" man. Of course the final revelation of her virginity plays into this image of women and sexuality by showing the spectator that the fallen woman is not fallen.

The effect of all these different identities—laborer, prodigal, child, mother, ingenue, seductress, trollop, virgin—is to create a field of choices for Jamie. Ironically a primary function of these choices is to allow Josie to function as a replacement for two absent women: the two significant female identities in Jamie's life—a whore on a train and a madonna-mother named Mary. With her Jamie might and almost does reenact the episode with the "blonde pig," or he might find forgiveness in his mother's arms. Josie might be one or the other to him. She cannot, however, be both. For Jamie the two terms are self-exclusive. The effect of Jamie's choice upon our perception of Josie is profound and representative of the way in which American domestic drama severely limits the functions of its female characters. The text wipes out, at least momentarily, a series of identities scattered throughout the play to present the spectator with a single image, a particularly strong and apparently authentic one. Josie, madonna-mother, holds Jamie in her arms throughout the night, forgiving him for visiting the blonde pig. She forgives him in his mother's name and in her place for his sins: "As *she* forgives, do you hear me! As *she* loves and understands and forgives!"[31] Out of the various identities available only two signify at this moment: the figure who forgives and the one who makes forgiveness necessary.

In this respect Josie seems finally to represent not so much a person as a dramatic function of forgiveness, the need for its presence or at least the illusion of its presence. This functionality, this identify contingent upon and shaped by the needs of a man, is itself, of course, an effacement of identity, another form of the absences already marked in *Iceman* and *Journey*.[32] Josie defines the term "functional other." Yet unlike some examples of the type, Josie also possesses an awareness of herself as a conventional figure, as an actor, as a "functional other," a role that she chooses, in Tyrone's case, for a night and as an act of love. This self-consciousness about the role she will play and the obviously transient nature of its assumption pushes up against the convention. At best, it asks the spectator to think of the "grace" figure as a role to be picked-up and put down. As with Hickey (the prodigal) in *Iceman*, O'Neill takes the convention of the "functional other," pushes it to an extreme, and forces its reconsideration. If we perceive Josie's playing of the mother as a revelation of her essence (one strategy that the play invites), then we find a foreclosure of possibilities. If, on the other hand, we perceive her playing of the mother as one among many roles she might choose to play in the course of a day or a life, then we find the basis for a subjectivity within this play in addition to Jamie's.

GENDER

In addition to these degrees of idealization, failure, and disguise, a second major factor is at work among this set of dramatic figures in the presences of both male and female sources of forgiveness. Of course, male "grace" figures may also be idealized (Nat Miller in *Ah, Wilderness!*), disguised (Big Daddy in *Cat*—for all his gruffness and crudity, he labors to bring the prodigal home), or failed/exhausted (Willy in *Salesman*—in Biff's, if not Happy's perception of him). My interest here, however, is not in these parallel examples but in briefly exploring some potential differences within American drama between the manifestation of male "grace," the form found in the parable, and the manifestation of female "grace," the form most often found in American drama. First of all male patience and forgiveness, usually present only in father/son relationships within these plays, often recalls the parable in its emphasis on financial concerns, in the presence, in one form or another, of an inheritance: in *Horn* Alan and Buddy's role in the wax fruit business; in *Salesman* Biff's ability or inability to make his way in the world of commerce; and in *Cat*, Brick's fitness to inherit the family estate. With female forgiveness these concerns shift. With mothers the focus is often on the inheritance of not a financial but a moral and spiritual legacy. In *Raisin*, for example, even though Mama Younger has control of the insurance check, it has essentially come from the father. What Mama passes on is not money but a lineage of dignity and integrity. With wives as well, the primary articulated concern is usually the spiritual or moral welfare of the husband, then, secondarily, the economic survival of the family. Money and morality are often present and important in both contexts (male forgiveness and female), but when fathers forgive sons, economic considerations are generally more significant. Indeed as noted above, a possible explanation for the decline in male "grace" figures is the relative unimportance of inherited wealth within the middle-class milieu of nineteenth- and twentieth-century America.

An additional inheritance from the father, one that may also explain to some degree the preponderance of female "grace" figures in American drama, is that of prodigality itself. A convention of Elizabethan drama (e.g., Old Flowerdale of *The London Prodigal*) is for the father of the prodigal to acknowledge his own youthful prodigality as a phase that he has outgrown and that presumably his son will also leave behind. In American drama, however, fathers do not always complete this process, so that fathers with some frequency represent not a model of maturity and forgiveness but of weakness and appetite: Willy in *Salesman* or, more recently, the persistent image in Shepard of a drunken, prodigal father, trying to run a farm (*Curse of the Starving Class*) or living alone in the desert (*True West, A Lie of the Mind, Fool for Love*). This model emphasizes the bifurcation of the self (father/appetite; mother/control), as opposed to an image of maturation, the balancing of these forces in the life of a single self, male or female. The double standard, of course, reflects this bifurcation: the sense that forgiveness is a female trait; that the need for forgiveness and, ironically, the demand for justice or a rigid standard (for women anyway), are male traits.[33]

The male "grace" figure—man as patient and forgiving—is perhaps more notable for his failures, than his successes. Biff in *Salesman* finds it difficult, if not impossible, to forgive his father. *All My Sons* deals with a similar problem. Quentin, in *After the Fall* (1964), ultimately runs out of patience in trying to deal with his wife, Maggie. In another Miller play, *The Price* (1968), Victor, the brother who had stayed behind with the father, finds it almost impossible to forgive the brother who went off to pursue a career as a surgeon but then later refused to lend him money so that he, too, could go to school. Jamie tells Edmund that he cannot yet forgive Mary for her latest relapse, while *Journey*, as a whole, builds on the sense of how difficult it is for three men to offer a woman the kind of endurance and patience that women conventionally offer men in American drama. Finally I would note again the general unwillingness of the men to hear Hickey's confession in *Iceman*, as well as Larry's almost brutal rejection of any relationship—particularly as father or "grace" figure—with Parritt. Larry, we are also told, was unable to accept or forgive Rosa's promiscuity. Indeed his relationship with her is, in this sense, the inverse of Evelyn's relationship with Hickey. Men are then potential "grace" figures, but in general, male "grace" is in American drama often a contradiction in terms. The role of the "functional other," at least in the body of plays included within this study, is usually reserved for female characters.[34]

Finally the shift from one man (a father) forgiving another (a son) to a woman (wife or mother) forgiving a man (husband or son) allows for a full eroticization of the paradigm, often along oedipal lines. This mixture of forgiveness and Eros will receive further consideration in the second half of this chapter in a discussion of responses to the prodigal's return. For the moment I want to simply register its presence as a significant facet in the predominance of female "grace" figures in American drama. Indeed if the son is perceived as constituting a threat to the father, it is to the father's advantage that he not be forgiven, that he not come home. Oedipus was, after all, also a son who returned from a far country.

This discussion of gender and idealization has purposely not addressed each example from the above inventory of characters with which this chapter began. To do so would be tedious. It has, however, tried to establish a field of possibilities in which these various characters are located, some bunched near the center of this character set, others near its periphery, all drawing, in varying degrees, on the energy of this convention. I conclude this section, as I did that on the figure of the prodigal, with Albee's *Woolf*, not as a central example but as one that reveals these conventions functioning near the limits of their visibility. To the extent that George and Martha both function as prodigals, they also serve as sources of patience and forgiveness for one another. The initial impression is that they exhaust or have exhausted whatever fund of forgiveness they once mutually shared. The play's final act, however, reverses this impression by suggesting that the ability to forgive, to accept the failures and weaknesses of the other, has not been completely depleted, that drunkenness and verbal abuse have disguised the presence of grace. It also inverts the conventional expectation that women must always be forgiving and good, while men should be forgiven and wild. It reverses these conventional charges and then uses these reversals to move the play forward.

As noted above "functional others" conventionally perform three distinct services: they wait for the prodigal to come home; they frame the narrative of his adventures by being its principal listener; they respond to the need for forgiveness and a return to the family. In the following section, I use these three elements to clarify further the nature of this character (its matter), but also to consider how these actions contribute to a play's dramatic or presentational functions (its manner).

To Wait

Josie is sitting on the steps before the front door. She has changed to her Sunday best, a cheap dark-blue dress, black stockings and shoes. . . . There is an expression on her face we have not seen before, a look of sadness and loneliness and humiliation.[35]

Although Josie is neither a spouse nor a parent, at the beginning of act 2 she is doing what fathers, mothers, and wives must continually do in American family drama: she is waiting at home for the prodigal's return, not knowing if or when he will come but ready if and when he does, just as Mary Follet waits for Jay in *All the Way Home* or Maggie and Big Daddy wait for Brick (even though he is already there) or Linda (*Salesman*), Cora (*Dark at the Top of the Stairs*), and Evelyn (*Iceman*) wait for their traveling-salesman husbands. In act 3 of *Ah, Wilderness!* the entire family sits waiting for the return of their son. In *Salesman* and *Horn*, Willy and Mr. Baker wait for their sons to find themselves and come home to their versions of the American dream. *Look Homeward, Angel* opens with the expectation of a father's drunken homecoming. Tyrone and Edmund wait for Jamie's return in *Journey*, just as Mary waited for Tyrone's drunken return from the hotel bar while they were still on their honeymoon. This play ends with three men, each holding a drink in their hand, waiting for a wife and mother, whose ability to function for others has been exhausted.

These images have their lighter counterparts in the television sitcoms in which mom and the kids greet dad at the door as he returns from work. They have their nineteenth-century counterparts in temperance melodramas in which mother and the children wait, grieving and poverty stricken, for the return of their drunken father from the local tavern or inn. They also find their parallels in evangelical invitation hymns such as this one:

> Softly and tenderly Jesus is calling,
> Calling for you and for me;
> See! at the portals He's waiting and watching,
> Watching for you and for me.
>
> Come home, . . . come home, . . .
> Ye who are weary come home;

Earnestly, tenderly, Jesus is calling,
Calling, "O sinner come home!"[36]

The Jesus imaged in this hymn is about as close as the Protestant
church comes to the equivalent of the Catholic Mary. He is a figure
who calls "softly and tenderly," not the harsh voice of an Old Testament or Calvinist god but the sweet and lovely voice of a sorrowing
mother. Ironically and effectively revivalist preachers often locate this
image of Jesus at the end of a sermon that promises hell's fires to
anyone who does not respond to these gentle supplications. The Jesus
of the hymn is not, however, the god who sends men to hell. He is
instead more like a male incarnation of the waiting wives and mothers
who inhabit American domestic drama. Indeed Ann Douglas in *The
Feminization of American Culture* argues that this Jesus was a creation
of the nineteenth century, brought to life by the same forces that
destroyed Puritan culture and created Little Eva. In contrast she
quotes the words of an old-fashioned Puritan minister (Nathaniel Emmons) on the death of his son (Erastus). Emmons speaks of his son
without sentimentality, without feeling the need to forgive and understand. The emphasis is not on bringing the prodigal home at any cost
but on a frank and, by contemporary standards, rigorous appraisal of
behavior, an emphasis on justice not grace:

> He lived stupid, thoughtless and secure in sin, until he was brought to
> the very sight of death. . . . But whether he did ever heartily renounce
> the world and choose God for his supreme portion cannot be known in
> this world. In his own view he had become reconciled to God. . . . But
> it is more than possible that like others on a sick-bed, he built his hopes
> upon a sandy foundation.[37]

In opposition to the severity of these words, the "grace" figure
activates a sense of time as positive duration, time that will wait for
the son or husband to come home. Through characters like Josie,
Maggie, or Cora, the spectator understands how time functions in
Misbegotten or *Cat* or *Dark at the Top of the Stairs*. If someone is still
waiting for the other to return, then time represents the possibility
of a hopeful outcome, a happy end, the chance that all will work out.
Waiting also allows the prodigal time away from home. Structurally
it facilitates his narrative of departure, journey, and return by provid-
ing a time in which it can occur. Even more importantly this positive
notion of time presupposes a particular attitude toward human nature
and the significance of duration. It posits a nature essentially good,
albeit potentially flawed, that will, given enough time and compassion, come to itself. Duration then is on the side of reformation,

reconciliation, and maturation. This final element comes into play whenever texts remind the spectator that the prodigal is still in some sense a child, still in the process of growing up, even if he is in his thirties. This element is evident in Simon's *Horn*, Miller's *Salesman*, Hansberry's *Raisin*, even in Williams's *Cat* and O'Neill's *Journey*— all plays in which we encounter the convention of an adult child. Although these plays stretch our faith in time's effectiveness by focusing on adult children for whom time has not done its work, in the end these works usually attest to the progress of maturation and the ultimate soundness of each adult child's fundamental nature. Willy chafes at time in *Salesman:*

> *Willy:* In the beginning, when he was young, I thought, well, a young man, it's good for him to tramp around, take a lot of different jobs. But it's more than ten years now and he has yet to make thirty-five dollars a week!
> *Linda:* He's finding himself, Willy.
> *Willy:* Not finding yourself at the age of thirty-four is a disgrace![38]

In the end Biff does grow up, even though the self he finds is different from the one Willy expected. Hansberry's *Raisin* represents a similar process, although in this instance Walter Lee's mother duly notes time's success and the revelation of her son's essentially good nature:

> *Mama: (Quietly, woman to woman)* He finally come into his manhood today, didn't he? Kind of like a rainbow after the rain . . .
> *Ruth: (Biting her lip lest her own pride explode in front of MAMA)* Yes, Lena.[39]

In *Horn*, Alan Baker, as the prodigal who has now come home, makes a similar observation:

> *Alan:* Dad, I don't know how to say this to you . . . but . . . well, you were right about so many things. . . . I was a bum. . . . I guess every boy's got to be a bum even for a little while. I just ran into overtime.[40]

Although he ultimately despairs, at one point James Tyrone even expresses some hope in the processes of time and maturation for his eldest son, Jamie:

> *Tyrone:* You're young yet. You could still make your mark. You had the talent to become a fine actor! You have it still. You're my son—![41]

Ultimately *Journey* and *Misbegotten* show Tyrone to be right, although, as in *Salesman*, the final terms differ from what the father had imagined. Tyrone's final assessment of Jamie is as a "waste," a "wreck, a drunken hulk, done with and finished,"[42] but this is not, I think, the spectator's final assessment after listening to the end of the play. As important as the differences between all of these texts and their respective dénouements are, these are finally differences of degree, not kind: each, to one extent or another, brings the prodigal home.

Williams's *Cat* is illustrative because it contrasts this more positive notion of duration with its opposite. Brick has time while Big Daddy waits for him to talk and Maggie waits for him to come to bed. Eventually he does talk and, in at least the Broadway version of *Cat*, we assume he probably will end up in bed with Maggie. This play, however, also carries another image of time, one that is less benign: as a cancer growing in the belly of the father, killing him from the inside out. Big Daddy's illness is another way of telling time, not as an opportunity for positive change, but as a process of growth that is, in Maggie's words, both "malignant" and "terminal."[43] Gooper describes it in these terms as well:

> *Gooper:* Big Daddy is dying of cancer, and it's spread all through him and it's attacked all his vital organs including the kidneys and right now he is sinking into uremia, and you all know what uremia is, it's poisoning of the whole system due to failure of the body to eliminate its poisons.[44]

The reference to poisons also suggests that this physical metaphor reflects a spiritual or moral problem: the problem of evil, of whatever it is within man that is dark and threatening, so that, just as texts tend to link a positive sense of time with essential goodness, so do they connect a more negative sense of time's progress to a darker image of human nature.

Even though death creates in *Cat* a powerful, perhaps overwhelming counterrhythm to positive duration, those who wait can and often do overpower death itself. Mary Follet (*All the Way Home*), unlike the Puritan father cited above, brings the prodigal home, even after his death, by allowing her perception of him to change. In this instance she experiences the growth that texts usually reserve for the prodigal. In *Misbegotten*, Jamie's mother (his putative "grace" figure) has died, but Josie takes her place so that she can extend to Jamie, at least temporarily, the forgiveness and reconciliation that Mary's death had seemed to deny him. Death is a formidable barrier, but "grace" can, on occasion, surmount even it.

To Listen

A primary function of the inhabitants of Harry Hope's bar is just to listen to one another and, in particular, to Hickey, to be the ones to whom the prodigal tells his story for the final time, to take the place of Evelyn who before had always listened and forgave. They listen to Hickey's long confessional narrative, just as Josie listens to Jamie's in *Misbegotten*. In *Wilderness*, Muriel also listens to a prodigal's recitation of his adventures, as does Tyrone to Edmund's in the final act of *Journey*. Edmund himself has already heard his father's narrative; later he will hear Jamie's. Because Mary can no longer hear them, they must exchange roles among themselves, listening, then speaking, then listening again. In *Cat*, Big Daddy pushes and prods his son into speaking, into telling his story, so that again a prodigal talks while another listens. *Salesman* begins with Willy talking, telling of his journey, and listening in turn to his son's story as told by the mother. In a later Miller work, *The Price*, much of the play focuses on telling the story of the son who left home, he who now wants to return and find forgiveness.

I would add here, almost parenthetically, that the autobiographical resonances of most American domestic dramas contribute to the perception that the *playwright* is or should be a "grace" figure of some sort, one who uses the process of writing a play to "come to terms with" or "make peace with" or "understand" (all ways of saying *forgive*) the members of his or her family. Often the onstage presence of an author surrogate, attending to these voices, makes this process even clearer, as with Tom in *The Glass Menagerie* (1945), Quentin in *After the Fall* (1964), Alan in Lanford Wilson's *Lemon Sky* (1970), Jerome in *Brighton Beach Memoirs* (1985) and *Broadway Bound* (1986), or Matt in Durang's *The Marriage of Bette and Boo* (1985). In other instances that presence may be more ambiguous. Arthur Miller, for example, disclaims a direct link between the Franz (*Price*) and Miller brothers. In still others enough is known from the author's own comments and other clues to assume that the play does represent an attempt similar to that of the "grace" figure's: an endeavor to somehow order or understand the narratives of a family's past. What is more important to me than whether or not this is what actually happens is the conventional opinion that this is what does or what should happen, a notion that valorizes the processing of family history as a compassionate, redemptive, quasi-heroic, socially valid task. Of course *Journey* is the ultimate model of this process and its dedication, known almost as well as the play itself, its canonical statement:

Dearest: I give you the original script of this play of old sorrow, written in tears and blood. . . . I mean it as a tribute to your love and tenderness which gave me the faith in love that enabled me to face my dead at last and write this play—write it with deep pity and understanding and *forgiveness* for all the four haunted Tyrones.[45]

These words define the playwright as one who listens (i.e., faces his "dead"), then writes ("in tears and blood," just as the "grace" figure weeps for the lost), and finally "forgives." Indeed one can almost not be an American playwright without a family to forgive. Tennessee Williams once stated this pre-requisite in an interview:

I don't think I would have been the poet I am without that anguished familial situation. . . . I've yet to meet a writer of consequence who did not have a difficult familial background if you explored it.[46]

Williams's statement is significant not so much for its insight into what makes a good writer but for the way in which it reflects a perception of a natural relationship between writing and family, one perhaps not shared by citizens of fifth-century Athens or Elizabethan England or even by contemporary playwrights in England or Germany.

Returning to the texts themselves, the narrative of the prodigal— the equivalent of the speech that the Lukan son prepares for his father—varies in shape from play to play. In some instances (e.g., *Iceman, Misbegotten*), it takes the shape of an extended monologue. In others (e.g., *Cat* or *Dark at the Top of the Stairs*), it assumes a more fragmented, dispersed form. In still others (e.g., *Salesman* or *Horn*), this spoken narrative is almost nonexistent, because the direct representation of action has made it unnecessary. In *Misbegotten*, Jamie tells Josie about his experience with the prostitute, but in *Salesman* the spectator actually sees Willy with the other woman through a flashback, and in *Horn*, Buddy progresses from innocence to prodigality in the dramatic present. With regard to the ways in which texts choose to represent prodigal experience, as monologue, as fragmented narrative, as flashback, as action in the dramatic present, two observations are relevant. First regardless of the method, contemporary adaptations of the parable, like their historical antecedents, generally enjoy elaborating in one way or another on the picaresque adventures of the protagonist. A prodigal life is more interesting dramatically than a virtuous one, unless like Augustine or the revivalist preacher, a period of vice has preceded the virtue. Second as in the *Confessions* or the evangelist's sermon, plays within this paradigm often, although not always, make prodigal behavior an event in the past in order for it to be forgiven: existent in memory but no longer viable in the dramatic present. The extended monologue, in particular, represents a process of sorting and ordering the past, a reification that implies control over and separation from the self of the narrative, a process that distances prior prodigality and enables the granting of forgiveness. Conventionally if the past can be articulated, it can be left behind. That Hickey with Evelyn can accomplish this articulation, but then not leave his life of drinking and womanizing is, of course, the tragic joke of the play. Husband and wife fulfill the rubrics of the convention, but their efforts are for nought. They keep repeating the magic ritual, but for them it never works.

On another level the prodigal's narrative performs a somewhat more mundane, yet nevertheless important function: it serves as an important means of delivering information to the spectator. In some ways this device resembles the dialogue between servants at the beginning of a realistic drama that texts use to set the scene. In other ways it is reminiscent of the messenger speech in Greek drama, a device also used to reveal crucial information, although often at a later point in the drama. In either event, the process of recitation and reception so often central to the process of coming home and being forgiven is an excellent structure for the revelation of information to the spectator at any point in the play, particularly if a writer is working within presentational conventions that do not allow dramatic figures to directly address an audience. Indeed without Josie, Jamie's past does not, in some sense, exist. It takes her listening presence to activate him, to unlock his words. Listening may seem a passive activity, but it also entails a degree of power, in this case, to begin or end speech. O'Neill's plays, particularly those written prior to *Mourning Becomes Electra*, do, of course, employ other means to reveal information about a character (masks, asides, thought monologues, alter egos), but in his later, more conventionally realistic plays, other methods must take their place. One of the more important, along with the use of alcohol, is this device of the one who listens to another who confesses.

Josie listens so that the audience can hear Jamie's story. I explore later the ways in which this process tends to turn the audience itself into a "grace" figure, but for the moment I want to examine its opposite: Josie's role as an audience member and Jamie's as a performer. The parable itself suggests the role of performance within this narrative. It shows the prodigal rehearsing the speech he will give to his father upon his return. What this suggests is that the prodigal's recitation of his history functions as a performance for a specific audience (i.e., the "grace" figure) with the intent of creating a specific response. This theatrical metaphor of a play within a play seems appropriate, because of the division of functions between listener/spectator (the "functional other") and speaker/performer (the prodigal) and because of the link, implied or stated, between the effectiveness of a performance and its reception.

Jamie's status as a performer, a professional actor, as well as his awareness of his rhetorical facility, makes the analogy even more apt. Furthermore *Misbegotten* is a work that constantly draws attention to the ways in which characters move in and out of various roles: Jamie's putting on a face when he comes up the road to Hogan's; Josie and Hogan's show for Harder; Josie's "brazen-trollop act"; Hogan's feigned drunkenness in act 2; Jamie's scene before his mother's coffin ("Once a ham, always a ham! So I put on an act.").[47] Yet the essence of the confessional speech is the impression of an event without self-consciousness, one that does not manipulate or evade, one that reveals the true self: unvarnished, naked, exposed. It also assumes, at least in this case, that the character is revealing a content so personal and so painful as to make artifice impossible. The mask comes off. O'Neill's stage directions reinforce this perception by calling for the removal of the mask, by having Jamie empty his face of any expression before he begins, giving up the tools of an actor:

> He makes his face expressionless. His voice becomes impersonal and objective, as though what he told concerned some man he had known, but had nothing to do with him. This is the only way he can start telling the story.[48]

For reasons appropriate to the character, this may be the "only way" in which Jamie can tell his story, but this clearing away of rhetorical devices also serves to establish the presence of an unmediated, artless self. Presentationally, however, he has merely exchanged the artifice of the stage and a melodramatic style of acting for that of film and the Method. What follows is, in Strasberg's terminology, Jamie's own private moment. Its objective is the impression that one is seeing pure truth.

In *Journey*, Edmund reveals his awareness of this dichotomy between authenticity and performance when, in response to an impassioned speech by his father, he replies, "That's a grand curtain."[49] Tyrone, however, does not reject this metaphor of life as performance. Instead, he accepts and extends it: "That's right, laugh at the old fool! The poor old ham! But the final curtain will be in the poorhouse just the same, and that's not a comedy!"[50] On another occasion, however, he, like Jamie in *Misbegotten*, tries to remove the mask to set his story apart from any performance. Before beginning the tale of his childhood years, he tells Edmund, "There was no damned romance in our poverty."[51] What follows is offered as an honest, open, unper-

formed narrative of both justification and confession. Yet the shape
of the story, its subject matter, the closing quotation of his mother's
words ("Glory be to God, for once in our lives we'll have enough for
each of us!"),[52] the wiping away of tears from the eyes—all indicate
the excellent enactment of a Victorian melodrama. Tyrone's attempt
to separate this story from performance, first indicates the father's
awareness of these elements in everyday life, an awareness that Tyrone
himself would find in the Shakespearean metaphor of man as a player
on a great stage. At the same time, Tyrone wants Edmund to believe
that this moment is different, that for a time the "acting" has
stopped.[53]

We are also aware of this tension in Hickey's last long monologue
in *Iceman*. On the one hand, we sense that these words reflect from
one moment to the next the truth for this character as he knows it,
that Hickey is not performing a self, so much as he is simply, painfully, and sincerely revealing one. His listeners reflect this perception
in their unwillingness to attend to this agonizing process of honesty
and exposure. Yet again the long monologue calls for and, in Robards's performance anyway, received a virtuoso performance. Indeed we perceive Hickey's act 4 confession as something of a play
within a play and anticipate it as such, wondering just how the actor/
character will accomplish it. With Hickey we are, if anything, even
less sure than with Tyrone and Jamie as to where the authenticity
begins and the salesman/revivalist leaves off, particularly since Hickey
seems so personally convinced of what he is selling/preaching and
because the salesman/revivalist is at the height of his or her performance at the moment when one is most convinced that a performance
is not taking place. Indeed *Iceman* finally exploits this ambiguity in
a way that *Journey* and *Misbegotten* do not by raising at the end of
this penultimate speech the question of the speaker's sanity and by
suggesting that the voice we have been hearing is not that of the
"real" Hickey but of an impostor that has usurped his place.

A tension exists then in *Iceman*, *Journey*, and *Misbegotten* between
the implied sincerity of the prodigal's confession and its status as a
performance, a tension that other works such as Williams's *Cat* dissi-
pate in various ways: by breaking the set speech into a series of smaller
units, by extending it over a greater period of dramatic time, by
making the speaker a less willing participant, by substituting a game
of questions and answers for a prolonged narrative. The long confessional speeches of Jamie, Tyrone, and Hickey seem to emerge hon-
estly and directly, without composition for effect. Yet because of their
status as set speeches performed for a listening audience, they cannot
help but reveal an intricacy of structure and a virtuosity of delivery.

In each instance the effectiveness of the moment, indeed of the play as a whole, apparently relies on the spectator's perception that the dramatic figure is not enacting a role but that the play within the play has stopped and the mask has come off. At least in these instances, we are reminded that the Lukan prodigal first rehearsed his speech before he performed it, and that to some extent, the performance never stops while an audience is present. Furthermore I wonder if this almost hidden awareness of the illusive within the "real" does not add to the power of these moments by raising beneath or above or beside them the faintest shadow of a question mark.

To Respond

Finally Josie tries to stop Jamie from saying any more, she tries to end her role as a listener ("Jim! For the love of God. I don't want to hear!"),[54] but to no avail. Her services as a listener are no longer needed; the story has been told. Having waited and listened, she must now respond. Both she and Jamie have, however, anticipated her response from before he began his story. Indeed the telling depended on it:

> *Josie (Puzzled)*: You said you'd tell me about the blonde on the train.
> *Tyrone*: She's part of it. I lied about that. (*He pauses—then blurts out sneeringly*) You won't believe it could have happened. Or if you did believe, you couldn't understand or forgive—(*Quickly*) But you might. You're the one person who might. Because you really love me. . . .
> *Josie (Hugging him tenderly)*: Of course I'll understand, Jim, darling.[55]

Having heard, however, Josie's reaction initially defies their expectations: instead of embracing the sinner, she pulls away. Jamie then threatens to leave, to find a "speak open and some drunk laughing."[56] If Josie will pull away from him, then he will pull away from her. Faced with this threat, she overcomes her disgust and offers forgiveness and acceptance:

> *Josie:* I'm proud you came to me as the one in the world you know loves you enough to understand and forgive—and I do forgive![57]

The Richard/Muriel scene in act 4 of *Wilderness* parallels this action, as does the perpetual victory of "grace" over disgust in the world of Hickey and Evelyn:

> *Hickey:* Anyway, she forgave me. The same way she forgave me every time I'd turn up after a periodical drunk. You all know what I'd be like

at the end of one. You've seen me. Like something lying in the gutter that no alley cat would lower itself to drag in—something they threw out of the D.T. ward in Bellevue along with the garbage, something that ought to be dead and isn't! . . . *I could see disgust having a battle in her eyes with love. Love always won.*[58]

This action of forgiveness winning out over disgust completes a process that began with separation and ends in reunion unless, of course, as in *Iceman* the prodigal and the "fixed" figure repeat the process again and again. Hickey's comings and goings serve as a metaphor for the way in which American drama has continually rehearsed this paradigm by repeatedly sending husbands and sons out of their homes and then bringing them back again.

I now want to consider three specific aspects of these scenes. First of all just as brother pairs function as devices for the juxtaposition of self-interest and brotherly love, so do "grace" figures and prodigals function as devices for the juxtaposition of two contradictory impulses: on one hand, the will, need, or desire to punish; on the other, the will, need, or desire to understand and forgive. Second I want to examine the role of animosity toward a third character so frequently a part of these scenes: the "other" woman. Finally I am interested in the eroticization of forgiveness, particularly in plays involving male prodigals and women who wait for their men to come home, in the slightly veiled sexuality of these moments that anticipate or enact a consummation of desire. After briefly considering each of these functions, this chapter concludes with a consideration of some parallels between the status of the "grace" figure and the status of the spectator, focusing in particular on the effect these parallels have on these plays in performance.

TO RESPOND: PUNISHMENT AND FORGIVENESS

The "grace" figure and the prodigal serve a popular dialectic, one frequently rehearsed in American thought and drama, that between punishment and forgiveness. I would, however, immediately qualify this statement by noting that in most instances very little tension actually exists between these two alternatives, for the underlying message of this paradigm is the need for understanding and the power of love. Nevertheless for love and forgiveness to manifest themselves, the possibility or at least the memory of an alternate system must still have some presence, even if the eventual outcome is almost always a foregone conclusion.

In *Misbegotten* this conflict occurs within both the prodigal and "grace" figure. Jamie is caught between a desire to be forgiven for what he has done and an inability to forgive himself. Josie also experiences this tension between forgiveness and condemnation, at least in her initial response to Jamie's story, but then goodness exerts itself: Josie is able to understand and forgive Jamie, and to some degree he is then able to forgive himself. *Salesman* represents this dichotomy in the tension between the difficulty Biff has in forgiving his father and Linda's apparent ability to forgive almost anything. *Cat* uses it to contrast Big Daddy and Maggie to Gooper and Mae: the first pair want to bring Brick home, albeit for different reasons; the latter want to hold him in exile and accountable. The final act of *Journey* is almost wholly given over to the search for forgiveness and issues of accountability between Tyrone and Edmund, then Edmund and Jamie. In *All the Way Home*, what Mary struggles to find is an understanding that will allow her to accept the husband according to standards other than those of an orthodox Catholicism. *Iceman*, above all, focuses on the tension between these two systems (forgiveness and accountability) by making Evelyn the personification of forgiveness. Ironically this only makes Hickey more and more aware of his own guilt, so that he ultimately becomes the voice of complete accountability that refuses to understand all the excuses men make for themselves and women make for them, creating more tension between these opposing forces than almost any other character in American drama.

A central facet of this dichotomy is a split between two different modes of perception: one, based upon reason, upon a logic that calculates the worth of an individual in terms of a particular moral standard; the other, based on emotion and the promptings of the heart that defies logic by extending to the sinner a "grace" that goes beyond understanding. In general emotional or felt understanding supplants intellect and the law.[59] Just as texts may use alcohol to introduce a form of irrationality into the apparently logical structures of dramatic realism, so also does the "grace" figure introduce the irrationality of "the heart." As the action of the story progresses, it may move not so much from drunkenness to sobriety as from one form of drunkenness or irrationality (alcoholic) to another (emotional). If we perceive intoxication as a state that diminishes or depresses rationality, then in some sense the "grace" figure is as inebriated as the drunkard. The point is perhaps an obvious one: these plays occupy a world of feeling and sensation whether we are with the prodigal or the one who welcomes him home. The only sober voices are those of the elder brothers who cannot understand the inconsistencies of it all. Those voices never will understand, because they represent a dramatic function different from the one under which prodigals and those who forgive them operate.

To Respond: Hatred of the Other

Fulfilling a second function, the "grace" figure's response to the prodigal locates blame and hatred; it finds a scapegoat for those deeds that are forgiven him. One solution is to blame "demon rum" itself, an approach that helped animate the temperance movements of the nineteenth and twentieth centuries. Another, as noted above, is to perceive the problem as a function of immaturity or, in some cases, as a conflict between two selves within a single consciousness. This latter method applies to Jamie in both *Journey* and *Misbegotten*, as well as several other prodigal figures caught up in their own psychomachias: Frank Elgin (*Country Girl*); Doc (*Sheba*); Rubin Flood (*Dark at the Top of the Stairs*). The maneuver that most interests me, however, because it most contradicts the general tone of understanding and forgiveness, is the attack on the other woman. In *Wilderness*, for example, Richard brags about/confesses his experience as a prodigal: his trip to a "low dive," his drinking and drunkenness, his kissing affair with Belle of the "yellow hair—the kind that burns and stings you."[60] His only excuse is that he believed his relationship with Muriel was over, that she was dead to him, that the visit to the tavern and the whore was born of sorrow at a great loss and a desire for revenge on one who had deserted him and caused so much pain. His story of sin and shame disgusts and unnerves her, but for love of him, Muriel will "forgive and forget" if only he will swear that the thought of the prostitute was and is as disgusting now to him as to her. Richard, of course, has little difficulty with this request. He has already told Muriel how he "hated" Belle and that she "wasn't even pretty!"[61] In the moonlight Richard and Muriel finally share a kind of consummation of their desires, a moment of peace and union and pure bliss, fully dependent upon their shared hatred of another, the one with the yellow hair, the "blonde pig."

That, of course, is what Jamie in *A Moon for the Misbegotten* calls the prostitute whom he had met on the train going East. For Jamie the other woman does not even have a name or, for that matter, human status: the animal image recalls the Lukan prodigal and the scene among the swine. O'Neill's texts do not always attack the prostitute or other woman with a vehemence akin to that found in these two plays. At times in *Iceman*, *Journey*, and "*Anna Christie*," for example, the attitude is at least more relaxed and affectionate. Nevertheless Hickey's efforts at reform finally suggest a process similar to that of Richard and Muriel in *Wilderness* and Jamie and Josie in *Misbegotten*—a process that grounds forgiveness in the exclusion of an other. This process creates a solidarity of animosity similar to that described by Girard in *Violence and the Sacred* with the other woman functioning as what he calls the *monstrous double*.[62] When this system breaks down, as it does, for example, in *Iceman*, then anger, hatred, and violence must find another outlet. In this instance Hickey turns it upon himself and finally, when he can stand it no longer, on the "grace" figure herself, on Evelyn.

In O'Neill's work, this ambivalence and occasional violence toward women—mothers, wives, and whores—is often prominent. Other American domestic dramas may not contain it at all, at least in this form, or they may mute it in various ways. But its presence is evident whenever texts deny the other woman, whether she is a "fallen" woman or a "grace" figure, a specific identity, turning her instead into a function of male identity or desire, only present when a particular dramatic function, only when a set of quotation marks, needs filling. In Miller's *Salesman,* for example, the cast list refers to Willy's Boston acquaintance simply as "The Woman." When Biff intrudes upon her and his father, Willy quickly pushes her out of the room and just as quickly gives his son the conventional reassurances of her personal unimportance: "She's nothing to me, Biff."[63] Her characterization as a whole reinforces this insubstantiality: her most pressing concern is whether or not she will receive the stockings that Willy has promised her; her most distinguishing quality is a grating laugh. Beyond this the text grants her no more personality or identity than her generic status demands. In this instance hate may seem too strong a word. What the text creates is not a person but an object, and the attitude toward that object is essentially negative, even antagonistic. The violence, however, comes not so much from Willy as it does from the convention itself and the characterization that accompanies it.

Of course plays of prodigality do not always demand the presence of another woman and among those that do, she is not always pilloried. Axelrod's *Itch*, for example, while retaining the generic title, "The Girl," plays off the norm by making her a sexual innocent, available and willing, without any sense of personal guilt on her part. She suggests an escape from the confines of middle-class morality or at least the illusion of an escape, while ultimately the play itself reaffirms that morality's worth by returning the husband to his wife and child. *Cat* makes the other woman a man, whom we are more inclined to pity (not because he is gay, but because he cannot accept himself) than to hate. As noted in chapter 3, *Fences* by August Wilson creates in the offstage presence of Alberta, Troy Maxson's other woman, a more sympathetic character. To do so, however, it must emphasize that she gives more to Troy than her body, that she gives him a new sense of life: joy and freedom. Furthermore it must make her a mother and then have her die in childbirth. In other words she must be to some extent desexualized and then victimized to counter the conventional antipathy toward this dramatic figure.[64] The lengths to which Wilson's text must go to achieve this more positive, but still marginal, image of the other woman indicate the strength and persistence of a convention that more regularly makes this figure an object of hatred and blame.

Plays give this exclusion a particularly concrete form whenever this other woman (or man) is absent from the final scene or scenes of the play. This disappearance is, for example, a convention of *Wilderness, Misbegotten, Salesman,* and *Cat.* These others are made to disappear, dramaturgically murdered, so that those onstage may speak of and about them without any fear that they will speak back. The force of this convention becomes even clearer if we try to imagine for a moment what all these "functional others," these *monstrous doubles,* might say if they came back in the final scene of the play to break out of the constricted identities that texts impose on them; for example for the "blonde pig" to say that it was not at all as Jamie described it and then to go on to tell her story, which, of course, O'Neill did try to do in *"Anna Christie."* My point, of course, is not that characters have lives of their own beyond their dramatic functions or that we need any more stories of good-hearted prostitutes, but merely the extreme narrowness of the other woman's function in most of these plays: like alcohol a sign of male desire; like alcohol a convenient target for blame.

TO RESPOND: FORGIVENESS AND EROS

A third facet of the "fixed" figure's response is the way in which it frequently anticipates, implies, or substitutes for sexual intercourse. Perhaps this is because the narrative of the prodigal is about distances, particularly the literal and metaphorical distance between the prodigal and those from whom he has estranged himself. Regardless of the specific relationship between the prodigal and the figure who waits for the prodigal's return (parent/child, husband/wife, or a surrogate for one or the other), the narrative conventionally moves toward an elimination of distance, toward an embrace in which two, at least momentarily, become one, as in *Wilderness* after Richard has confessed to Muriel and been forgiven for the affair with Belle: *"He kisses her tremblingly and for a moment their lips remain together. Then she lets her head sink on his shoulder and sighs softly."*[65] A similar moment occurs in *Misbegotten*, after Jamie has confessed to Josie and been forgiven for the affair with the "blonde pig": *"His face is convulsed. He hides it on her breast and sobs rackingly. She hugs him more tightly and speaks softly, staring into the moonlight."*[66]

Perhaps this representation of union operates because the story of the prodigal also seems to be about the filling of a series of empty spaces: he fills a temporal space with his confession of what he has done during his absence from home; he fills an emotional and sociological space in his return to the abandoned role of husband or son; he returns to his place at the table; he sleeps again in his old bed; what had been incomplete without him is now made whole. The identification of the one who waits with this space is so complete ("You could be a home for me") that the listening ear, the home that lodges, and the body of the one who waits all become contiguous presences, vessels to be filled by the prodigal's homecoming. When he and that person who patiently waits are husband and wife, the last stage in this process is usually, implicitly or explicitly, sexual, that is, the end of a journey, a literal reunion with the body that was left behind, a final eradication of emptiness and distance.

Some works, of course, only hint at this aspect of homecoming. For example the final tableau of the *The Drunkard* is of a family united: the father, recently reformed, is seated, but in prayer, with his hand on his Bible and his wife at his side, "leaning upon his chair."[67] The scene is certainly chaste but extremely sensual as well: "The sun is setting over the hills at the back of landscape"; there is an elegant "table . . . with an astral lamp," as well as "flower-stands, with roses, myrtles, etc. . . . Bird-cages on wings, R. and L."[68] Suffusing it all is the sound of music. Just prior to assuming the positions described above, the father plays on the flute "Home, Sweet Home," while Julia, the drunkard's daughter, sings the first verse, the "burthen is then taken up by chorus of villagers behind" with accompaniment, building to a "crescendo, forte" and then subsiding to a slow air: "Music till curtain falls—Picture[.] The End."[69] The rise and fall of the music, the sensuality of the setting, and the focus on groupings (who stands, who sits, who kneels, where and by whom) create an emotional climax that has strong sexual parallels. Indeed just as *The Drunkard* explores in its fashion the tension between sobriety and drunkenness or between control and release, so does this final tableau represent a similar tension in its juxtaposition, on the one hand, of neatness, stillness, and order created by the convention of the tableau itself and its manifestation: stage directions note that all is "entirely neat, and in keeping." On the other hand, a disorder of emotions is created by this display of a happy end and the pathos/bathos of the musical accompaniment. The melodrama appears to resolve these conflicts, but in some ways it only rearranges them.

The distance between this ending and that of Inge's *Dark at the Top of the Stairs* is not, I would argue, that great:

> (*Cora starts up the stairs to her husband, stopping for one final look at her departing son. And Sonny, just before going out the door, stops for one final look at his mother, his face full of confused understanding. Then he hurries out to Reenie, and Cora, like a shy maiden, starts up the stairs, where we see Rubin's naked feet standing in the warm light at the top*)
> *Cora:* I'm coming, Rubin. I'm coming.
> CURTAIN[70]

Inge's dénouement makes obvious what *The Drunkard* implies: forgiveness is a sexual, as well as a spiritual and emotional process; forgiveness and coitus are often equivalent. Williams's *Cat* makes this context even clearer by bringing the empty bed onstage. Maggie in turn leaves no doubt as to what she wants: a return to that bed. Her reasons for wanting it filled are also clear: her own love and desire for Brick and the hope that if she has a child by him, it will guarantee them a sizable portion of Big Daddy's estate.

Turning again to O'Neill's late plays, *Iceman* reminds the spectator of this link between forgiveness and Eros at the crucial moment: when Hickey tells his listeners that he had infected Evelyn with a venereal disease. The infection is not just a product of Evelyn's repeated willingness to forgive Hickey. It also indicates that a sexual reunion has accompanied each manifestation of "grace." *Wilderness*, of course, functions on a different level of intensity, but nevertheless Richard and Muriel consummate their desire after he returns to her, although in this case, a kiss or two is all that is required. The interior setting of *Wilderness*, which the father and mother inhabit, also suggests this physical intimacy as they retire into the "darkness of the front parlor" and from that darkness to bed.[71] In *Misbegotten* the relationship between forgiveness and desire is more complex. Jamie and Josie spend the night together, but they do not share a bed. As noted earlier a critical decision takes place just prior to Jamie's confession, when they choose which set of roles they will enact: that of a "blonde pig" and her John or of a mother and her son. This choice is not, however, between desire and its absence but rather between two ways of perceiving desire and the self or perhaps two ways of satisfying desire: one is unalterably linked in the mind of the protagonist to shame and guilt; the other is just as unalterably linked to forgiveness and love. Josie's function is to allow Jamie this second option to find forgiveness and a consummation of desire without guilt, even if only for a night. To do so Jamie and Josie must play out his return not inside the house, but in front of it, on steps as opposed to in a bed. The intimate interior space of the home is not used in the final scenes of the play— their relationship is totally intimate and yet totally chaste, a homecoming that never crosses the threshold, an accommodated intimacy.[72]

In chapter 1 I suggest that alcohol functions as a form of sexual appetite, as its enactable substitute. So, too, does the scene of forgiveness as it anticipates and to some extent even represents a consummation of desire. This is not, of course, a complaint. Forgiveness as an erotic experience has a rather long lineage, one that religious and biblical imagery recognizes. My point is that plays of prodigality frequently take advantage of this eroticism and that this obviously constitutes much of their appeal. The irony, of course, is that we generally perceive the prodigal's return as a turning away from desire and sensuality, when in fact it is also a running toward it. The parable embodies this movement toward a fulfillment of desire in the luxurious sensuality of the prodigal's reception: the embrace, the kiss, the robe and sandals, the killing of the fatted calf, the feast with its music and dancing, as if the father had turned hedonist. American domestic drama, with its substitution of female for male "grace" figures, allows this fulfillment of desire one expression in the tears and embracings of the mother, another in the husband's return to the marriage bed, in Stanley and Stella's return to the darkness of their flat.

THE DUAL RESPONSE: THE GRACE FIGURE AND THE SPECTATOR

In considering all of these functions—waiting, listening, responding—it seems particularly important to stress the connection between she (or he) who waits, listens, and forgives and another who participates in similar activities: the spectator. What particularly interests me is an alignment between these two that tends to turn the latter into a version of the former: a major function of works such as *Misbegotten, Iceman, Cat, Sheba, Dark at the Top of the Stairs,* and *Raisin* is to make "grace" figures of spectators. The basis of this process is the similarity of their situations: both waiting, both confined to a fixed space, both listening and processing the prodigal's narrative, both called upon to respond in ways more emotional than rational.

Just as texts often confine these characters to a particular dramatic space, *the home*, so does theatrical convention regularly confine audience members to a particular theatrical space, *the house*. When Jamie, for example, goes off to the inn, both Josie and the spectator are left behind. "Grace" figure and spectator wait together for him to return, even as the spectator earlier waited in his seat for the play to begin. Much the same might be said for any number of plays (*Sheba, Journey, Dark at the Top of the Stairs, Raisin, All the Way Home*) in which *home* is mimetically present and *not home* or the place to which the prodigal goes is mimetically absent, embodied only in the words of the text and the mind of the character or the spectator. The character who is able to leave the space of representation is free in a way that the spectator and the character who stays behind are not. On a banal level, the actor playing Jamie can literally go across the street and have a cup of coffee at the beginning of act 2, while Josie and the audience wait together for his return. The audience waits and watches at home with the Lindas and Coras and Lolas and Marys of American domestic drama, confined with them to a concrete world of things, to the space of representation, while prodigals move into worlds of their own making, worlds of freedom and imagination. As usual *Iceman* reverses these coordinates, while at the same time it reaffirms them. We wait for Hickey to come not home but back to the bar, which has become a second home for him and the others, and then later we listen with its occupants to Hickey's confession, as spectators transformed along with Harry's patrons into "grace" figures, "functional others." We also wait with Maggie and Big Daddy for Brick to come home, although in this case, a broken ankle has for once confined the prodigal to the same space in which "grace" figure and spectator abide.

Of course in the process of waiting for the prodigal to return, the "fixed" figure and spectator also listen together to his story. Works like *Misbegotten, Cat,* and *Iceman* increase the bond between these listeners whenever neither knows how the story being told will end, whenever the information contained in the narrative is new to both parties. This means that the onstage listener and the audience member must process the story simultaneously. Like the reader of a mystery story and the detective within it, together they must compile its various bits of information into some sort of total narrative, projecting and revising along the way, making story (*fabula*) out of plot (*sjuzet*). This is evident, for example, in the various ways in which the inhabitants of Harry's bar try throughout the drama to complete Hickey's story before he has a chance to finish it. Their process of projecting various meanings and endings based on information they have collected up to that point in the play both mirrors the spectator's simultaneous processing of that same narrative material and at the same time often guides him or her toward one response or another.

As already noted the conventional end of this waiting and listening is understanding and forgiveness grounded in love, that is, in felt experience, not analysis or logic. For the prodigal this means a reconstitution of the self based on another character's perception of him. For Jamie this other is, of course, Josie, but also, to some extent, the audience itself. Furthermore just as the prodigal relies on this "functional other" for a new perception of himself, so does this character often guide the spectator in his response to the one who needs or wants forgiveness.

This transformation of audience members into "grace" figures is, I think, the basis of a literature of forgiveness and understanding for which the paradigm of the prodigal is a central example (see epilogue). In chapter 3 I argued that potentiality was a distinguishing characteristic of the prodigal. By that I meant that he or she must be potentially forgivable. An interesting feature of plays that reflect this literature of forgiveness is their tendency continually to expand its boundaries. In a sense a mark of technical excellence within this genre is how far a text can stretch an audience's capacity to forgive, how far the prodigal can go astray and still be brought home, not only to the one who waits and listens but also to those who wait and listen in the house, the audience. The high water marks of this genre are not too difficult to perceive. For Jamie in *Misbegotten*, of course, it is the following lines, "I bribed the porter to take a message to her and that night she sneaked into my drawing room. She was bound for New York, too. So every night—for fifty bucks a night—"[73]; for Hickey in *Iceman*, it is these, "I picked up a nail from some tart in Altoona. . . . The quack I went to got all my dough and then told me I was cured and I took his word. But I wasn't, and poor Evelyn—."[74] With Brick it is, at least within the context of the midfifties, the father's perception that Brick might be a gay man. *Sheba, Dark at the Top of the Stairs,* and, more recently, Sam Shepard's *A Lie of the Mind* ask us to understand and forgive men who physically abuse women. The motto for this genre might be taken from a biblical text: "where sin abounded, *grace* did much more abound."[75]

The irony, one that has certainly not been lost on feminists and other critics, is that in the midst of all this love for the prodigal we find this hatred of that other woman. Just as texts invite the spectator to join the "grace" figure in forgiving and understanding the prodigal, so is he or she frequently invited to share in this hatred of that even more othered character, of one almost always excluded from the final scenes of the play, denied access to the new community formed by prodigal, "grace" figure, and spectator. Not only in the processes of waiting, listening, and forgiving but also in the process of hating do "grace" figure and spectator potentially move through the play as one.

These and other characteristics make these plays particularly problematic for many contemporary critics. They are, as am I, skeptical of the cultural work theater performs as part of a hegemonic culture: White, male, middle-class, heterosexual. This ongoing reexamination of the relationship between theater and society potentially entails a whole range of critiques: of theatricality itself, often in terms of its structural principles (e.g., the male gaze and processes of objectification); of the role of presence within the theatrical event; of representation as a form of presence; of realism as a species of representation; of domestic drama as the favored venue of realism; of sentimentalism as a type of domestic drama; of gendered (and in some instances class- and race-typed) roles for men and women as an aspect of sentimentalism; and of the kinds of roles connected with plays of prodigality as vehicles for this stereotyping process.[76] This critical discourse is lively, multifaceted, and ongoing. Two of the most powerful statements on these matters belong to Hélène Cixous and Sue-Ellen Case. In "Aller à la mer," Cixous asks the following question:

> How, as women, can we go to the theatre without lending our complicity to the sadism directed against women, or being asked to assume, in the patriarchal family structure that the theatre reproduces *ad infinitum,* the position of victim. . . . It is always necessary for a woman to die in order for the play to begin. Only when she has disappeared can the curtain go up; she is relegated to repression, to the grave, the asylum, oblivion and silence. When she does make an appearance, she is doomed, ostracized or in a waiting-room.[77]

In *Feminism and the Theatre,* Case writes, "The portrayal of female characters within the family unit—with their confinement to the domestic setting, their dependence on the husband, their often defeatist view of the opportunities for change—makes realism a 'prisonhouse of art' for women, both in their representation on stage and in the female actor's preparation and production of such roles."[78] Based on much that has been said within this chapter, these are fit words for its closing. Case and Cixous concisely recapitulate many of the conventions described above.

The final pages of this study consider the persistence of this paradigm in contemporary drama, its role within a number of plays by women, its dispersion in the mass media, and, finally, its relationship to what I call the "sentimental spectator." In doing so I continue to consider both the persistence of homecomings and a refusal of them, ways in which drunkards and prodigals both fulfill conventional expectations and, on occasion, invite their reexamination.

6

Persistence, Variation, Dispersion

Prodigal son. The world will wipe its dirty hands all over you.
—Roy Cohn, *Angels in America, Part One: Millennium Approaches*

In the summer of 1994, a feature on National Public Radio's *All Things Considered* told of the successful youth ministry of an urban, predominantly African-American church. Central to the report was an account of the parable of the prodigal son that the church's drama group enacted at one of their services. Not surprisingly given its history, the parable lent itself to adaptation, to a contemporary retelling. The prodigal was a drug dealer; his language was not Hebrew, New Testament Greek, or the King James Bible but the language of the streets: "I told you boys you could make a lot of money. Easy money. You can't beat the fringe benefits. The hours. The security of being in a close-knit family. Now tell me, what more could you ask for?"

The news report also provided the often present biographical and autobiographical connections. It told of a group of young men ("looking cool and tough") who "sauntered" into church during the service: "Rev. Lucas spotted them as they entered and ran down the aisle to greet them, as if they too were prodigal sons, returning to the arms of their father." The pastor challenged them to "be leaders" like they "were meant to be": "Not just to play basketball, but to be a leader, a business entrepreneur." The report also introduced testimonies by young people who attend the church, male and female, who spoke as prodigals who had found a home. The seventeen-year-old actor who played the drug-dealing prodigal, like William H. Smith in *The Drunkard* or Jason Robards in *Long Day's Journey*, plays a role he is "familiar with in real life." A young woman told of friends headed towards trouble, and confessed that she was "one of those kids," that "it really was" for her a "life or death situation."[1] Wilder's *Happy Journey* (as do many of the other plays and characters discussed throughout this study) finds its echo here, in a different culture, in a different time, in a different place, but one nevertheless connected to them by the prodigal's journey. Here then are some further examples of the persistence, variation, and dispersion of this paradigm, of the prodigal moving toward a new millennium.

Spalding Gray

The first time I saw wine was when my Uncle Tinky brought two bottles of Great Western sparkling burgundy to Gram and Gramp Horton's for Thanksgiving. I sat next to Gram Gray, who didn't like sparkling burgundy all that much, so she took only a few sips and left the rest for me. That meant I had almost two glasses, and that sparkling burgundy made me so happy I wanted more.[2]

In *Swimming to Cambodia* (1985), Spalding Gray sits in front of a map of Southeast Asia and tells the audience of his adventures in a faraway land: Thailand in particular, a place of pleasure, perhaps the place of pleasure in the Anglo-American mind (i.e., good drugs, cheap sex), the South Sea Islands of the post-Vietnam era, both created by and foreign to the Judeo-Christian consciousness of middle-class, White America. Paradigmaticly Gray's text establishes a tension between this distant land and home: in general, America; in particular, a house in upstate New York in which a woman, Renée, waits patiently for Gray to return. And he eventually does go home after he has had his "perfect moment," and after he has, like the prodigal, come to himself in a far-off land:

And when I got to Athol Fugard, he turned to me and said, "So, Spalding. You're leaving Paradise?"
"Athol (oh!) Athol (I!) uh, Athol (uh!), I—was thinking that maybe I should (oh!) eh, uh, wait a minute, Athol, you really think I, uh. . . ."
"Return to Renée. She's a lovely lady. Go back, Spalding! Take what you've learned here and go back. It's all the same, you know."
I wanted to believe him.[3]

Gray's monologues chronicle the adventures of an American prodigal, the conventions of prodigality reflected even in their titles: *Sex and Death to the Age of 14; Booze, Cars, and College Girls; Nobody Wants to Sit Behind a Desk*. Part of the appeal is in the intimacy of these autobiographical narratives: the chance to listen in on confession. In some ways they are extensions of Hickey and Jamie's long final act monologues in *Iceman* and *Moon*, as if their speeches had

grown and taken over the entire play. Another part of their appeal is
their freedom from a guilt and pain that O'Neill's work only occasionally escapes, as in *Ah, Wilderness!* Gray (the persona created by text
and performance) epitomizes the Good Bad Boy of Fiedler's *Love and
Death*. We never doubt, for all his talk of drink and sex and drugs,
that Spalding will one day come home, that he is, as both Thornton
Wilder and American drama in general would understand, a "good
boy after all." This finally is much of his appeal, this voicing of the
intimate and forbidden within the reassuring context of almost palpa-
ble goodness, sensitivity, and decency, all elements germane to the
conventions of the prodigal. If we want to know what happened to
Wilder's Arthur of Newark, New Jersey, we need look no farther
than to Spalding Gray of Barrington, Rhode Island. He has grown
up and is now telling us the story of his life. Fittingly *Gray's Anatomy*
(1993) concludes with a marriage: Spalding, now in his fifties and
feeling his mortality, marries Renée Shafransky. His next piece, he
informs a reporter, will involve following his taxes to Washington: an
occupation more appropriate to elder sons or, in any event, sons who
have come home.

STILL LIFE

> I walked in the door and sat everything down.
> I was home.
> My dad looked at me, my mom looked at me.
> I sat down. Said:
> Could I have some coffee?
> That's when my mother started raggin' on me
> about drinking coffee.
> The whole thing broke down.[4]

In Emily Mann's *Still Life* (1981), Mark tells the story of returning
from Vietnam to his home and parents. No one killed the fatted calf;
no one put a ring on his finger or sandals on his feet. Instead he asked
for a cup of coffee, and his mother started "raggin'" on him.[5] Coffee
takes the place of a feast that is asked for, not offered; carping takes
the place of the embrace and welcome he might have expected. This
episode makes one wonder to what degree the story of the prodigal
formed the sense of loss that Vietnam veterans felt on their return.
In addition to the newsreels of returning vets from World War II, the
story of a son who went away and then came back to overwhelming
love and acceptance was, for them, part of a fantasy that never
came true.

Still Life asks whether the prodigal, who has supposedly gone too far and who, like the apprentice in *The London Merchant* or Hickey in *Iceman,* has committed murder, can be reformed, whether or not, by some act of grace, he might still come home. *Still Life* and *for colored girls* (see below) are similar in that they both use the deaths of children to shock and horrify. In Shange's texts these deaths function as surprises, as twists at the end of an O. Henrylike short story. In Mann's text one of their functions is to create suspense and give structure to a purposefully fragmented narrative. To use a crude metaphor, they are like the teasers that local stations use in the middle of prime time to induce viewers to stay up for the eleven o'clock news, a process that begins with the following lines, early in the first act of Mann's play:

Mark: I thought:
If I gave *you* the information,
I couldn't wash my hands of the guilt,
because I did things over there.
We all did.[6]

This is the first clue that the play contains some dark secret, some revelation of an atrocity (like Hickey's) too horrible to voice, but that someone will eventually reveal. These references accumulate until it becomes clear that the play is moving toward a confession involving Mark's complicity in the deaths of some children, a confession that is finally both horrifying and, in a sense, fascinating. In a fundamental way, *Still Life* uses, exploits, or explores (each word connotes a different value judgment) this horror and fascination to structure itself and to hold the spectator's attention.

This question of response goes to the core of the paradigm and its use here. Cheryl (his wife) listens; Nadine (the other woman) listens; Emily Mann listened (the play is based on interviews that Mann conducted); and now the spectator listens, like the "grace" figure of the parable, to the story of what happened in a distant land:

The Lukan Prodigal: Father, I have sinned against heaven, and before thee, And am no more worth to be called thy son: make me as one of thy hired servants.[7]

Mark: I don't know . . .
I don't know . . .
if it's a terrible flaw of *mine,*

then I guess deep down I'm just everything that's
bad.[8]

Cheryl voices one potential response to the inclination to forgive:

Cheryl: There was a time when a man would confess to me,
"I'm a jerk,"
at a private moment
and I would smile
sweetly
and try to comfort him.
Now I believe him.[9]

Nadine's response is different and, in terms of the plays on which
this study has focused on, more typical:

Nadine: Through him [Mark]—I've come to understand the violence
in myself . . . and in him, and in all of us.
And I think if we can stay aware of that,
hold on to that knowledge,
maybe we can protect ourselves
and come out on the other side.[10]

Of course to place violence in the woman as well as the man is to
revise the paradigm, to allow for the figure of a female prodigal. But
more fundamentally to understand is to forgive, and in this Nadine's
words are typical of efforts made to bring the prodigal home.

Following Nadine's speech, Mark tells the audience that he is after
all "just a regular guy."[11] He then goes on to recite the names of
friends who died in the war and its aftermath, a litany that creates
finally a more sympathetic image of Mark, an action that finally emphasizes not judgment or accountability, but understanding and sympathy. I may be making Mann's text less ambiguous than it is at this
point, but it seems to me that its final accomplishment is to bring the
prodigal home, even though, in this instance, we know that he has
murdered three children. That this apparent attempt even partially
works is a rather amazing testament to the continued vitality of this
paradigm and the ethos that empowers it.

FOR COLORED GIRLS

somebody
went & tol crystal that beau was spendin alla his

money
on the bartendin bitch down at the merry-
go-round cafe/
. . . now he hadta get alla that shit outta
crystal's
mind/so she wd let him come home[12]

In "a nite with beau willie brown" from Ntozake Shange's *for colored girls who have considered suicide / when the rainbow is enuf* (1976), the Lady in Red tells of a relationship between a man, a woman, and their two children. At one point the narrated image is of the man, Beau Willie Brown, on one side of the room and the woman, Crystal, on the other. She is holding onto her two children so that they will not run to their father. For his part the father seems to want to come home, to marry the mother of his children, to hold them in his arms, to be forgiven for his behavior, for wasting his money on the girl at the bar, for almost killing Crystal in a drugged or drunken rage: "willie came in blasted & got ta swingin chairs at crystal."[13] But now Beau Willie wants to come home and so he stands opposite his children and their mother "all humble & apologetic," waiting for Crystal to relent.[14] Four hundred years of dramatic convention predict the response. First the daughter pushes away from the mother and runs to her father "cryin / daddy, daddy come back daddy," and then Crystal gives in: she lets Kwame go to his father; she lets Beau Willie come home.[15] But instead of tableau and "Home, Sweet Home," Beau Willie drops his children out a fifth story window. By challenging conventional expectations—forgiven husbands do not usually commit infanticide—Shange's text spotlights the unspoken assumption that women should be "grace" figures, should be "functional others." Indeed the story serves as a cautionary tale on the dangers of forgiveness, as a warning not to play the role that dramatic and social conventions dictates, a point also made, albeit less dramatically in an earlier piece (appropriately titled, "sorry") in which women refuse to accept men's excuses and apologies. The prodigal who goes beyond prodigality to acts of violence and murder is not, however, aparadigmatic (see chapter 3): he exists as a constant alternative to the movement toward reformation.

Shange's choreopoem, like many of the plays discussed within this study, engages in a dialogue with the figure of the prodigal. Subjectivity shifts from the prodigal to the "other." Although the story's focus on Crystal is clear from the start, the final line dramatically underscores that shift as the narrator exchanges third for first person: "i stood by beau in the window."[16] Here notions of *rupture* and *potential* are stood on their heads. Rupture, the creation of a space between Crystal and Beau Willie, represents a positive value: it offers the promise of a safe place for mother and children. Potential resides less in the promise of a homecoming than in the loss of potential figured in the deaths of the children. These deaths join others discussed earlier in this study. They recall the ways in which the parable has adopted the child as a fundamental device. In American drama Kwame's death descends from that of Mary Morgan in *Ten Nights in a Bar-Room*.

THREE VARIATIONS: OLD AND NEW

The Traveler Returned (1796), an early American drama by Judith Sargent Murray (1751–1820), features the return of a husband to a family he had left nineteen years earlier. He departed, however, not because of his prodigality but his wife's. She confesses to her daughter: "I engaged in a round of dissipation—I continued the most censurable pursuits; and at length *imagined* myself tenderly attached to a person, who was every way the *inferior* of your father."[17] Unlike the long-suffering wife, the husband does not stay at home. As a "grace" figure, he is, however, eventually willing to forgive his wife and reconstitute the family. Even though that forgiveness comes no less than nineteen years after his wife's "dissipations," this play still stands as an early and significant example of how women writers might rewrite this set of conventions. In this instance the author creates a place for a female prodigal and a kind of homecoming that plays usually reserve for men only.

More recent and well known, Sophie Treadwell's *Machinal* (1928) also represents a response to the figure of the prodigal, although one not so optimistic as *The Traveler Returned*. *Machinal* uses expressionism to explore the progress of its female protagonist (Helen Jones or the Young Woman) from office girl, to wife, to mother, to lover, to murderer. The last role results from an attempt to find freedom from a loveless marriage. The play contains image after image of containment, suffocation, gagging, and claustrophobia in the Young Woman's life. For her, life is like "drowning."[18] Containment in turn contrasts with another set of images connected with a man whom the Young Woman meets and loves. He has many of the features of a male prodigal: always on the move, not committed to the idea of family, linked with far countries or places (Spain, Mexico and "Frisco"), with mountains, riding, ships, and nature. He would be at home in a play by Shepard or O'Neill. He tells the Young Woman that he once killed two men to secure his freedom. For that he suffered no consequences. When the Young Woman repeats his act by killing her husband to gain her freedom, she receives the death penalty. The play ends with her execution. Treadwell uses the figure of the prodigal (Gable played the role in the original production) to underscore the gendered disparity that women experience in their efforts to fulfill the most basic of human needs, the need for a space in which to breath. Treadwell's play, like Shange's, uses the tradition to question its assumptions.

A more recent example, Cherríe Moraga's *Shadow of a Man* (1990), explores the life of the Rodríguez family living in the Los Angeles area during the spring of 1969. Its members include Lupe, a twelve-year-old daughter; Leticia, a seventeen-year-old daughter; Hortensia, their mother; Manuel, their father; Rosario, their aunt; Conrado, their father's compadre; and an unseen brother, Rigo, who is leaving home to marry a *gringuita*. The father and son both share qualities of the male prodigal: both pull out and away from the nuclear family; absence, more than presence, defines them (the son's absence from his father; the husband's from his daughter and wife). The father mourns the loss of his son, who now prefers a handshake to an embrace. The father also makes the conventional journey from home to tavern and back. The bottle marks him. He dreams, however, of a more extravagant prodigality, a dream echoed in many of the plays this study has examined from Renaissance prodigal son plays to Sam Shepard's family dramas: "One of these days, I'm gonna get in the car, buy me a couple six packs and hit the road and I'm not gonna stop until I reach the desert."[19] He also articulates as well as almost any character in American drama the conventional phenomenology of drinking: "I am a lonely man. I bring the bottle to my lips and feel the tequila pour down behind my tongue, remojando the back of my throat. Corre down la espina, until it hits my belly and burns como madre in there. For a minute, I am filled up, contento . . . satisfecho."[20]

A double standard seemingly exists for the two Rodríguez daughters. The mother allows the son to come and go as he pleases, but does not want the older daughter Leticia to "hang out . . . on the street."[21] Leticia, however, like Treadwell's Young Woman, wants to be "free like a man."[22] Moraga's playscript, however, like Shange's, also counters conventional expectations. For the younger daughter Lupe, Mary Magdalene serves not as the negative half of a double standard but as an almost mythic, heroic figure: "I loved how she jus' walked right through all those phony baloney pharisees, right up to the face of Jesus."[23] The daughters play out the scene of Mary

Magdalene's forgiveness, enacting their version of a prodigal's home-coming while one does the other's nails, enjoying the moment, sa-voring its sensuality and its ironies:

> *Lupe:* Can you imagine what it musta felt like to have this woman with such beautiful hair wiping it on you? (*Plays with the strands of Leticia's hair.*) It's jus' too much to think about. And then Jesus says . . . (*Pulling up Leticia as "Magdalene."*) "Rise woman and go and sin no more," (*After a beat.*) Now that's what I call forgiveness. That's . . . relief.[24]

A later scene between mother and daughter mirrors this one. Parent and child, like father and prodigal son, meet on a porch in the "wee hours" of the morning. Leticia tells her mother that she has, in her mother's words, given her "virginidad" away":

> *Leticia:* I was tired of carrying it around . . . that weight of being a woman with a prize. Walking around with that special secret, that valuable com-modity, waiting for some lucky guy to put his name on it. I wanted it to be worthless, Mamá. Don't you see? Not for me to be worthless, but to know that my worth had nothing to do with it.
> *Hortensia:* You protect yourself, hija? (*Hortensia goes to her.*)
> *Leticia:* Yeah. I'll be alright. (*They embrace.*)[25]

The "prodigal" (although like Shange, Moraga might well reject this term) comes home, now a daughter not a son, to a mother, not a father. The mother's concern finally becomes, as in the parable, not so much with the nature of the voyage but with the safety of the voyager: elder brothers worry about morality and commodities; the father, like Hortensia, only cares that his child has been restored to him. Moraga's play, like Shange's and Treadwell's, takes the paradigm and dances with it, moving it in ways it has not been wont to go. *Shadow of a Man* begins and ends with an image of female subjectivity and objectivity, of the younger daughter Lupe looking into a mirror and looking into herself: the man is the shadow here; the reflection in the mirror is a woman's.[26]

DISPERSION

In addition to the *persistence* and *variation* of the prodigal in twentieth-century American theater, this figure and the narratives that accompany it also continue to *disperse* themselves throughout popular culture in an ongoing weave of social conditions and narrative conventions that makes it difficult if not impossible to tell where one leaves off and the other begins. For the most part, this study has avoided film versions of the drunk and prodigal as generally outside its focus, but one somewhat idiosyncratic example will serve to introduce this theme of dispersion. In the popular film, *Mrs. Doubtfire*, Robin Williams plays the role of the prodigal. His prodigality does not literally involve drunkenness or philandering. Indeed Williams's character does not want to leave home (in particular, his children), but contrives to return to it in the guise of the woman (the sweet but stern English nanny of the title) that his estranged wife hires to care for their children. His prodigality revolves around an inability to maintain regular employment and his disruptiveness to the order of the house. On the day in which he loses his job, he throws an anarchic birthday party for one of his children that resembles nothing less than a kind of juvenile bacchanalia complete with animals, food mess, and dancing on the table tops. Williams's character is the child who will not grow up, who refuses to take seriously his responsibilities as a parent and an adult. Sally Fields's character at first resembles the professional woman that contemporary films regularly demonize, but she also has traits often associated with the patient wife. She cares for her children and the well-being of the family. She tells about the times she was forced to clean-up after the husband's messes, just as wives of drunken husbands compensate for their spouses' shortcomings. The differences are that the patient wife has now run out of patience and that the end of the film refuses the full return of the prodigal: he will see his children on a regular basis, but the marriage itself is not totally reconstituted. The film ends with a reply to the persistent force of the prodigal's return and the consequent reification of the traditional nuclear family, with Williams as Mrs. Doubtfire (the persona now serves as a host for a children's television show) reassuring children that families come in many different shapes and sizes, including single-parent families, families to whom some husbands or wives will never return.

Of course the subjectivity of the film is still fundamentally male: Williams's character literally borrows a female identity to work out his own. The movie itself is clearly within the tradition of heartwarming family films. But even though the family remains technically divided, the protagonist has indeed reformed himself. He has gotten a job and grown up, learned to take care of the house and the home, learned to pick-up after himself and cook nutritious homemade meals. The ending, even with its affirmation of familial variety, clearly mourns the loss of this particular nuclear family and seems to yearn for its full reunion. None of this should be particularly surprising, but the refusal of a completely conventional closure, and the movie's attempt to broaden at least nominally the notion of family highlights a national dialogue about the role of family in American life. This film is just one example, among many, of the dispersion of the prodigal, of ways in which popular culture continues to play with this figure in the final quarter of the twentieth century.

For example remarkable parallels exist between the recovery movements of the 1980s and many of the dramatic conventions described in the preceding pages. As in the parable, recovery often deals with the relationship between an individual whose life is marked by a sort of riotous living (i.e., "addictive behavior") involving alcohol, drugs, gambling, eating, sex, or even compulsive shopping and other individuals, usually family members, whose identities are shaped by the addict ("co-dependents" in the nomenclature of recovery, roughly akin to the father and the elder brother of the parable). As noted in the discussion of potentiality in chapter 3, these behaviors lend themselves to processes of forgiveness and reform: they are misdemeanors, not felonies. Appropriately, most of them also appear in illustrations from the Middle Ages to the present of the prodigal's dissipations in images of drinking, eating, gambling, spending, and womanizing. The recovery movement, rooted in the traditions of Alcoholics Anonymous, also emphasizes a moment of self-realization similar to the prodigal's, involving an acceptance of one's failures and weaknesses along with a consequent notion of rebirth and homecoming. Being "in denial" has now become a cliche, but it underscores the importance of a moment of recognition similar to that experienced by the prodigal among the swine. Also as in the parable, confession plays a central role in recovery. Autobiographical experience represents the surest form of truth. The child, in this instance the "inner child" of the adult in recovery, stands, as in the temperance melodrama, as the epitome of innocence and grace.

John Bradshaw, a leading figure in the recovery movement, entitles one of his books: *Homecoming: Reclaiming and Championing Your Inner Child*. With Bradshaw's assistance readers can play both the role of the prodigal and the role of the one who welcomes the prodigal home. They must acknowledge their weaknesses but also come to terms with their own "toxic shame"; they must find acceptance and healing in themselves. Writers like Bradshaw model this process by taking on different roles within their own narratives. On occasion they play the "grace" figure: they enable homecomings; they facilitate forgiveness and healing. Bradshaw, in particular, resembles the wise and benevolent figure of Rencelaw in *The Drunkard*, a character like the father in the parable, but one who was also once far from home: in Bradshaw's case a reformed alcoholic. Bradshaw writes, "In my early teens,

I ran with other fatherless guys. We drank and whored to prove our manhood. From ages 15 to 30, I drank and used drugs in an addictive manner. On December 11, 1965, I put the cork in the bottle."[27] For Bradshaw, however, the end of drinking did not mean an immediate homecoming. That came some years later, not as a son, but as a father and a husband, after a period of raging and screaming at his family that left him sitting "alone and ashamed" in a "crummy motel room": a contemporaay equivalent of the prodigal among the swine. Bradshaw had gotten in the car and literally left his family in the middle of their vacation: "I had gone away emotionally before—but I had never gone away physically." It is at this point—at the age of forty—that he finally experiences, like the prodigal, the moment of understanding and awareness that eventually allows the homecoming he had been moving toward for some years.[28]

Charlotte Davis Kasl, another mainstay of recovery literature, concludes *Women, Sex, and Addiction*—a book for women struggling with issues of "sex addiction" and "sexual codependency"—with a section entitled, "Recovery: The Journey Home." Although she does not use the word *prodigal*, Kasl's book makes available to women who wish it a homeward journey similar to that which men have traditionally enjoyed, although I am not at all sure that she, any more than Shange, would want to activate the phrase, *prodigal daughter*. Kasl relies more on other individual case histories (biography and anecdote as opposed to autobiography), but the section of the book dealing with homecomings begins with an account of her own "journey" into "codependency and addictiveness" that climaxes with a scene of tears and forgiveness. This instance inverts the parable: the daughter must forgive the mother, now deceased, to end the addictive behavior.[29] Ironically another key moment of realization comes on a chiropractor's table: "My back needed adjustment after a night when I had been more sexually involved than I truly wanted to be. . . . As she worked on my back I said to myself, 'Charlotte, have you got the message yet?'"[30] A moment of realization follows a kind of riotous living.

These stories of recovery, prodigality, and reform are played out not only in books on recovery and in their related seminars but also in other forms of mass media: newspapers, weekly magazines (especially those that feature celebrity and human interest stories such as *People*), supermarket tabloids, television shows with magazine formats, television talk shows, and movies of the week. Conventionally, the story focuses on the reform of an actor, musician, politician, or athlete who has a problem with drinking or drugs. It usually includes a detailed account of the wayward behavior (often in the form of confessional autobiography), culminating in a bottoming out experience that leads to the turn toward home. The individual might then take his or her story to others, such as groups of high school students, in an effort to save them from a similar fate. An alternate narrative recalls the rake's or harlot's progress, as well as those temperance melodramas in which the protagonist self-destructs. These stories end with the death of the celebrity figure at the end of a long downward spiral, as in the demise of John Belushi. *Potentiality* in these stories takes the form not of a homecoming but of laments for the loss of talents, as in "S/he had so much potential." As with temperance melodramas, however, the story of the prodigal who makes it home most pleases.

A newspaper headline reads, "Kennedy Admits Personal 'Frailties,' Vows to Fight On." The article itself notes "allegations of heavy drinking and womanizing," as well as Kennedy's pledge to "reform his lifestyle." Kennedy's speech of realization could have been written by the author of the parables: "I recognize my own shortcomings— the faults in the conduct of my private life. I realize that I alone am responsible for them, and I am the one who must confront them."[31] Of course these errors fall within the range of potential for reform. Chappaquiddick, however, has been the lapse that the public could not quite forgive and forget. It went beyond prodigality. The death of Mary Jo Kopechne created a rupture in confidence that Kennedy has never been able fully to close: confusion surrounding the nature of his actions blocked the potential for understanding and reconstitution of a pre-Chappaquiddick image.

No less paradigmatic is a newspaper article entitled, "Daddy was *the* playboy" that features a large photo of *Playboy*'s founder Hugh Hefner with wife Kimberley and his two young sons framed by two ragged halves of a photo featuring Hefner and his bunnies. Text to one side of the photo notes, "Life for Hugh Hefner isn't what it once was. After more than three decades as a fancy-free single [i.e., prodigal], he's a model husband and father." Like the prodigal who, in the eyes of the father has come back from the dead, so has Hefner had his own little death, a stroke in 1985 that "initially left him partly paralyzed . . . and unable to speak," an experience, like the prodigal's sojourn among the swine that he used "to reevaluate his life." That reevaluation led to a homecoming for the "King of Libertines" (now "Father's Day pin-up") described with a circularity that would make Abrams happy: "I am in the best place that I've ever been. Because I've come full circle. I'm in the safe harbor, having ridden the waves." Hefner, a once "emotionally repressed Methodist," admits that he "had a longer adolescence than most," and in words that again mirror the parable, he describes his newfound domesticity as being like "coming home." The man who, according to Barbara Ehreneich, epitomized middle-class, male wanderlust in the fifties now also completes the narrative, comes home again. Kennedy and Hefner, two somewhat sad and aging prodigals, represent near parodies of the genre, so late are they in their returns and so unconvincing in their new personae. They remind us more of Hickey than any character out of a Wilder play.[32]

A final, somewhat more extended mass media example concerns Drew Barrymore and her picture on the cover of a *People* magazine in January of 1990. Inside is the story of her journey into a far country of addiction, of her coming to herself, of the attempt to come home, of what seems to be a narrative of prodigality with young Drew standing in for Wilder's young Arthur with whom this study began. Of course in Arthur's case the "speak-easies and night-clubs" are only imagined ends, while in *People* we are shown Drew at age seven in *Ma Maison* with what looks like a half-dozen empty margarita glasses in front of her. The caption tells us, however, that she is not drunk, only "tired and bored": those are probably only fancy water glasses after all. But the caption also informs the reader that within two years Drew will be a "veteran party girl," which is, of course, what we might expect of someone who actually grows up in Babylon, in Hollywood, the ultimate prodigal destination.

Prominent in several photos accompanying the article is a tiny cross hanging from a chain around Drew's neck: in addition to jewelry, it is a symbol of salvation, redemption, homecoming. Barrymore also has that moment of anagnorisis and despair, that moment when she hits bottom. Her words could almost go directly into the mouth of the son who found himself among the swine in a foreign land, even though the tone is more petulant and her body image contrasts sharply with the conventional image of an emaciated prodigal: "I thought, 'My dad hates me, I'm fat, ugly, I've got no money, I'm living on my own, nobody likes me, I can't stand this!'"[33] The "grace" figure will not, however, be the mother who raised her as a single parent: she is either a co-victim or even a villain, the one who "largely ignored the early signs of her daughter's smoking and clubs where her bad habits began."[34] Nor is Drew's "functional other" her father, John Barrymore, Jr., an old-fashioned, O'Neill style, Shepardian prodigal who according to the article calls Drew to ask for money. *People* pushes this figure, more at home in a temperance melodrama, to the side. His picture does not even make it into the magazine. His daughter has apparently taken over his role, both as prodigal and as heir to the Barrymore theatrical legacy. In this piece singer David Crosby plays the role of the benevolent patriarch, who, like Rencelaw in *The Drunkard*, is also a reformed addict. *People* shows him and his wholesome-looking wife sitting with Drew between them on a porch, on a white wicker love seat dressed in cutoffs and shorts: a California-happy, nuclear family reconstituted. Crosby becomes the missing piece of the puzzle, that person who makes Drew complete, who as surrogate parent helps her turn her life around.

On the final page of the story, Drew sits astride a beautiful horse at sunset, literally back in the saddle again, but not headed away from home. The article notes that she will now be returning to work as an actor, that she is reading scripts again.[35] The prodigal has, like so many others, come home to the nine-to-five world of regularity and industriousness:

> Drew has changed her hours, her crowd, her hangouts and has stopped cutting classes at her private school. On a typical weekend of the past, she says, "I'd wake up about 3 o'clock, 4 o'clock in the afternoon, watch some TV, around 7 we'd go out to dinner, get high, go out to a club, get loaded, go dance, you know." And now? "We go to the movies, go out to lunch, go out to an AA meeting."[36]

Crosby is cautiously optimistic: "It's kind of like watching your baby walk off into traffic. . . . But I have a feeling she'll make it."[37]

Drew might well represent an opening for the future, the natural-ization of the prodigal daughter. Yet the tentativeness of this new role reveals itself in the magazine's use of Drew's fourteen-year-old sexuality to sell itself. It shows Drew in her bedroom surrounded by pictures of Monroe. In the cover photo, the tiny cross is ultimately swallowed-up by the bright red lips above it, just as Drew's status as reformed subject seems threatened by her status as available sexual object, as Marilyn's heir, ripe for consumption and death. Despite Crosby's optimistic words, the magazine's banner headline returns us to that persistent paradigm in which redemption is probable for men, problematic for women; all in caps across the magazine's cover—"NO HAPPY END"; at the bottom of the page, "The truth is you're never fully mended." Strangely enough these words do not seem to apply to the reformed Crosby. He seems to have mended fairly well. At best the article represents some part of a shift; at worst it reifies objectification and the double-standard.

The Christian Terence dramas of the sixteenth century, the prodigal son comedies of the English Renaissance, the temperance melodramas of the nineteenth century, and even the American domestic dramas of the immediate post–World War II era may now seem relics of another time. To the extent that theater as a whole no longer speaks to or for the majority culture, this may hold true. But clearly many of the conventions this study describes persist, although they now disperse themselves to a mass audience. They provide roles and play-scripts for a kind of environmental theater project more extensive than Richard Schechner ever imagined.

This study began with Arthur and his mother in their Chevrolet, with a journey from the front seat to the back, with a reunion over hot dogs, with a miniature version of an old story that at least some part of American culture wants to hear again and again, like some child's favorite bedtime story. It might well end with Joe Pitt on the phone from New York to his mother in Salt Lake City. Act 2, scene 8 of *Angels in America, Part One* is not so far from the encounter between *Happy Journey*'s mother and son with its fears of "speak-easies and night-clubs and places like that," although the son has now grown-up and finds himself where his mother feared he would one day go:

> *Hannah:* Joe, you haven't . . . have you been drinking, Joe?
> *Joe:* Yes ma'am. I'm drunk.
> *Hannah:* That isn't like you. . . . Why are you on the street at four AM? In that crazy city. It's dangerous. . . . Drinking is a sin! A sin! I raised you better than that.[38]

Later in the play, Roy Cohn, as a kind of perverse and ironic father figure, hugs Joe to himself and gives him a name: "Prodigal son." Harper, Joe's wife, experiences the conventional enclosure of those who wait, but she also fantasizes with a Mr. Lies (International Order of Travel Agents) of a journey to Antarctica. Yet another central character, Louis, agonizes about whether or not he should depart from his AIDS-stricken lover and companion, Prior, while Belize, former drag queen and a grace figure (without quotation marks) massages this dying man's body. I cannot here begin to analyze the complex ways (ironic and not so ironic) in which *Angels* plays with the figure of the prodigal and those who accompany him, but this study should make such an analysis more possible for others, should help make clearer the ways in which Kushner's play is indeed a gay fantasia on national themes.

My central goal in the preceding chapters has been to read a number of midcentury American domestic drama as manifestations of Arthur's story and to then explore the nature of these continuities in terms of dramatic form and function. Without apology this study has sought out the figure of the drunk and the prodigal to the neglect of many other significant aspects of these playscripts. With respect to the whole, my own ambivalence is, I am sure, by now painfully clear. The prodigal has exhausted theatrical time and energy that might well have been directed toward other concerns. Our infatuation with family matters keeps us from recognizing and responding to problems that we encounter as communities. In many instances despite radical ruptures, these works move toward a confirmation of the status quo. Finally as can be said for much of Western literature, plays of prodigality, with but a few exceptions to date, have spoken primarily to and for certain versions of male subjectivity. Women have been in effect absent: silenced, othered, turned into a function.

So why study one more set of images from a dominant culture and ideology already too well known by those who find no place within it. For me the initial answer is simple: I saw a certain recurrence within a set of playscripts I had chosen to read, playscripts on the family in American drama, and I wanted to explore it. From the beginning ambivalence marked and empowered that desire. I would not have undertaken this study were I not in some way, at some level, attracted to these figures and their exploits, an attraction that I understand to be historically and culturally conditioned by the same forces that have kept the prodigal near the center of the American stage: the dynamics of the family drama; the tension between, on the one hand, home and its securities and, on the other, the mythos of the open road with its freedoms and dangers; an obsession with departures and returns; the fantasy of great sinning and of even greater forgiveness; the illusion of an immersion in sexuality and the counterillusion of an escape from sexuality into an uncomplicated homosocial world; the self-importance of epiphany, autobiography, and confession; the hunger for presence and the real; a longing for circularity and continuity; the desire to die and live again, to be given the best robe, an embrace, and a feast. All of these elements, to a lesser or greater degree, speak to an imaginative set of which I am a part. That imaginative set might be described as White, middle-class, male, heterosexual, and dominant, but I am not qualified nor would I presume at this moment to de-limit it in one way or another, to presume to judge its appeal or lack of appeal to other groups or individuals with respect to race, gender, class, or any other qualifier. To my mind the fundamental need is to see the paradigm as such, to see it moving in and about domestic drama in a number of ways; to appreciate, when appropriate, the complexity of the forms it takes along with its more or less naive persistence; to use an awareness of conventionality to read against the naturalizing, self-affirming, truth claims of realism and autobiography so central to American theater; to understand that our narratives have a history, that in some degree

O'Neill's late plays (to take one set of examples) find their foreshadow-
ings not only in the author's life experiences but also in certain
nineteenth-century temperance melodramas, some Renaissance comedies, the stained glass windows of Chartres Cathedral, and Augustine's *Confessions*.

What is left is an epilogue that takes one step back from the immediate concerns of this study. It steps away from all these prodigals to
consider a figure upon whom they depend, without whom they might
not have a life: the "sentimental spectator."

Epilogue: The Sentimental Spectator

. . . the virtuous person in sentimental plays enjoys the satisfaction of humiliating his opponents, and of taking them captive by converting them to his own ideas.

But while all this is happening onstage, what should the spectator be thinking? *Of course* he is on the side of virtue and presumably believes himself virtuous. Therefore he begins to identify with the hero or heroine; and the dramatist encourages him by always showing the hero or heroine in a favorable light, no matter how unsavory the implications of his actions might appear to an unbiased judge.

—Paul Parnell, "The Sentimental Mask"; emphasis added.

In "The Sentimental Mask," Paul Parnell constitutes an audience: he describes with almost sublime certainty the relationship between a group of people and a group of plays. He constructs for his readers an image of what I would call "the sentimental spectator." Parnell, of course, is not alone. Few audiences have been drawn with more certainty by critics than this one. Indeed the "sentimental spectator" may well be the most important spectator of the twentieth century. In this epilogue to a study of the prodigal, I first want to quickly review some features of this spectator, basing my composite view not so much on what we see when we go to the theater but on what we have been told by critics like Parnell we should expect to see if we were to meet one of these individuals face to face. After my totalization of what I take to be a totalizing process, I consider why this constituted spectator has been so important to us and how we might further use her or him.

DISTINGUISHING FEATURES

The sentimental spectator is, first of all, a spectator given to optimism: human character and behavior may not be perfect, indeed, it may be highly problematic at times, but it is amenable to positive change, to reformation, to recovery. Goodness, as a descriptive term,

177

has meaning. No less importantly tears mark the sentimental specta-tor, pleasurable tears that confirm this goodness and optimism. This spectator, as Parnell noted, is also given to self-approval (a function of optimism) and so is a spectator in love with his/her own image, a narcissistic spectator. According to Parnell "tears show an intense preoccupation with oneself."[1] Also because this spectator only exists as a member of a mass audience, this narcissism will, of necessity, lead to a contemplation, even celebration of the normal, the regular, the average, which, as Douglas notes, is the "trademark of mass culture."[2] As Bertolt Brecht, Michael Fried, and others note, this is a spectator absorbed in the proceedings at hand, which in turn sug-gests a spectator not fully conscious of his/her own self as a spectator, that is, a spectator who may not realize, for example, that sympathy for the victim may mask a degree of delight in the victim's pain, a spectator who does not perhaps realize the extent to which he or she feeds on distress, takes an almost sensual pleasure in it.[3] Furthermore with respect to third person singular pronouns, critics constitute the sentimental spectator more often as a woman than as a man and if as a man, then as a "nice guy," a "sensitive man," a "man of feeling," who is open to the gendered charge of effeminacy. This same specta-tor, male or female, believes in and values sincerity, the real, testi-mony and confession, the autobiographical incident.[4] The domestic scene entrances this audience member, and at the heart of that scene, we often find a male prodigal (son, husband, father) and a long-suffering woman (mother, wife). Within that world we also find the victim and the child, often conjoined. In particular the sentimental spectator has an affinity for partings and reunions, particularly within the family, and so might watch over and again various enactments of the parable of the prodigal, so well does it capture many of the ele-ments just mentioned: domesticity, benevolence, optimism, testi-mony, tears. (Without the sentimental spectator, the story of the prodigal would not have played the role it has in American drama.) Critics often cast this audience member as a consumer (literally and metaphorically) or banqueter, as one who purchases and eats. Beyond these qualities, we often define this figure by what she (or he) is not, by a series of absences: a spectator with neither wit nor sophistication; a spectator lacking toughness and intellectual rigor; a spectator who represents an absence of "theology" and "dogma";[5] a spectator who stands over and against the Stoics, the Hobbesians, the Calvinists, the Puritans, the Hebrew Bible, and the Protestant Old Testament: "There is no room in sentimentalism [nor, by implication, the senti-mental spectator] for the awareness of sin and the real sense of humil-ity that Christianity is ordinarily thought to demand. Neither has sentimentalism room for theology, dogma, or ethical speculation. All that has been swept away and replaced with the sentimentalist's own virtue."[6] Finally and most importantly, a sentimental spectator is a spectator who should be ashamed of herself (himself). Before the critique of the domestic scene, before the critique of "the real," and before the critique of presence and representation, the sentimental spectator was there, in anticipation of them all, the mother (or father) of them all, still today, more tainted than any of these others.

One of the most recent constitutions of this sentimental spectator occurs in Wendy Kaminer's mass market book with the unfortunate title, *I'm Dysfunctional, You're Dysfunctional*. Kaminer critiques the recovery movement, its mindset, and its rhetoric: dysfunctional, co-dependent, denial, shame, and so forth. All of the features of senti-mental spectatorship mentioned above are in play within this move-ment. The sentimental spectator purchases and reads volumes of recovery or self-help literature; watches *Donohue, Oprah*, and *Sallie Jessie;* and participates as a player in a burgeoning number of self-help groups built on the AA or twelve-step model. Kaminer appreciates the important role such groups play in people's lives but is clearly skepti-cal about what she perceives as an entire society's apparent need to cast itself in what theater history would probably call a sentimental comedy. Although Kaminer does not directly make the connection, Phil Donohue is clearly our man of feeling and benevolence, while Oprah Winfrey is our woman of feeling and (at times) feminine victim as well. Their afternoon and morning shows are the form that middle-class sentimental comedy has taken in late twentieth-century Ameri-can culture.

Kaminer's examination of sentimental consumption belongs to an American critique of native sentimentalism that includes such major studies as Leslie Fiedler's *Love, Death, and the American Novel* and Ann Douglas's *The Feminization of American Culture*, studies that constitute the sentimental spectator I have been describing. Parnell's essay participates in this American critique. Even though he writes about English plays of the seventeenth and eighteenth centuries that most of his readers have never seen performed, his account of these works and his constitution of the sentimental spectator functions as a cautionary tale for a twentieth-century audience. The real threat is not Steele or Cumberland but their American descendants.

I asserted above that this sentimental spectator, more or less as I have reconstituted her (him) here, is the most important spectator in the twentieth century. I base this assertion on the number of signifi-cant functions that she (he) fills. Through her, her constituters make explicit a set of values—economic and gendered—that they find at work in middle-class culture. Also through her they challenge the status of these values. For Douglas the "sentimentalization of theological and secular culture [i.e., the creation of a nation of sentimental spectators] was an inevitable part of the self-evasion of a society both committed to laissez-faire industrial expansion and disturbed by its consequences." It "provided the inevitable rationalization of the economic order."[7] Fiedler, describing the gendered consequences of what he calls the Sentimental Love Religion, has even harsher words: "The demand that every woman act out the allegorical role of Womanhood is like the contemporary pressure on all Negroes to play The Negro; and the Clarissa image, when degraded from archetype to stereotype, is analogous to the current image of Uncle Tom."[8]

But this is not quite all. This sentimental spectator compensates also for certain other absences that cause discomfort. In the highly relativistic world of academic criticism, antisentimentalism still has for many an almost absolute value. Indeed "sentimental" as a pejorative term may signal a longing for moral absolutes like *good* and *evil*, *true* and *false*, *right* and *wrong*, words that do not easily spring from the lips of contemporary critics and that now are subsumed by a single pejorative: sentimental. Another part of the sentimental spectator's job is to keep other spectators in line: who wants to be like her or him, that naive, middle-class dolt. She also provides a basis for the creation of an American dramatic and literary canon: whatever she likes will be automatically excluded. She maintains the status of the critic and the teacher, bolsters the rationale for a good graduate school education. She will be reeducated, learn what to spurn and what to love.

THE SENTIMENTAL SPECTATOR RECONSIDERED

Jane Tompkins was one of the first poststructuralist critics to recognize and challenge this last set of functions. She writes, "What first made me uncomfortable about this story [modernism's heroic battle with sentimentalism] was not only all its heroes were men and its scapegoats women, but also its characterization of the reading public as an 'undiscriminating mass' whose fears could easily be pacified with pious clichés."[9] Tompkins also uses the sentimental spectator but for purposes different from those just outlined. Her moves take us in several different directions: an examination of those historical circumstances that led critics to create the sentimental spectator and the American literary canon (Thompkins constitutes the constituters), a more positive appraisal of the cultural work that sentimental dis-

courses perform in the material world, and a valorization of the sentimental spectator as someone more interesting and more radical than
usually thought.[10]

Poststructuralism created a discursive space in which Thompkins
could embrace (a sentimental terms, perhaps) the spectator that modernism used to define itself: *it* (modernism) was what that spectator
was *not;* *it* valued what she could *never* understand or appreciate,
"psychological complexity, moral ambiguity, epistemological sophistication, stylistic density, formal economy."[11] The "sentimental spectator" and the modernist critic were incommensurate entities. As
Suzanne Clark writes in *Sentimental Modernism,* "The horror of the
sentimental helped to define the good male poet as the prostitute once
defined the good woman."[12] And again "as an epithet, *sentimental*
condenses the way gender still operates as a political unconscious
within criticism to trigger shame, embarrassment, and disgust"; the
sentimental spectator is abject, diseased, wholly other.[13]

So what should we do with this fictive person? Embrace her or
excoriate her? Perhaps we might on occasion try to identify with, as
well as against, this figure, realizing full well that the effort to identify
will in itself push us in her direction, for identifying is one of the
activities at which sentimental spectators excel. But how might we do
this, those of us who have practiced so long the doctrines of antisentimentalism? We might begin with the thought that if sentimentalism
anticipates realism, then it, too, might possess Barthes's "reality effect," that because it eschews theatricality as it invites sympathy and
absorption, it might be most at work when it is least evident; that
what we usually regard as sentimental is conventionalized sentimentalism or perhaps lower middle-class sentimentalism as opposed to our
own upper middle-class academic versions; and that sentimentalism's
"self-approving joy" need not always be as public and demonstrative
as we might imagine it. Along with the sentimental self-awareness
that tears produce, there is also a process of being drawn in, of forget-
ting.[14] This is why defining sentimentalism as "unearned emotion"
seems not only totally subjective but also patently inadequate: sentimental effects only seem "unearned" when they are no longer working
for their audiences, when they are out-of-date or inept. Of course this
notion of an elusive sentimentalism also gives antisentimentalists a
kind of "self-approving joy." It gives them a mission to seek out the
hidden and make it manifest, a mission that can lead to an inquisi-
tional search for sentimental tendencies, one moving in an ever
tightening spiral, seeking a kind of purity of heart in an absence of
heart, a search that can never end because the search itself is a kind
of self-examination perpetuated by narratives with sentimental reso-

nances: the pure of heart shall see God. Similarly what Alice Rayner in *Comic Persuasion* refers to as the rhetoric of sincerity seems so central to the sentimental impulse that any effort to rid ourselves of sentimentalism based on its insincerity is bound to reproduce the paradigm we are trying to escape.[15]

With the sentimental spectator, I wonder as well about hidden narratives of goodness: Why, for example, do academics speak? To earn tenure; to hear the sounds of their own voices; to see their words in print; to climb above somebody else on the ladder of success. Of course. Many academic and nonacademic Americans are happy to admit their utilitarianism. They are proudly unsentimental about what they do. As academics we sometimes employ the language of business to describe university life, and the rhetoric of business itself possesses a certain "reality effect." For academics some assurance that they own a place in "the real" is often welcome. Furthermore if we follow Ann Douglas's explanation of the feminization of American culture, our initial disavowal of sentimental discourse was perhaps primarily motivated by the desire to separate from those irreal and fundamentally powerless members of nineteenth-century society who first articulated that discourse: women, liberal Protestant ministers, and men of letters (the university's ancestors).

I suspect, however, that more subtle narratives of benevolence and good feeling (not necessarily arising from an essential human nature, but present all the same) are also at work in our writing and teaching. Like uncharted undersea currents they affect our movements, but remain unnamed, because to name them without entering a sentimental discourse is almost impossible. They are like relatives unmentioned at family dinners, secrets from a past we would just as soon not remember. Perhaps these hidden narratives should remain closeted. But I wonder if this does not lead to more than a degree of confusion about the projects we undertake, the agendas we set.

Finally with the sentimental spectator, we might examine our own comings and goings. As noted above we are near the center of sentimental spectatorship when we encounter and respond to scenes of arrival and departure: E.T. says good-bye; a child returns a mended animal to the wild (eagle, deer, dolphin); Bambi's mother dies; the soldier goes to war and does or does not come home to wife and child; Linda says good-bye to Willy; Tom says one long good-bye to Amanda and Laura; Lear holds Cordelia in his arms for one last time; Clov heads toward the door. Evangelical invitational hymns ("Softly and Tenderly," "Just As I Am") draw strongly on images of departure and return. They also reflect, according to Ann Douglas, a fundamental aspect of the feminization/sentimentalization process in nineteenth-century America: the turning of colonial Puritanism into mush. Nevertheless the valorization of Puritan ideals found in anti-sentimentalist literature itself suggests a yearning for a return, a nostalgia for the good old days of rigor and guilt, a nostalgia I sometimes expect is felt by individuals who never had the opportunity to experience a dogmatic ideology during their own formative years.

Finally with that sentimental spectator still by our side, what should we make of this domestic scene of a child abandoned by its mother, now alone and playing with a makeshift toy, with a wooden reel and a piece of string perhaps: fort/da; presence/absence; departures/returns; lack: I think she would be moved. Academia spurns lower- and middle-class sentimentalism, yet near the center of current critical discourse is a prolonged meditation on the dynamics of presence and absence. Among its central images are dramas of separation articulated in narratives such as the one alluded to above in which Freud describes his grandson playing with a toy that he made disappear and appear, playing out either his mother's departures (Freud) or his own processes of self-alienation (Lacan).[16] Although Derrida undercuts the metaphysics of presence, his work still foregrounds a certain sense of a permanently delayed homecoming captured in the signifier that always eludes us, that is never quite here, that is endlessly caught up in a play of difference and deferral. These figures appeal to the sentimental spectator. Indeed therein lies a measure of their power.

If (caught in a sentimental, interior gaze) we find these or other aspects of that sentimental spectator within ourselves, then we have a decision to make. We might calculate that these examples are not so egregious as to deserve reprimand, that they are allowable under the law and that therefore we are not touched by the general charge, that what we experience is "earned emotion" not the "unearned emotion" of the sentimental spectator, healthy emotion in and of the present, not some nostalgia for the past. Or, we might determine that the sentimental spectator is not so wholly other as we thought, that at different times and places, we are her. We might agree with Clark that "modernism rejected the sentimental, because modernism *was* sentimental."[17] Perhaps we will want to change her name and start the process of constitution all over again, or we might in an act of sympathy accept her name as our own, at least on some occasions, without quite the shame or embarrassment more recently felt.

Appendix A: The Parable

AND he said, A certain man had two sons:

And the younger of them said to *his* father, Father, give me the portion of goods that falleth to *me*. And he divided unto them *his* living.

And not many days later the younger son gathered all together, and took his journey into a far country, and there wasted his substance with riotous living.

And when he had spent all, there arose a mighty famine in that land; and he began to be in want.

And he went and joined himself to a citizen of that country; and he sent him into his fields to feed swine.

And he would fain have filled his belly with the husks that the swine did eat: and no man gave unto him.

And when he came to himself, he said, How many hired servants of my father's have bread enough and to spare, and I perish with hunger!

I will arise and go to my father, and will say unto him, Father, I have sinned against heaven, and before thee,

And am no more worthy to be called thy son: make me as one of thy hired servants.

And he arose, and came to his father. But when he was yet a great way off, his father saw him, and had compassion, and ran, and fell on his neck, and kissed him.

And the son said unto him, Father, I have sinned against Heaven, and in thy sight, and am no more worthy to be called thy son.

But the father said to his servants, Bring forth the best robe, and put *it* on him; and put a ring on his hand, and shoes on *his* feet:

And bring hither the fatted calf, and kill *it;* and let us eat, and be merry.

Now his elder son was in the field: and as he came and drew nigh to the house, he heard musick and dancing.

And he called one of the servants, and asked what these things meant.

And he said unto him, Thy brother is come; and thy father hath killed the fatted calf, because he hath received him safe and sound.

And he was angry, and would not go in: therefore came his father out, and intreated him.

And he answering said to *his* father, Lo, these many years do I serve
thee, neither transgressed I at any time thy commandment: and
yet thou never gavest me a kid, that I might make merry with
my friends:

But as soon as this thy son was come, which hath devoured thy living
with harlots, thou hast killed for him the fatted calf.

And he said unto him, Son, thou art ever with me, and all that I have
is thine.

It was meet that we should make merry, and be glad: for this thy
brother was dead, and is alive again: and was lost, and is found.[1]

Appendix B: Alcohol and the Prodigal: Some Significant Dates

397–400 CE: Augustine employs the figure of the prodigal in his *Confessions*

9th Century: illuminated manuscript depicts the "return of the prodigal"[1]

11th to 13th centuries: early illuminated, stained glass, sculptural, and dramatic versions of the parable, including twenty-two stained glass scenes at Chartres Cathedral[2]

ca. 1496: Albrecht Dürer, *The Contemplation of the Prodigal Son*

1516: Hieronymus Bosch, *The Prodigal Son*

1529: William Fullonius (Gnapheus), *Acolastus* (published in' Antwerp); perhaps the most popular Renaissance version of the story[3]

1540: *Acolastus* translated into English by John Palsgrave[4]

1597–98: William Shakespeare, *Henry IV, Parts I and II*

ca. 1665: Rembrandt van Ryn, *The Return of the Prodigal Son*

1690: British government removes restrictions on production of gin to create "a market for low-grade corn";[5] contributes to a marked increase in drunkenness among the urban poor; creates a concern early in the eighteenth century for the effect of drunkenness on the family

1698: Jeremy Collier, "A Short View of the Immorality and Profaneness of the English Stage"

1704: Colley Cibber, *The Careless Husband*

1731: George Lillo, *The London Merchant*

1734: William Hogarth, *A Rake's Progress*

1736: George Lillo, *The Fatal Curiosity*

1751: British government sets controls on the sale of gin in response to abuse of the drink, particularly among the poor; Hogarth, *Gin Lane* and *Beer Street*

1755: Le Clerc designs prodigal prints in England that portray the characters in modern dress[6]

1774: Anthony Benezet, "The Mighty Destroyer Displayed" (pamphlet): the "first full-scale assault on American drinking habits"[7]

1784: Dr. Benjamin Rush (early American advocate of temperance), "An Inquiry into the Effects of Ardent Spirits on the Mind and Body";[8] Quakers and Methodists begin to ask members "to abstain from hard liquor and to take no part in its manufacture or sale"[9]

1789: bourbon first produced in Bourbon county Kentucky[10]

1795: prints of the parable of the prodigal produced in America[11]

Early nineteenth-century America: disestablishment of churches; urbanization and industrialization; the doctrine of separate spheres for men and women (male/public/workplace; female/private/home); "for more and more people a commercial drinking context" replaces a "domestic or community setting";[12] drink (purchased rather than produced) begins to compete for family earnings

1811: Presbyterian general assembly denounces drinking in America[13]

1820s: a whiskey glut, caused in part by surplus of grain west of the Appalachians, makes distilled alcohol more readily available; by 1830 annual per capita consumption of absolute alcohol is at 7.1 gallons, as compared with 5.8 gallons in 1790 and 2.45 in 1970;[14] polluted water supplies, as well as the expense or unavailability of coffee, tea, and milk also contribute to an increase in alcohol consumption[15]

1826: founding of American Society for the Promotion of Temperance, advocating abstinence from distilled spirits[16]

1828: Douglas Jerrold, *Fifteen Years of a Drunkard's Life* (London)

1836: American Temperance Union recommends total abstinence

1838: *The Drunkard's Warning* (New York)

1844: W. H. Smith, *The Drunkard; or, The Fallen Saved* (Boston Museum; 140 performances)

1851: sale of beverage alcohol prohibited by law in Maine

1879: Zola, *L'Assommoir* (Paris)

1920: Constitutional prohibition begins

1933: Constitutional prohibition repealed

1940: John D. Rockefeller, Jr., holds dinner on behalf of Alcoholics Anonymous and contributes to the "publication of a book about the lives of the first generation of alcoholics who had recovered through the programme"[17]

1940: E. M. Jellineck creates *The Quarterly Journal of Studies on Alcohol*

1941: *Saturday Evening Post* article on Alcoholics Anonymous increases national awareness of AA

1943: Yale Summer School in Alcohol Studies begins[18]

1946: General Assembly of the northern Presbyterian church adopts disease model of alcoholism[19]

1954: American Medical Association declares alcoholism a disease[20]

1956: New York premiere of *Long Day's Journey into Night*

Notes

Chapter 1. The Bottle

1. Thornton Wilder, *The Happy Journey to Trenton and Camden*, in *The Long Christmas Dinner and Other Plays in One Act* (New York: Harper and Row, 1931), 102.

2. Ibid., 98.

3. Ibid., 98.

4. Ibid., 99.

5. Ibid., 99.

6. These are, of course, locales (fictional and real) from the worlds of O'Neill, Miller, and Williams.

7. Wilder, *Journey*, 99.

8. Ibid., 103.

9. Ibid., 110.

10. For related discussions of this phenomenon, see Steven F. Bloom, "Empty Bottles, Empty Dreams: O'Neill's Use of Drinking and Alcoholism in *Long Day's Journey into Night*," in *Critical Essays on Eugene O'Neill*, ed. James J. Martine (Boston: Hall, 1984), 159–77; Steven F. Bloom, "Empty Bottles, Empty Dreams: O'Neill's Alcoholic Drama" (Ph.D. diss., Brandeis University, 1982); Thomas B. Gilmore, "*The Iceman Cometh* and the Anatomy of Alcoholism," in *Equivocal Spirits: Alcoholism and Drinking in the Twentieth-Century* (Chapel Hill: University of North Carolina Press, 1987), 48–61; Donald W. Goodwin, "O'Neill: Alcohol and the Irish," in *Alcohol and the Writer* (Kansas City: Andrews and McMeel, 1988), 123–37; Robin Room, "A 'Reverence for Strong Drink': The Lost Generation and the Elevation of Alcohol in American Culture," *Journal of Studies in Alcohol* 45 (1984): 540–45; Robert Whitman, "O'Neill's Search for a 'Language of the Theatre,'" in *O'Neill*, ed. John Gassner (Englewood Cliffs, N.J.: Prentice, 1964), 160–64.

11. Edward Albee, *Who's Afraid of Virginia Woolf?* (New York: Atheneum, 1962), 106.

12. Some other American plays in which alcohol plays a prominent role are *The Boys in the Band* (Mart Crowley, 1968); *The River Niger* (Walker, 1973); Sam Shepard's family plays such as *Curse of the Starving Class* (1978); *Buried Child* (1978); *True West* (1980); *Burn This* (Lanford Wilson; 1987); *New Music*, a trilogy of plays by Reynolds Price (*August Snow*, 1989; *Night Dance*, 1990; *Better Days*, 1990); and *The Orphan's Home Cycle*, Horton Foote's nine-play family saga.

13. Sheila Hickey Garvey, "Recreating a Myth: *The Iceman Cometh* in Washington, 1985," *The Eugene O'Neill Newsletter* 9 no. 3 (1985): 21.

14. Ibid., 22.

15. Roland Barthes, "The Reality Effect," in *The Rustle of Language*, trans. Richard Howard (New York: Hill, 1986), 142.

16. Ibid., 141.

17. In "Universals of Performance," Herbert Blau makes the distinction between

"do" and "ado." The latter signals consciousness. Drinking as an activity corresponds to the first category; drinking as an index corresponds to the second. For Blau's essay, see *The Eye of Prey* (Bloomington: Indiana University Press, 1987), 161–88.

18. The distinction between icon, index, and symbol comes, of course, from semiotician Charles S. Peirce. Keir Elam, among others, makes the connection to theater and drama: *The Semiotics of Theatre and Drama* (London: Methuen, 1980), 21–27.

19. Clifford Odets, *The Country Girl* (New York: Viking Press, 1951), 74.

20. Eugene O'Neill, *Long Day's Journey into Night*, in *Eugene O'Neill: Complete Plays, 1932–1943* (New York: Library of America, 1988), 796.

21. Richard Moody, introduction to *The Drunkard, or The Fallen Saved*, by W.H. Smith in *Dramas from the American Theatre: 1762–1909* (Cleveland: World, 1966), 280.

22. Ketti Frings, *Look Homeward, Angel*, based on the novel by Thomas Wolfe in *Best American Plays*, ed. John Gassner, Fifth Series: 1957–1963 (New York: Crown, 1963), 254.

23. From Robert Brustein's *The Theatre of Revolt: An Approach to Modern Drama* (Boston: Atlantic Monthly Press-Little, 1962), 142.

24. Bloom, "Empty," 167; Bloom also points out in his dissertation on the subject that drunken speech is not always truthful speech, that each instance must be judged separately. This observation is valid, but in terms of dramatic convention, drunkenness usually signals revelation, not obfuscation. See also the Whitman article (perhaps the earliest sustained discussions of O'Neill's use of alcohol as a dramatic device), as well as the following: John Henry Raleigh, *The Plays of Eugene O'Neill* (Carbondale: Southern Illinois University Press, 1965), 173, 183–84, 203; Timo Tiusanen, *O'Neill's Scenic Images* (Princeton: Princeton University Press, 1968), 279–280; Egil Törnqvist, *A Drama of Souls: Studies in O'Neill's Super-naturalistic Technique* (Uppsala, Sweden: Almqvist and Wiksells, 1968), 149.

25. Travis Bogard, *Contour in Time: The Plays of Eugene O'Neill* (New York: Oxford University Press, 1972), 430–31.

26. O'Neill, *Journey*, 820.

27. John A. Ewing, and Beatrice A. Rouse, "Drinks, Drinkers, and Drinking," in *Drinking in American Society—Issues and Current Research*, ed. John A. Ewing and Beatrice A. Rouse (Chicago: Nelson-Hall, 1978), 6.

28. Compare Bloom's juxtaposition (in both his dissertation and the essay on *Journey*) of two different perceptions of drink at work in O'Neill's late plays: one of transcendence and romanticism; the other of reality and cynicism. See also Gilmore's *Equivocal Spirits* and David C. McClelland et al., *The Drinking Man* (New York: Free Press, 1972).

29. William James, *The Varieties of Religious Experience: A Study in Human Nature* (London: Collier-Macmillan, 1961), 304–5.

30. Mark Edward Lender, and James Kirby Martin, *Drinking in America: A History* (New York: Free Press, 1982), 39.

31. Ibid., 1.

32. Ibid., 45–46.

33. Ibid., 2.

34. Harry Gene Levine, "The Alcohol Problem in America: From Temperance to Alcoholism," *British Journal of Addiction* 79 (1984): 110.

35. In addition to Lender and Levine, see, for example, Jack S. Blocker, Jr., *American Temperance Movements: Cycles of Reform* (Boston: Twayne, 1989); W. J. Rorabaugh, *The Alcoholic Republic: An American Tradition* (New York: Oxford Uni-

versity Press, 1979); John W. Frick, "'He Drank from the Poisoned Cup'": Theatre, Culture, and Temperance in Antebellum America," *The Journal of American Drama and Theatre* 4 no. 2 (1992): 22.

36. Blocker traces five temperance movements over the past two centuries from 1784 to the present. The reoccurrence of these movements indicates the persistence of underlying issues that refuse closure.

37. Odets, *Country Girl*, 107.

38. Tad Mosel, *All the Way Home*, based on the novel *A Death in the Family* by James Agee (New York: Ivan Obolensky, 1961), 161.

39. O'Neill, *A Moon for the Misbegotten*, in *Eugene O'Neill: Complete Plays, 1932–1943* (New York: Library of America, 1988), 926.

40. Bloom makes a similar point in his article, "Empty Bottles," 159. Other examples of women who drink would include Maggie in *After the Fall* (Miller, 1964); Claire in *A Delicate Balance* (Albee, 1966); Halie in *Buried Child* (1978) (she enters in act 3 with a Protestant minister and a bottle of whiskey); Grandma Wilhemina Brown in *The River Niger;* and Billie Holiday in *Lady Day at Emerson's Bar & Grill* (Robertson, 1986).

41. See Norman K. Denzin's discussion of the female alcoholic in film in *Hollywood Shot by Shot: Alcoholism in American Cinema* (New York: Aldine de Gruyter, 1991); see also Judith Harwin and Shirley Otto, "Women, Alcohol and the Screen," in *Images of Alcoholism*, ed. Jim Cook and Mike Lewington (London: British Film Institute and Alcohol Education Centre, 1979), 37–49.

42. O'Neill, *Journey*, 820.

43. Frick, "'He Drank,'" 223.

44. Lender and Martin, *Drinking*, 196–97. See also Lender and Martin, "Metamorphosis: From 'Good Creature' to 'Demon Rum,' 1790–1860," *Drinking*, 41–86; Blocker, "The First Temperance Movement (1784–1840)," in *American Temperance*, 1–29.

45. Whether this morality of the home represented a softening or feminization of Puritan morality or an ideology more radical and confrontational (as manifested, for example, in the work of the Women's Christian Temperance Union and the writings of Harriet Beecher Stowe) is a matter of debate among scholars of the period. For the first view, see Ann Douglas, *The Feminization of American Culture* (New York: Anchor Press, Doubleday, 1988); for the latter, see Jane Tompkins, *Sensational Designs: The Cultural Work of American Fiction, 1790–1860* (New York: Oxford University Press, 1985).

46. For discussions of the rise of the modern nuclear family, the division of spheres, and accompanying notions of masculine and feminine roles, see, among others, Carl N. Degler, *At Odds: Women and the Family in America from the Revolution to the Present* (Oxford: Oxford University Press, 1980); Ann Douglas, *Feminization;* Barbara Ehreneich, "Introduction: Why Women Married Men," in *The Hearts of Men: American Dreams and the Flight from Commitment* (Garden City, N.Y.: Anchor Press, Doubleday, 1983), 1–13; Barbara Epstein, *The Politics of Domesticity: Women, Evangelism, and Temperance in Nineteenth-Century America* (Middletown, Ct.: Wesleyan University Press, 1981); Julie A. Matthaei, "Women's Work and the Sexual Division of Labor Under the Cult of Domesticity," *An Economic History of Women in America: Women's Work, the Sexual Division of Labor, and the Development of Capitalism* (New York: Schocken Books, 1982), 101–232; Steven Mintz and Susan Kellogg, "The Rise of the Democratic Family," *Domestic Revolutions: A Social History of American Family Life* (New York: Free Press, Macmillan, 1988), 43–65.

47. Of course Euripides's *Bacchae* reminds us that the desire to control female energy is not restricted to nineteenth-and twentieth-century America.

48. Lender, *Drinking,* 117–18.

49. The increase in gin consumption in England and of distilled spirits in America a few years later helped to spur changes in attitudes toward drinking behaviors, particularly as they affected families (poor, working, and middle class). Both instances were to some extent triggered by an increase in inexpensive alcohol, occasioned by agricultural surpluses.

50. Related professions, as Denzin notes, would be "actress, singer, or entertainer, occupations typically reserved for 'tainted' women who had turned their back on their proper place in the family" in Denzin, *Hollywood,* 71.

51. O'Neill, *"Anna Christie,"* in *Eugene O'Neill: Complete Plays, 1913–1920,* 968; O'Neill, *Journey,* 818.

52. O'Neill, *Ah, Wilderness!* in *Eugene O'Neill: Complete Plays, 1932–1943,* 51.

53. O'Neill, *The Iceman Cometh.* In *Eugene O'Neill: Complete Plays: 1932–1943* (New York: Library of America, 1988).

54. Tennessee Williams, *A Streetcar Named Desire,* vol. 1 of *The Theatre of Tennessee Williams* (New York: New Directions, 1971), 266.

55. Caryl Churchill, *Top Girls* (London: Methuen, 1984), 1.

56. Ibid., 2.

57. Ibid., 29.

58. Denzin, *Hollywood,* 242.

59. Sarah Crichton, "Sexual Correctness: Has It Gone too Far?" *Newsweek,* 25 October 1993, 54.

60. Froma I. Zeitlin, "Playing the Other: Theater, Theatricality, and the Feminine in Greek Drama," in *Nothing to Do with Dionysos?* ed. John J. Winkler and Froma I. Zeitlin (Princeton: Princeton University Press, 1990), 85.

61. Appropriately the kinds of visions experienced in a delirium episode, reptilian hallucinations, for example, in *The Drunkard,* are not so far from the imagery found in Greek tragedies, as in the Furies of the *Oresteia.*

62. For one discussion of this process, see James Hillman, "On Psychological Femininity," in *The Myth of Analysis: Three Essays in Archetypal Psychology* (Evanston, Ill.: Northwestern University Press, 1972), 215–98.

63. Richard Stivers, *A Hair of the Dog: Irish Drinking and American Stereotype* (University Park: Pennsylvania State University Press, 1976).

64. Jane Tompkins, *West of Everything: The Inner Life of Westerns* (New York: Oxford University Press, 1992), 127.

65. John Gassner once wrote that American drama seemed more interested in "growing up" than "grown-ups"; also relevant are the observations of critics such as Benedict Nightingale and Martin Esslin who, from European perspectives, look with some dismay/amazement/despair on American drama's obsession with the family: Benedict Nightingale, *Fifth Row Center: A Critic's Year On and Off Broadway* (New York: Times Books-Random, 1986), 128–35; Martin Esslin, "'Dead! and *never* called me mother!'" *Studies in the Literary Imagination* 21 no. 2 (1988): 23–33.

66. See also Joseph R. Gusfield, *The Symbolic Crusade: Status Politics and the American Temperance Movement* (Urbana: University of Illinois Press, 1963).

67. Epstein, *Domesticity,* 103; emphasis added.

68. Lender and Martin, *Drinking,* 41–86.

69. Judith N. McArthur, "Demon Rum on the Boards: Temperance Melodrama and the Tradition of Antebellum Reform," *Journal of the Early Republic* 9 (1989): 518.

70. Frick, "'He Drank,'" 24.

71. On temperance melodrama, see Michael R. Booth, "The Drunkard's Progress: Nineteenth-Century Temperance Drama," *The Dalhousie Review* 44 (1964): 205–12; Frick, "'He Drank'"; McArthur, "Demon Rum"; Frank Rahill, "The Delirium Tremens Drama," in *The World of Melodrama* (University Park: Pennsylvania State University Press, 1967), 240–46.

72. Moody, *American Theatre: 1762–1909*, 279.

73. Don L. Hixon, and Don A. Hennessee, *Nineteenth-Century American Drama: A Finding Guide* (Metuchen, N.J.: Scarecrow Press, 1977), 566–68.

74. See Degler, *At Odds*, 316–317; Epstein, *Domesticity*, 102–3; Frick, "'He Drank,'" 31.

75. Frick, "'He Drank,'" 31.

76. Ibid., 25.

77. Ibid., 25–26.

CHAPTER 2. PRODIGAL SONS, PRODIGAL HUSBANDS: A PARTICULAR LINEAGE

1. O'Neill, *Iceman Cometh*, 694.

2. H. Colin Slim, *The Prodigal Son at the Whores': Music, Art, and Drama*, Distinguished Faculty Lecture: 1975–1976 (Irvine: University of California, 1976), 2. Slim discusses the relationship of the parable to the music, as well as the art and drama, of the sixteenth century.

3. In visual representations of the parable, the inheritance was, however, usually lost through the trickery of gamblers or prostitutes.

4. O'Neill, *Iceman*, 563.

5. Ibid., 577–78.

6. Alcoholics Anonymous, *Twelve Steps and Twelve Traditions* (New York: Alcoholics Anonymous, 1981), 21–23.

7. Vernon E. Johnson, *I'll Quit Tomorrow*, rev. ed. (San Francisco: Harper and Row, 1980), 114–25.

8. Ibid., 123.

9. O'Neill, *Iceman*, 697.

10. See, for example, Beck's discussion of this issue in his examination of the prodigal: Ervin Beck, "Terence Improved: The Paradigm of the Prodigal Son in English Renaissance Comedy," in *Renaissance Drama*, ed. Alan C. Dessen, New Series 6: Essays on Dramatic Antecedents (Evanston: Northwestern University Press, 1973), 110.

11. For the only other booklength study of the prodigal in modern drama, see Leah Hadomi, *The Homecoming Theme in Modern Drama: The Return of the Prodigal, "Guilt to be on Your Side"* (Lewiston, N.Y.: Edwin Mellen Press, 1992).

12. Daryl Tippens, "Shakespeare and the Prodigal Son Tradition," *Explorations in Renaissance Culture* 14 (1988): 58.

13. For one overview of studies on biography and conventionality, see Norman K. Denzin, *Interpretive Biography*, Qualitative Research Methods, vol. 17 (Newbury Park: Sage, 1989).

14. Tippens, "Prodigal Son," 58.

15. Emile Mâle, *Religous Art in France: The Thirteenth Century, A Study of Medieval Iconography and Its Sources*, Bollingen Series, no. 90 (Princeton: Princeton University Press, 1984), 199, 204, 205.

16. Ibid., 205.

17. David Kunzle, *History of the Comic Strip*, vol. I: *The Early Comic Strip, Narrative Strips and Picture Stories in the European Broadsheet from c. 1450 to 1825* (Berkeley: University of California Press, 1973), 2–3.

18. Alan R. Young, *The English Prodigal Son Plays: A Theatrical Fashion of the Sixteenth and Seventeenth Centuries*, Jacobean Drama Studies 89 (Salzburg: Institut für Anglistik und Amerikanistik, 1979), 291–317.

19. Tippens, "Prodigal Son," 63–72.

20. Using relatively unambiguous references to scenes of departure, riotous living, feeding with the swine, and the return, I count around ten departures, thirty-five riotous livings, ten feeding with the swine, and thirty-five returns. This does not take into account multiscene works.

21. Edwin Wolf, II, "The *Prodigal Son* in England and America: A Century of Change," in *Eighteenth-Century Prints in Colonial America: To Educate and Decorate*, ed. Joan D. Dolmetsch (Williamsburg, Va.: Colonial Williamsburg Foundation, 1979), 154.

22. Ibid., 152, 155.

23. Ibid., 151.

24. William H. Halewood, *Six Subjects of Reformation Art: A Preface to Rembrandt* (Toronto: University of Toronto Press, 1982), 53. According to David Kunzle, Hogarth first "intended to start the *Rake* by marrying him to a rich old woman," but in the "completed version . . . reverted to the idea of a foolish young man, like the Prodigal of old, taking possession of his patrimony," in Kunzle, *History*, 308–9.

25. Tom Cheesman, "The Return of the Transformed Son: A Popular Ballad Complex and Cultural History, Germany 1500–1900," *Oxford German Studies* 18/19 (1990): 60–91.

26. Ibid., 65.

27. Ibid. H. Colin Slim supports Cheesman's position. He notes that by "the late fifteenth century and throughout the sixteenth century, especially in countries of Northern Europe, dramatic and visual presentations of the parable reach flood-like proportions." See "The Prodigal Son at the Whores'," 1.

28. Cheesman, "The Return," 65.

29. Ibid., 65, 68.

30. Ibid., 65.

31. Ibid., 68.

32. For studies of the Christian Terence tradition and the prodigal, see W. E. D. Atkinson, appendix, *Acolastus: A Latin Play of the Sixteenth Century* (London, Ontario: University of Western Ontario, 1964); Genevieve Kelly, "The Drama of Student Life in the German Renaissance," *Educational Theatre Journal* 26 (1974): 291–307; Marvin T. Herrick, *Tragicomedy: Its Origin and Development in Italy, France, and England*, Illinois Studies in Language and Literature 39 (Urbana: University of Illinois Press, 1955) 37–46; see also Boas, Herford, and Schelling cited below.

33. Earlier dramatizations include *Courtois D'Arras*, late twelfth or early thirteenth century (France); Castellano Catellani's *Rappresentazione del Figliuol Prodigo*, late fifteenth or early sixteenth century (Italy), and *L'Enfant Prodigue*, fifteenth century (France). See Atkinson's appendix to Gnapheus's *Acolastus*, 207. One of the earliest recorded versions dates from the 1470s in Italy: the author was a woman, Antonia Pulci. See Konrad Eisenbicher, «From *Sacra Rappresentazione* to *Commedia Spirituale;* Three 'Prodigal Son' Plays», *Bibliothètheque D'Humainsme et Renaissance* 45 (1983): 107–13.

34. Herrick, *Tragicomedy*, 17.

35. Tippens, "Prodigal Son," 59.

36. Felix Schelling, *Elizabethan Drama: 1588–1642*, 2 vols. (Boston: Houghton, 1908), I: 63; Herrick, *Tragicomedy*, 37.

37. Eisenbichler, "Three 'Prodigal Son' Plays," 109.

38. For studies relevant to this phenomenon, see, in addition to those already cited, the following: John Doebler, "Beaumont's *The Knight of the Burning Pestle* and the Prodigal Son Plays," *Studies in English Literature: 1500–1900* 5 (1965): 333–44; Robert Hapgood and Robert Y. Turner, "Dramatic Conventions in *All's Well That Ends Well*," *Publications of the Modern Language Association of America* 79 (1964): 177–82; Leanore Lieblein, "Thomas Middleton's Prodigal Play," *Comparative Drama* 10 (1976): 54–60; James E. May and Calhoun Winton, "The 'Prodigal Son' at Bartholomew Fair: A New Document," *Theatre Survey: The American Journal of Theatre History* 21 no. 1 (1980): 63–72; Robert Y. Turner, "Dramatic Conventions in *All's Well That Ends Well*," *Publications of the Modern Language Association of America* 75 (1960): 497–502. For brief references within the context of larger studies, see, Frederick S. Boas, *An Introduction to Tudor Drama* (Oxford: Clarendon, 1933), 40–41; Muriel C. Bradrook, *The Growth and Structure of Elizabethan Comedy*, new ed. (London: Chatto and Windus, 1973), 127–33; C. F. Tucker Brooke, *The Tudor Drama: A History of English National Drama to the Retirement of Shakespeare* (Boston: Houghton, 1911), 123–29; Charles H. Herford, *Studies in the Literary Relations of England and Germany in the Sixteenth Century* (Cambridge: Cambridge University Press, 1886), 84–88, 149–64.

39. Young, *Prodigal Son Plays*, 319–21.

40. Beck, "Terence Improved," 107–8; Tippens, "Prodigal Son," 76. Susan Synder argues convincingly for the centrality of the prodigal to an understanding of *King Lear* in "*King Lear* and the Prodigal Son," *Shakespeare Quarterly* 17 (1966): 361–69. Richmond Noble finds nine references in Shakespeare: *Shakespeare's Biblical Knowledge* (London: SPCK, 1935), 277–78.

41. Beck, "Terence Improved," 107.

42. Ibid., 121.

43. Ibid., 109; format altered for clarity.

44. Ibid., 116–17; format altered for clarity.

45. Arthur Hobson Quinn, introduction to *The Faire Maide of Bristow*, Publications of the University of Pennsylvania, Series in Philology and Literature 8.1 (Philadelphia: Ginn, 1902), 27.

46. Bradbrook, *Elizabethan Comedy*, 133.

47. Beck, "Terence Improved," 116.

48. Ibid., 112.

49. Northrop Frye, *The Anatomy of Criticism: Four Essays* (Princeton: Princeton University Press, 1957), 164–73; Beck, "Terence Improved," 114.

50. See, for example, Richard Bevis, *The Laughing Tradition: Stage Comedy in Garrick's Day* (Athens: University of Georgia Press, 1980), 50–52.

51. Gotthold Ephraim Lessing, *Miss Sara Sampson: A Tragedy in Five Acts*, trans. G. Hoern Schlage (Stuttgart: Akademischer Verlag Hans-Dieter Heinz, 1977), 5.

52. Edward Moore, *The Gamester*, in *Eighteenth Century Tragedy* (London: Oxford University Press, 1965), 164.

53. Rahill, *Melodrama*, 57.

54. Ibid., 240.

55. McArthur, "Demon Rum," 522.

56. Rahill, *Melodrama*, 246.

57. For cinematic analogues, see Denzin, *Hollywood*, in particular his discussions of films like *The Lost Weekend*, *Days of Wine and Roses*, and *Clean and Sober*.

58. Lender and Martin, *Drinking*, 74–78.

59. Frick, "'He Drank,'" 29.

60. Maud and Otis Skinner, *One Man in His Time: The Adventures of H. Watkins, Strolling Player, 1845–1863, from His Journal* (Philadelphia: University of Pennsylvania Press, 1938), 70.

61. See Booth, "Drunkard's Progress," 207.

62. Smith, *Drunkard*, 300–301.

63. Ibid., 298.

64. See note no. 46, chapter 1.

65. Mintz and Kellogg, *Revolutions*, 54–55.

66. Tom Scanlan, *Family, Drama, and American Dreams*, Contributions in American Studies, no. 35 (Westport, Ct.: Greenwood, 1978), 27.

67. Ibid., 26.

68. Ibid., 34, 121.

69. Ibid., 42.

70. Ibid.

71. Arthur Miller, *Death of a Salesman*, in *Arthur Miller Collected Plays* (London: Secker and Warburg, 1958), 183.

72. Scanlan, *Family*, 42, 94.

73. Ibid., 42.

74. Mintz and Kellogg, *Revolutions*, 44.

75. Eisenbicher, "Three 'Prodigal Son' Plays," 108, 113; May and Winton, "'Prodigal Son,'" 63, 69; Schelling, *Elizabethan Drama*, 61; Joseph B. Spieker, "The Theme of the Prodigal Son in XVII Century Spanish Art and Letters," *Hispanic Journal* 5 (1984): 29, 36; Tippens, "Prodigal Son," 59.

76. Herrick, *Tragicomedy*, 39; Lieblein, "Prodigal Play," 58; Spieker, "Prodigal Son," 32–33.

77. Herrick, *Tragicomedy*, 24.

78. Erich Auerbach, *Mimesis: The Representation of Reality in Western Literature*, trans. Willard R. Trask (Princeton: Princeton University Press, 1953), 246.

79. Auerbach, *Mimesis*, 249–50.

80. For Auerbach, Racine is perhaps the most extreme example of the opposite tendency, of a tradition that eliminated details of "everyday living, references to sleeping, eating and drinking, the weather" from the realm of the serious or sublime.

81. The impetus for this statement comes from Leslie Fiedler on Richardson: "through Richardson a whole class cries: We will be raped and bamboozled no more!" In *Love and Death in the American Novel*, rev. ed. (New York: Scarborough Book, Stein and Day, 1966), 72.

82. O'Neill, *Misbegotten*, 907.

83. Lawson A. Carter, *Zola and the Theater* (Westport, Ct.: Greenwood Press, 1963), 108–18.

84. Ibid., 108, 118.

85. Sarcey, as quoted by Carter, *Zola*, 112; translation by Jan Weldin.

86. Jack Gelber, *The Connection* (New York: Grove Press, 1957), 85.

87. Richard C. Kostelanetz, "*The Connection*: Heroin as Existential Choice," *The Texas Quarterly* 5 (Winter 1962): 159.

88. Kostelanetz, "*The Connection*," 159–60.

89. Gelber, *Connection*, 70.

90. See Slim, "The Prodigal Son at the Whores'."

91. George E. Wellwarth, "Hope Deferred—The New American Drama: Reflec-

tions on Edward Albee, Jack Richardson, Jack Gelber, and Arthur Kopit," *The Literary Review: An International Journal of Contemporary Writing* 7 no. 1 (1963): 25.

92. Gelber, *Connection*, 31.

93. Auerbach, *Mimesis*, 518.

94. M. H. Abrams, *Natural Supernaturalism: Tradition and Revolution in Romantic Literature* (New York: Norton, 1971), 146.

95. Abrams, *Natural Supernaturalism*, 147.

96. See, for example, Michel Foucault, "Rarity, Exteriority, Accumulation," in *The Archaeology of Knowledge and the Discourse on Language*, trans. by A. M. Sheridan Smith (New York: Pantheon Books, 1972), 118–25; Roland Barthes, "From Work to Text," in *Textual Strategies: Perspectives in Post-Structuralist Criticism*, ed. Josué V. Harari (Ithaca: Cornell University Press, 1979), 73–81; Hayden White, "The Absurdist Moment in Contemporary Literary Theory," in *Tropics of Discourse: Essays in Cultural Criticism* (Baltimore: Johns Hopkins University Press, 1978), 261–82.

97. Abrams, *Natural Supernaturalism*, 194. Kaja Silverman points out the centrality of a similar metaphor to Lacanian psychoanalytic theory in *The Subject of Semiotics* (New York: Oxford University Press, 1983), 151–57.

98. Lorraine Hansberry, *A Raisin in the Sun* (New York: Random, 1959), 92–93.

99. Abrams, *Natural Supernaturalism*, 166.

100. Abrams, *Natural Supernaturalism*, 167.

101. Quoted by Abrams, *Natural Supernaturlism*, 167.

102. For one discussion of male identity as threatened by the family, see Ehrenreich, *The Hearts of Men*.

CHAPTER 3. PRODIGAL SONS, PRODIGAL HUSBANDS: RUPTURE AND POTENTIAL

1. Tennessee Williams, *The Glass Menagerie*, in vol. 1 of *The Theatre of Tennessee Williams* (New York: New Directions, 1971), 145.

2. William Inge, *The Dark at the Top of the Stairs*, in *Four Plays by William Inge* (New York: Grove Weidenfeld, 1958), 228.

3. Ibid., 278.

4. Sam Shepard, *True West*, in *Sam Shepard: Seven Plays* (New York: Bantam-Macmillan, 1981), 5.

5. Mosel, *Home*, 20–21.

6. Ibid., 22.

7. On images of the family, the prodigal, the pilgrim, and American identity, see Jay Fliegelman, *Prodigals and Pilgrims: The American Revolution Against Patriarchal Authority, 1750–1800* (Cambridge: Cambridge University Press, 1982); also Fiedler, *Love and Death*, particularly on the roles of men and women in American fiction.

8. Mosel, *Home*, 159–60; emphasis added.

9. O'Neill, *Iceman*, 696.

10. Mosel, *Home*, 160.

11. Raleigh, *O'Neill*, 173.

12. Ibid.

13. O'Neill, *Iceman*, 563.

14. In *El hijo pródigo*, Lope de Vega, as do various visual artists, gives the prodigal a horse for his departure. Spieker, "Prodigal Son," 33.

15. Cheesman, "The Return," 66–67.

16. Ibid., 67.

17. Frye, *Anatomy*, 166.

18. See also discussion of Shange, Treadwell, and Moraga in chapter 6.

19. Ehreneich, *Hearts of Men*, 20, 26, 50, 170, 172, 182.

20. Ibid., 49.

21. Nancy Corson Carter, "The Prodigal Daughter: A Parable Re-Visioned," *Soundings* 68 (1985): 89.

22. Raleigh, *O'Neill*, 163.

23. Matthew 12:31, RSV.

24. In *Journey*, we also find the examples of the two grandfather's and in *Salesman*, the interesting figure of Willy's brother, Ben. The latter is a related, although slightly peripheral variant. Mary and Tyrone's fathers are typical male prodigal figures.

25. Fiedler, *Love and Death*, 270; see also John Frick, "'He Drank,'" 30, 33.

26. Quoted in Fiedler, *Love and Death*, 290.

27. For an example that makes this transition from prodigal to rebel/criminal the initial action of a drama, see the opening scenes of Schiller's *Die Räuber* (1781).

28. George L. Aiken, *Uncle Tom's Cabin*, based on the novel by Harriet Beecher Stowe, in *Dramas from the American Theatre: 1762–1909*, ed. Richard Moody (Cleveland: World, 1969), 393.

29. Turner, "Dramatic Conventions," 499.

30. O'Neill, *Iceman*, 701.

31. Cheesman, "The Return," 67; Beck, "Terence Improved," 112; Lieblein, "Prodigal Play," 59.

32. Beck, "Terence Improved," 115.

33. Victor Turner, "Liminal to Liminoid, in Play, Flow, and Ritual: An Essay in Comparative Symbology," in *From Ritual to Theatre: The Human Seriousness of Play* (New York: Performing Arts Journal, 1982), 20–59. Turner cites Arnold van Gennep's *Rites of Passage*.

34. Ibid., 24.

35. Ibid.

36. Ibid., 25.

37. Ibid., 26.

38. Ibid., 24.

39. Ibid., 24–25.

40. Ibid., 44; emphasis added.

41. Ibid., 31.

42. Ibid., 32.

43. See also Stivers, "Drinking as a Rite of Passage," in *Hair of the Dog*, 81–86.

44. To these examples, we might add several others: *The Long Voyage Home* (O'Neill; 1917), *Dynamo* (O'Neill; 1929), *The Glass Menagerie* (Williams; 1945), *Summer and Smoke* (Williams; 1948), *The Rope Dancers* (Wishengrad; 1957), *The Touch of a Poet* (O'Neill; 1958; written 1935–42), even *Arsenic and Old Lace* (Kesserling, 1941). I have, however, tried to keep this initial list relatively short and manageable.

45. Hebbel's *Maria Magdelena* (1844) demonstrates the same familiar double standard: the inability to forgive the prodigal daughter or wife.

46. We might also conceive of Stella as a prodigal: she has left home to come to a strange city. But her identity as wife and mother significantly obscures her prodigality.

47. O'Neill, *Journey*, 769.

48. Albee, *Woolf*, 131.

49. For one example of an attempt at imagining the prodigal daughter, see Carter,

"Prodigal Daughter," 88–105. See also Patricia Kane, "The Prodigal Daughter in Alice Walker's "Everyday Use," *Notes on Contemporary Literature* 15 (1985): 7; Alice Walker, "Everyday Use," in *In Love and Trouble: Stories of Black Women* (New York: Harcourt, 1967), 47–59. In chapter 6 I look more closely at reworkings of this structure by women playwrights.

50. Unlike the use of alcohol in American dra'ma, however, the *Kindermord* convention has more consistent parallels in European literature, as in Brecht, Ibsen, Chekhov, Shakespeare, Euripides, Aeschylus; on many of these instances and on Albee's *Woolf*, see Charles R. Lyons, "Some Variations of *Kindermord* as Dramatic Archetype," *Comparative Drama* 1 (1967): 56–71.

51. William Inge, *Come Back, Little Sheba* in *Four Plays by William Inge* (New York: Grove Weidenfeld, 1958), 33.

52. Christopher Durang, *The Marriage of Bette and Boo* (New York: Grove Press, 1985), 25, 81, 85, 107, 108.

53. Bonnie Marranca, "Robert Wilson: Byrd Hoffman School for Byrds," in *The Theatre of Images* (New York: Drama Book Specialists, 1977), 40. For contrasting views of Little Eva and the image of the dying child, see Fiedler, *Love and Death*, 266–69 (as sexual object); Douglas, "The Legacy of American Victorianism: The Meaning of Little Eva," in *Feminization*, 3–13 (as trigger for nostalgia and narcissism); Tompkins, *Sensational Designs*, 127–33 (as regenerative force).

54. See R. S. Crane, "Suggestions Toward a Genealogy of the 'Man of Feeling,'" in *The Idea of the Humanities and Other Essays: Critical and Historical*, 2 vols. (Chicago: University of Chicago Press, 1967), I: 188–213.

55. See, for example, François Bovon, "Julius Welhausen's Exegesis of Luke 15:11–32," in *Exegesis: Problems of Method and Exercises in Reading (Genesis 22 and Luke 15)*, published under the direction of François Bovon and Grégoire Rouiller. trans. Donald G. Miller (Pittsburgh, Pa.: Pickwick, 1978), 118–22.

CHAPTER 4: THE BROTHER

1. Miller, *Salesman*, 133.

2. Michael Manheim discusses this tension in O'Neill's plays in terms of what he calls the "rhythm of kinship" in *Eugene O'Neill's New Language of Kinship* (Syracuse: Syracuse University Press, 1982), 8–11.

3. Fiedler, *Love and Death*, 206.

4. 1 Sam. 16:12, KJV.

5. Arthur Miller, *The Price*, in *Arthur Miller's Collected Plays, Vol. II* (New York: Viking, 1981), 329.

6. Sam Shepard, *True West*, in *Sam Shepard: Seven Plays* (New York: Bantam-Macmillan, 1981), 2.

7. O'Neill, *Journey*, 722–23.

8. Gen. 25:25–26, RSV; emphasis added.

9. J. Duncan M. Derrett, "Law in the New Testament: The Parable of the Prodigal Son," *New Testament Studies* 14 (1967): 68.

10. Ibid.

11. Ibid.

12. Ibid., 70.

13. Jill Robbins, "The Prodigal Son and Elder Brother: The Example of Augustine's *Confessions*," *Genre* 16 (1983): 323.

14. C. F. Keppler, *The Literature of the Second Self* (Tucson: University of Arizona Press, 1972), 22.

15. Keppler, *Second Self*, 216 n. 30.

16. Bruno Bettelheim, *The Uses of Enchantment: The Meaning and Importance of Fairy Tales* (New York: Vintage-Random, 1975), 108.

17. Ibid., 91.

18. Stith Thompson, *Motif-Index of Folk-Literature: A Classification of Narrative Elements in Folktales, Ballads, Myths, Fables, Mediaeval Romances, Exempla, Fabliaux, Jest-Books, and Local Legends*, rev. and enl. ed., 6 vols. (Bloomington: Indiana University Press, 1955–58), V: 6–9.

19. Bettelheim, *Uses*, 103.

20. O'Neill, *Journey*, 733.

21. Ibid., 820.

22. Neil Simon, *Come Blow Your Horn* (Garden City: Doubleday, 1963), 108.

23. O'Neill, *Journey*, 819.

24. Ibid., 821.

25. Ibid.

26. Ibid., 732.

27. René Girard, *Violence and the Sacred*, trans. Patrick Gregory (Baltimore: Johns Hopkins University Press, 1972), 143–68.

28. O'Neill, *Journey*, 721.

29. Ibid., 814.

30. Sheaffer notes that one reason O'Neill purportedly wrote *Misbegotten* was because he "had come to view *Long Day's Journey* as too severe on Jamie." This observation suggests O'Neill's own sense that the writing of *Journey* involved a degree of violence against his brother. Whether or not *Misbegotten* counters or continues that violence is, I think, an open question: Louis Sheaffer, *O'Neill: Son and Artist* (Boston: Little, 1973), 528.

31. Books and articles addressing these issues (the divided self and the related phenomenon of the double), in addition to those already mentioned, include the following: Clifford Hallam, "The Double as Incomplete Self: Toward a Definition of Doppelgänger," in *Fearful Symmetry: Double and Doubling in Literature and Film,* ed. Eugene J. Cook, Papers from the Fifth Annual Florida State University Conference on Literature and Film (Tallahassee: University Presses of Florida, 1981) 1–31; Otto Rank, *The Double: A Psychoanalytic Study*, trans. Harry Tucker, Jr. (Chapel Hill: University of North Carolina Press, 1971); Robert Rogers, *A Psychoanalytic Study of the Double in Literature* (Detroit: Wayne State University Press, 1970); Claire Rosenfield, "The Conscious and the Unconscious Use of the Double," in *Stories of the Double*, ed. Albert J. Guerard (Philadelphia: Lippincott, 1967); Törnqvist, *Drama of Souls*, 218–41; Stephen Watt, "O'Neill and Otto Rank: Doubles, 'Death Instincts,' and the Trauma of Birth," *Comparative Drama* 20 (1986): 211–30; Albert Wertheim, "Eugene O'Neill's *Days Without End* and the Tradition of the Split Character in Modern American and British Drama," *The Eugene O'Neill Newsletter* 6 no. 3 (1982): 5–9.

32. Bogard, *Contour*, 447.

33. Rank, *Double*, 76.

34. See Keppler, *Second Self*, 56–77, for a discussion of what he calls the "second self as tempter," a figure similar in many ways to what I call the mentor.

35. Bettelheim in *Uses* observes that elder siblings often function as displaced parent figures. In fact he argues that this may be a central reason for the convention

of the pair of elder siblings so often found in folk and fairy tales—a mother double and a father double—often opposed to a single younger daughter or son: 106.

36. O'Neill, *Journey*, 822.

37. In a sense the hypocritical elder brother (e.g., Williams's Gooper) also combines both of these attributes: desire and authoritarian control. He appears to operate under the strictures of the father, but beneath a façade of idealism, there exists a body of violent desire that manifests itself in animosity and greed.

38. Herbert Ashton, Jr., *Brothers* (New York: Samuel French, 1927), 3.

39. Watt, among others, discusses contrasting doubles in his essay, "O'Neill and Otto Rank," 219.

40. Tennessee Williams, *Cat on a Hot Tin Roof*, in vol.3 of *The Theatre of Tennessee Williams* (New York: New Directions, 1971), 17, 22.

41. Miller, *Price*, 295.

42. See Charles Lyons, "Character and Criticism," Paper for the Speech Communications Association (Denver, November 1985), 5–7.

CHAPTER 5: HE (OR SHE) WHO WAITS

1. Williams, *Streetcar*, 306–7.

2. Ibid., 312.

3. Ibid., 307.

4. This list is for the purposes of illustration. I have not tried to list every conceivable prodigal or "grace" figure in these plays.

5. As pointed out in chapter 3, Happy is also something of a prodigal, but Willy and Biff are clearly the central figures in terms of grace and forgiveness. Whether or not Linda knows about the "Boston woman," she still takes her place within the paradigm. It is enough that Willy and Biff perceive her as the long-suffering wife to whom the husband comes home. The son who encounters and must then come to terms with his father's prodigality is a less common but not particularly unusual inversion of the norm. It has become in recent years a staple of Shepard's family dramas.

6. Again, Helen's awareness or lack of awareness of her husband's affair is irrelevant to whether or not she fits within this structure. In an interesting variation on the convention, a psychiatrist hears Richard's confession as a kind of surrogate for the wife and then advises the husband that he and his wife will both be better off if she never knows what happened.

7. Maggie, of course, must also seek forgiveness from Brick for taking Skipper to bed and the part which that action played in his death. This behavior was, however, a function not of unfaithfulness or lust, but of loneliness and the desire to bring an absent husband home. We perceive it, therefore, not as an act of betrayal or female prodigality but as an act of love more reminiscent of the Lukan father than of the prodigal son.

8. Hannah, like Shannon, is an almost allegorical manifestation of the convention: she personifies a kind of "grace" that can accept even the peculiarities of the Australian salesman.

9. Cheesman, "The Return," 67.

10. Wendy Kaminer, *I'm Dysfuntional, You're Dysfunctional: The Recovery Movement and Other Self-Help Fashions* (New York: Vintage, Random House, 1993), 3. The title of Kaminer's book is unfortunate—it belies her insightful discussion of the ideology underlying the recovery movement in the eighties.

11. The suggestion purposely reflects Sue-Ellen Case's comments on Greek theater in *Feminism and Theatre* (New York: Methuen, 1988).

12. Mary Crapo Hyde, *Playwriting for Elizabethans: 1600–1605* (New York: Columbia University Press, 1949), 41.

13. See Scanlan's discussion of the "good woman" type, *Family*, 71–72.

14. Thornton Wilder, author's notes for *The Happy Journey* (New York: Samuel French, 1931), 4.

15. Odets, *Country Girl*, 114.

16. O'Neill, *Journey*, 818.

17. See Bette Mandl, "Absence as Presence: The Second Sex in *The Iceman Cometh*," *The Eugene O'Neill Newsletter* 6 no. 2 (1982): 10–15.

18. O'Neill, *Iceman*, 704.

19. Degler, *At Odds*, 298–327.

20. O'Neill, *Iceman*, 634.

21. Ibid., 579.

22. Ibid., 639, 678. The O'Neill concordance lists nineteen occurrences of the word *bitch* in his works; fourteen of them occur in *Iceman:* J. Russell Reaver, compiler, *An O'Neill Concordance*, 3 vols. (Detroit: Gale, 1969).

23. Mandl, "Absence," 10.

24. O'Neill, *Misbegotten*, 857.

25. Ibid., 860.

26. Hogan actually describes her as being as "big and strong as a bull": 864.

27. O'Neill, *Misbegotten*, 859.

28. Ibid., 868.

29. Ibid., 861.

30. Ibid., 924.

31. Ibid., 933.

32. For other more recent examples of the phenomenon of the failed or exhausted "grace" figure see Shepard's mothers and wives in *Buried Child, True West*, and *The Curse of the Starving Class;* for a reversal of this tendency, see Beth in *A Lie of the Mind.*

33. Studies of alcoholism and marriage may tend to confirm this convention. See Joan K. Jackson, "Alcoholism and the Family," in *Society, Culture, and Drinking Patterns,* ed. David J. Pittman and Charles R. Snyder (New York: John Wiley, 1962), 472–92.

34. For a discussion of some texts that attempt to break out of this double standard to portray images of more liberated women, see the following articles: Carol Billman, "Women and the Family in American Drama," *Arizona Quarterly* 36 (1980): 35–48; Deborah S. Kolb, "The Rise and Fall of the New Woman in American Drama," *Educational Theatre Journal* 27 (1975): 149–60; Yvonne B. Shafer, "The Liberated Woman in American Plays of the Past," *Players* 49 (1974): 95–100.

35. O'Neill, *Misbegotten*, 892.

36. Will L. Thompson, "Softly and Tenderly Jesus Is Calling," no. 178, *The Sunday School Hymnal with Office of Devotion* (Philadelphia: Heidelberg, 1902).

37. Douglas, *Feminization*, 131.

38. Miller, *Salesman*, 134.

39. Hansberry, *Raisin*, 141.

40. Simon, *Horn*, 131–32.

41. O'Neill, *Journey*, 731.

42. Ibid., 822.

43. Williams, *Cat*, 51.

44. Ibid., 152.

45. O'Neill, *Journey*, 714; emphasis added.

46. Cecil Brown, "Interview with Tennessee Williams," *Partisan Review* 45 (1978): 284.

47. O'Neill, *Misbegotten*, 930–31.

48. Ibid., 929.

49. O'Neill, *Journey*, 794.

50. Ibid.

51. Ibid., 807.

52. Ibid., 808.

53. For a further discussion of this scene, see Geoffrey S. Proehl, "Foucault on Discourse: O'Neill as Discourse: *LDJN* (4: 125–54) Tyrone and Edmund," *Journal of Dramatic Theory and Criticism* 4 no. 2 (1990): 51–62.

54. O'Neill, *Misbegotten*, 912.

55. Ibid., 928–29.

56. Ibid., 933.

57. Ibid.

58. O'Neill, *Iceman*, 697–98; emphasis added.

59. Ann Douglas explores this shift as a historical and cultural phenomenon in *The Feminization of American Culture*. See also Fiedler, *Love and Death*, 430–32.

60. O'Neill, *Wilderness*, 93.

61. Ibid., 95.

62. Girard, *Violence*, 161.

63. Miller, *Salesman*, 208.

64. These devices are similar to those employed to redeem fallen women in plays and novels of sensibility that date from the eighteenth century. See Janet Todd, *Sensibility: An Introduction* (London: Methuen, 1986), 81. In American drama examples range from Herne's *Margaret Fleming* (1890) to Simon's *Broadway Bound* (1986).

65. O'Neill, *Wilderness*, 96.

66. O'Neill, *Misbegotten*, 933.

67. Smith, *Drunkard*, 307.

68. Ibid.

69. Ibid.

70. Inge, *Dark*, 304.

71. O'Neill, *Wilderness*, 107.

72. Watt's excellent article on Rank and O'Neill suggests, if I read it correctly, that Jamie's choice is between the forces of *partialization/fragmentation* (usually connected with genital sexuality) and *totalization/wholeness* (usually connected with a return to the mother, to the womb, to unconsciousness, and death): "O'Neill and Otto Rank," 216.

73. O'Neill, *Misbegotten*, 931.

74. O'Neill, *Iceman*, 697.

75. Romans 3:20; emphasis added.

76. For example on *theatricality*, see Blau, "Universals," 161–88; Sue-Ellen Case, "Towards a New Poetics," in *Feminism and Theatre;* and Barbara Freedman, *Staging the Gaze: Postmodernism, Psychoanalysis, and Shakespearean Comedy* (Ithaca: Cornell University Press, 1991); on *representation* and *presence*, see Philip Auslander, "Towards a Concept of the Political in Postmodern Theatre," *Theatre Journal* 39 (1987): 20–34; Elinor Fuchs, "Presence and the Revenge of Writing: Re-thinking Theatre after Derrida," *Performing Arts Journal* 26/27 9 nos. 2 and 3 (1985): 163–73; Kate Linker, "Representation and Sexuality" and other essays in *Art After Modernism:*

Rethinking Representation, ed. Brian Wallis (New York: New Museum of Contemporary Art, 1984), 391–415; and Craig Owens, "The Discourse of Others: Feminists and Postmodernism," in *The Anti-Aesthetic: Essays on Postmodern Culture,* ed. Hal Foster (Seattle, Wash.: Bay Press, 1983), 57–82; on *realism,* see Barthes, "The Reality Effect"; and Sheila Stowell, "Rehabilitating Realism," *Journal of Dramatic Theory and Criticism* 6 no. 2 (1992): 81–88; on *sentimentalism,* see Suzanne Clark, *Sentimental Modernism: Women Writers and the Revolution of the Word* (Bloomington: Indiana University Press, 1991); Douglas, *Feminization;* and Jane Tompkins, *Sensational Designs;* on *domestic drama* and the encoding of *gender roles,* see "Playwrights Polemic: A Shortage of Themes" *West Coast Plays* 10 (1981): 75–100 (an exchange of letters and opinions that began with Martin Esslin's critique of American drama in terms of its obsession with family matters); also see again, Case's *Feminism and Theatre;* Case, ed., *Performing Feminisms: Feminist Critical Theory and Theatre* (Baltimore, Md.: Johns Hopkins University Press, 1990); Sharon Friedman, "Feminism as Theme in Twentieth-Century American Women's Drama," *American Studies* 25 no. 1 (1984): 69–89; numerous other books and articles, as well as essays cited earlier in this chapter by Billman, Kolb, Mandl, and Shafer. I have not tried to cite even the major critical documents in these discussions, but essays and books that provide entry points.

77. Hélène Cixous, "Aller à la mer," *Modern Drama* 27 (1984): 546.

78. Case, *Feminism,* 124.

CHAPTER 6: PERSISTENCE, VARIATION, DISPERSION

1. "Shekana Youth Chapel," Narr. Lynn Neary. *All Things Considered* (National Public Radio; WHYY, Philadelphia, 27 June 1994).

2. Spalding Gray, *Booze, Cars, and College Girls,* in *Sex and Death to the Age of 14* (New York: Vintage-Random, 1986), 36.

3. Spalding Gray, *Swimming to Cambodia* (New York: Theatre Communications Group, 1985), 102.

4. Emily Mann, *Still Life,* in *Coming to Terms: American Plays and the Vietnam War* (New York: Theatre Communications Group, 1985), 258.

5. Ibid.

6. Ibid., 223.

7. Luke 15:18–19.

8. Mann, *Still Life,* 270.

9. Ibid., 268.

10. Ibid., 271.

11. Ibid.

12. Ntozake Shange, *for colored girls who have considered suicide/when the rainbow is enuf* (New York: Macmillan, 1975), 56.

13. Ibid., 57.

14. Ibid., 58.

15. Ibid., 59.

16. Ibid., 60.

17. Judith Sargent Murray, *The Traveler Returned,* from a typed copy of the original in Brown University Library, 143.

18. Sophie Treadwell, *Machinal,* in *Twenty-Five Best Plays of the Modern American Theatre,* early series, ed. John Gassner (New York: Crown, 1949), 518.

19. Cherríe Moraga, *Shadow of a Man,* in *Shattering the Myth: Plays by Hispanic*

Women, selected by Denise Chávez, ed. Linda Feyder (Houston: Arte Publico Press, 1992), 24. This play was brought to my attention by Susan Haedicke.

20. Ibid., 38.

21. Ibid., 18.

22. Ibid., 43.

23. Ibid., 37.

24. Ibid., 38.

25. Ibid., 43–45; emphasis added.

26. Here are several more recent domestic dramas in which prodigals play a role: James Baldwin's *The Amen Corner* (1965); Lanford Wilson's *Lemon Sky* (1970); David Mamet's *Reunion* (1976); Sam Shepard's family plays, *The Curse of the Starving Class* (1978), *Buried Child* (1978), *True West* (1980); David Rabe's *Hurlyburly* (1984); August Wilson's *Fences* (1985); Eric Bogosian's *Drinking in America* (1986); Neil Simon's *Broadway Bound* (1986); Lanie Robertson's *Lady Day at Emerson's Bar & Grill* (1986); Horton Foote's *The Orphan's Home Cycle.*

27. John Bradshaw, *Homecoming: Reclaiming and Championing Your Inner Child* (New York: Bantam, 1990), 20.

28. Ibid., 7.

29. Charlotte Davis Kasl, *Women, Sex, and Addiction: A Search for Love and Power* (New York: Ticknor and Fields, 1989), 279–82.

30. Ibid., 280.

31. William J. Eaton, "Kennedy Admits to Personal 'Frailties,' Vows to Fight On," *Los Angeles Times,* 26 October 1991, sec. A, p. 1.

32. Carlin Romano, "Daddy Was *the* Playboy," *Philadelphia Inquirer* 19 June 1994, sec. M.

33. Jeannie Park and Robin Micheli, "Falling Down . . . and Getting Up Again," *People,* 29 January 1990, 58.

34. Ibid., 59.

35. Since the article's publication, Barrymore has indeed appeared successfully in several films.

36. Park and Micheli, "Falling Down," 61.

37. Ibid.

38. Tony Kushner, *Angels in America: A Gay Fantasia on National Themes; Part One: Millenium Approaches* (New York: Theatre Communications Group, 1993), 74–76.

Epilogue: The Sentimental Spectator

1. Paul Parnell, "The Sentimental Mask," *Publications of the Modern Language Association of America* 78 (1963): 533; see also, Douglas, *Feminization,* 4.

2. Douglas, *Feminization,* 4; also, for an excellent discussion of sentimental comedy, see Alice Rayner, "Cumberland and Steele's Aphorism: Use in Utopia," in *Comic Persuasion: Moral Structure in British Comedy from Shakespeare to Stoppard* (Berkeley: University of California Press, 1987), 81–103. Rayner's insights have been helpful in framing several of the issues within this chapter.

3. Michael Fried, *Absorption and Theatricality: Painting and the Beholder in the Age of Diderot* (Berkeley: University of California Press, 1980).

4. On the rhetoric of sincerity, see Rayner, *Comic Persuasion,* 84–85.

5. Parnell, "Sentimental," 534.

6. Ibid.

7. Douglas, *Feminization*, 12.
8. Fielder, *Love and Death*, 68.
9. Tompkins, *Sensational Designs*, 424.
10. See, for example, Tompkins, "Sentimental Power: *Uncle Tom's Cabin* and the Politics of Literary History," in *Sensational Designs*, 122–46.
11. Tompkins, *Sensational Designs*, xvii.
12. Clark, *Sentimental*, 10.
13. Ibid., 11. Incidentally Clark's use of the word *shame* connects her with the recovery movement. I am curious about the degree to which sentimentalism or its reconstitution requires as a precondition a rhetoric of shame or if it simply creates this rhetoric after the fact to justify itself.
14. David Marshall discusses this dialectic in *The Surprising Effects of Sympathy: Marivaux, Diderot, Rousseau, and Mary Shelley* (Chicago: University of Chicago Press, 1988).
15. Rayner, *Comic Persuasion*, 84–85.
16. Silverman, *Semiotics*, 167–72.
17. Clark, *Sentimental*, 7.

Appendix A: The Parable

1. Luke 15:11–32; King James Version. I have used this version not for its authenticity as a translation, but because of its status as a work of literature and its relative familiarity.

Appendix B: Alcohol and the Prodigal

1. Young, *English Prodigal Son Plays*, 291.
2. Ibid.; Slim, "Prodigal Son at the Whores'," 1.
3. A. Bronson Feldman, "Ghaphaeus in England," *Modern Language Notes* 67 (1952): 325–28.
4. Ibid., 326.
5. Norman Longmate, *The Waterdrinkers: A History of Temperance* (London: Hamish Hamilton, 1968), 14.
6. Wolf, "Prodigal Son," 152.
7. Lender and Martin, *Drinking*, 35.
8. Levine, "Alcohol Problem," 110.
9. Lender and Martin, "Drinking," 35.
10. Ibid., 33.
11. Wolf, "Prodigal Son," 146.
12. Blocker, *American Temperance*, 9–10.
13. Lender and Martin, "Drinking," 67.
14. Ibid., 196.
15. Blocker, *American Temperance*, 9–10.
16. Ibid., 12.
17. Levine, "Alcohol Problem," 116.
18. Ibid., 117.
19. Blocker, *American Temperance*, 149.
20. Levine, "Alcohol Problem," 117.

Works Cited

PRIMARY SOURCES

Anonymous. *The Faire Maide of Bristow*. Edited by Arthur Hobson Quinn. Philadelphia: Ginn, 1902.

————. *How a Man May Chuse a Good Wife from a Bad*. Edited by A. E. H. Swaen. Louvain: A. Uystpruyst, 1912.

————. *The Interlude of Youth*. *Two Tudor Interludes: The Interlude of Youth, Hick Scorner*. Edited by Ian Lancashire. Manchester, England: Manchester University Press, 1980.

————. *The London Prodigal*. [Amersham, England]: Tudor facsimile, 1910.

————. *Nice Wanton*. In *Chief Patterns of World Drama: Aeschylus to Anderson*. Edited by William Smith Clark. New York: Houghton, 1946.

Aiken, George L. *Uncle Tom's Cabin*. Based on the novel by Harriet Beecher Stowe. In *Dramas from the American Theatre: 1762–1909*. Edited by Richard Moody. Cleveland: World, 1969.

Albee, Edward. *A Delicate Balance*. New York: Atheneum, 1966.

————. *Who's Afraid of Virginia Woolf?* New York: Atheneum, 1962.

Ashton, Herbert, Jr. *Brothers*. New York: Samuel French, 1927.

Axelrod, George. *The Seven Year Itch: A Romantic Comedy*. New York: Random, 1953.

Bogosian, Eric. *Drinking in America*. New York: Vintage-Random, 1987.

Cibber, Colley. *Colley Cibber: Three Sentimental Comedies*. Edited by Maureen Sullivan. New Haven: Yale University Press, 1973.

Churchill, Caryl. *Top Girls*. New York: Methuen, 1984.

Cixous, Hélène. *Portrait of Dora*. In *Benmussa Directs*. Translated by Anita Barrows. London: John Calder, 1979.

Crowley, Mart. *The Boys in the Band*. New York: Farrar, Straus, and Giroux, 1968.

Cumberland, Richard. *The West Indian*. In *British Dramatists from Dryden to Sheridan*. Edited by George H. Nettleton and Arthur E. Chase. Boston: Houghton, 1939.

Durang, Christopher. *The Marriage of Bette and Boo*. New York: Grove, 1985.

Frings, Ketti. *Look Homeward, Angel*. Based on the novel by Thomas Wolfe. In *Best American Plays*. Edited by John Gassner. Fifth Series, 1957–63. New York: Crown, 1963.

Gelber, Jack. *The Connection*. New York: Grove, 1957.

Gnapheus, Gulielmus. *Acolastus: A Latin Play of the Sixteenth Century*. Translated by W. E. D. Atkinson. London, Ontario: University of Western Ontario, 1964.

Gray, Spalding. *Sex and Death to the Age of 14*. New York: Vintage-Random, 1986.

————. *Swimming to Cambodia*. New York: Theatre Communications Group, 1985.

Hansberry, Lorraine. *A Raisin in the Sun*. New York: Random, 1959.

Hebbel, Friedrich. *Maria Magdalena*. In *Chief Patterns of World Drama: Aeschylus to Anderson*. Edited by William Smith Clark. New York: Houghton, 1946.

Herne, James A. *Margaret Fleming*. In *Representative American Plays From 1767 to the Present Day*. Edited by Arthur Hobson Quinn. 5th ed. New York: Appleton, 1917.

Inge, William. *Come Back, Little Sheba*. In *Four Plays by William Inge*. New York: Random, 1958.

————. *The Dark at the Top of the Stairs*. In *Four Plays by William Inge*. New York: Random, 1958.

Jerrold, Douglas. *Fifteen Years of a Drunkard's Life*. New York: Samuel French, [prem. 1828].

Jonson, Ben, George Chapman, and John Marston. *Eastward Ho!* Edited by C. G. Petter. London: Ernest Benn, 1973.

Kennedy, Adrienne. *The Owl Answers*. In *Adrienne Kennedy in One Act*. Minneapolis: University of Minnesota Press, 1988.

Kesserling, Joseph. *Arsenic and Old Lace*. In *Best Plays of the Modern American Theatre*. Edited by John Gassner. Second Series. New York: Crown, 1947.

Kushner, Tony. *Angels in America: A Gay Fantasia on National Themes; Part One: Millenium Approaches*. New York: Theatre Communications Group, 1993.

Lessing, Gotthold Ephraim. *Miss Sara Sampson: A Tragedy in Five Acts*. Translated by Hoern Schlage. Stuttgart: Adademischer Verlag Hans-Dieter Heinz, 1965.

Lillo, George. *The London Merchant; or, The History of George Barnwell*. In *British Dramatists from Dryden to Sheridan*. Edited by George H. Nettleton and Arthur E. Chase. Boston: Houghton, 1939.

Mann, Emily. *Still Life*. In *Coming to Terms: American Plays and the Vietnam War*. New York: Theatre Communications Group, 1985.

Miller, Arthur. *Death of a Salesman*. In *Arthur Miller Collected Plays*. London: Secker and Warburg, 1958.

————. *The Price*. In *Arthur Miller's Collected Plays, Vol. II*. New York: Viking, 1981.

Moore, Edward. *The Gamester*. In *Eighteenth Century Tragedy*. London: Oxford University Press, 1965.

Moraga, Cherríe. *Shadow of a Man*. In *Shattering the Myth: Plays by Hispanic Women*. Selected by Denise Chavez. Edited by Linda Feyder. Houston: Arte Publico Press, 1992.

Mosel, Tad. *All the Way Home*. Based on the novel *A Death in the Family* by James Agee. New York: Ivan Obolensky, 1961.

Murray, Judith Sargent. *The Traveler Returned*, from a typed copy of the original in Brown University Library.

Odets, Clifford. *The Country Girl*. New York: Viking, 1951.

O'Neill, Eugene. *Ah, Wilderness!* In *Eugene O'Neill: Complete Plays: 1932–1943*. New York: Library of America, 1988.

————. *"Anna Christie."* In *Eugene O'Neill: Complete Plays: 1913–1920*. New York: Library of America, 1988.

————. *Dynamo*. In *Eugene O'Neill: Complete Plays: 1920–1931*. New York: Library of America, 1988.

————. *The Iceman Cometh*. In *Eugene O'Neill: Complete Plays: 1932–1943*. New York: Library of America, 1988.

————. *Long Day's Journey into Night*. In *Eugene O'Neill: Complete Plays: 1932–1943*. New York: Library of America, 1988.

————. *The Long Voyage Home*. In *Eugene O'Neill: Complete Plays: 1913–1920*. New York: Library of America, 1988.

————. *A Moon for the Misbegotten*. In *Eugene O'Neill: Complete Plays: 1932–1943*. New York: Library of America, 1988.

————. *The Touch of a Poet*. In *Eugene O'Neill: Complete Plays: 1932–1943*. New York: Library of America, 1988.

Pratt, William W. *Ten Nights in a Bar-Room: A Temperance Drama in Five Acts*. Based on the novel by T. S. Arthur. In *Hiss the Villain: Six English and American Melodramas*. Edited by Michael R. Booth. New York: Benjamin Blom, 1964.

Price, Reynolds. *New Music: A Trilogy (August Snow, Night Dance, Better Days)*. New York: Theatre Communication Group, 1990.

Robertson, Lanie. *Lady Day at Emerson's Bar & Grill*. New York: Samuel French, 1983.

Schiller, Friedrich. *The Robbers; Wallenstein*. Translated by F. J. Lamport. New York: Penguin, 1979.

Shange, Ntozake. *for colored girls who have considered suicide/when the rainbow is enuf*. New York: Macmillan, 1975.

Shepard, Sam. *Buried Child*. In *Sam Shepard: Seven Plays*. New York: Bantam-Macmillan, 1981.

————. *Curse of the Starving Class*. In *Sam Shepard: Seven Plays*. New York: Bantam-Macmillan, 1981.

————. *A Lie of the Mind*. New York: Plume-New American Library, 1986.

————. *True West*. In *Sam Shepard: Seven Plays*. New York: Bantam-Macmillan, 1981.

Sheridan, Richard Brinsley. *The School for Scandal*. In *British Dramatists from Dryden to Sheridan*. Edited by George H. Nettleton and Arthur E. Chase. Boston: Houghton, 1939.

Simon, Neil. *Brighton Beach Memoirs*. New York: Random, 1984.

————. *Broadway Bound*. New York: Random, 1987.

————. *Come Blow Your Horn*. Garden City: Doubleday, 1963.

Smith, W. H. *The Drunkard, or the Fallen Saved*. In *Dramas from the American Theatre: 1762–1909*. Edited by Richard Moody. Cleveland: World, 1969.

Steele, Richard. *The Conscious Lovers*. In *British Dramatists from Dryden to Sheridan*. Edited by George H. Nettleton and Arthur E. Chase. Boston: Houghton, 1939.

Taylor, T. P. *The Bottle*. In *The Minor Drama*. No. 20. New York: William Taylor [prem. 1847].

Treadwell, Sophie. *Machinal*. In *Twenty-Five Best Plays of the Modern American Theatre*. Early series. Edited by John Gassner. New York: Crown, 1949.

Vanbrugh, John. *The Relapse; or, Virtue in Danger*. In *British Dramatists from Dryden to Sheridan*. Edited by George H. Nettleton and Arthur E. Chase. Boston: Houghton, 1939.

Walker, Alice. "Everyday Use." In *In Love and Trouble: Stories of Black Women*. New York: Harcourt, 1967.

Walker, Joseph A. *The River Niger.* New York: Hill and Wang, 1973.

Wilder, Thornton. *The Happy Journey to Trenton and Camden.* In *The Long Christmas Dinner and Other Plays in One Act.* New York: Harper and Row, 1931.

———. Author's Notes for *The Happy Journey to Trenton and Camden.* New York: Samuel French, 1931.

Williams, Tennessee. *Cat on a Hot Tin Roof.* In *The Theatre of Tennessee Williams.* Vol. 3. New York: New Directions, 1971.

———. *The Glass Menagerie.* In *The Theatre of Tennessee Williams.* Vol. 1. New York: New Directions, 1971.

———. *The Night of the Iguana.* In *The Theatre of Tennessee Williams.* Vol. 4. New York: New Directions, 1972.

———. *A Streetcar Named Desire.* In *The Theatre of Tennessee Williams.* Vol. 1. New York: New Directions, 1971.

———. *Summer and Smoke.* In *The Theatre of Tennessee Williams.* Vol. 2. New York: New Directions, 1971.

Wilson, August. *Fences.* New York: Plume-New American Library, 1986.

Wilson, Lanford. *Burn This.* New York: Noonday Press, 1987.

———. *Lemon Sky.* In *Best American Plays.* Edited by Clive Barnes. Seventh Series: 1967–73. New York: Crown, 1975.

Wishengrad, Morton. *The Rope Dancers.* In *Best American Plays.* Edited by John Gassner. Fifth Series: 1957–63. New York: Crown, 1963.

SECONDARY SOURCES

Abrams, M. H. *Natural Supernaturalism: Tradition and Revolution in Romantic Literature.* New York: Norton, 1971.

Alcoholics Anonymous. *Twelve Steps.* New York: Alcoholics Anonymous, 1981.

Armens, Sven. *Archetypes of the Family in Literature.* Seattle: University of Washington Press, 1966.

Atkinson, W. E. D. Introduction and Appendix. *Acolastus: A Latin Play of the Sixteenth Century.* London, Ontario: University of Western Ontario, 1964.

Auerbach, Erich. *Mimesis: The Representation of Reality in Western Literature.* Translated by Willard R. Trask. Princeton: Princeton University Press, 1953.

Auslander, Philip. "Toward a Concept of the Political in Postmodern Theatre." *Theatre Journal* 39 (1987): 20–34.

Barthes, Roland. "From Work to Text." In *Textual Strategies: Perspectives in Post-Structuralist Criticism.* Edited by Josué V. Harari. Ithaca: Cornell University Press, 1979.

———. "The Reality Effect." In *The Rustle of Language.* Translated by Richard Howard. New York: Hill, 1986.

Beck, Ervin. "Terence Improved: The Paradigm of the Prodigal Son in English Renaissance Comedy." *Renaissance Drama.* Edited by Alan C. Dessen. New Series 6: Essays on Dramatic Antecedents. Evanston: Northwestern University Press, 1973.

Bernbaum, Ernest. *The Drama of Sensibility: A Sketch of the History of English Sentimental Comedy and Domestic Tragedy, 1696–1780.* Gloucester: Peter Smith, 1958.

Berson, Misha. "Playwrights' Polemic: A Shortage of Themes." *West Coast Plays* 10 (1981): 75–100.

Bettelheim, Bruno. *The Uses of Enchantment: The Meaning and Importance of Fairy Tales.* New York: Vintage-Random, 1975.

Bevis, Richard. *The Laughing Tradition: Stage Comedy in Garrick's Day.* Athens: University of Georgia Press, 1980.

Bigsby, C. W. E. *Albee.* Edinburgh: Oliver and Boyd, 1969.

Billman, Carol. "Women and the Family in American Drama." *Arizona Quarterly* 36 (1980): 35–48.

Blau, Herbert. "Universals of Performance; or, Amortizing Play." In *The Eye of Prey.* Bloomington: Indiana University Press, 1987.

Blocker, Jack S., Jr. *American Temperance Movements: Cycles of Reform.* Boston: Twayne, 1989.

Bloom, Steven F. "Empty Bottles, Empty Dreams: O'Neill's Alcoholic Drama." Ph.D. diss., Brandeis University, 1982.

———. "Empty Bottles, Empty Dreams: O'Neill's Use of Drinking and Alcoholism in *Long Day's Journey into Night.*" *Critical Essays on Eugene O'Neill.* Edited by James J. Martine. Boston: Hall, 1984.

Boas, Frederick S. *An Introduction to Tudor Drama.* Oxford: Clarendon, 1933.

Bogard, Travis. *Contour in Time: The Plays of Eugene O'Neill.* New York: Oxford University Press, 1972.

Booth, Michael R. "The Drunkard's Progress: Nineteenth-Century Temperance Drama." *Dalhousie Review* 44 (1964): 205–12.

Bovon, François. "Julius Welhausen's Exegesis of Luke 15:11–32." In *Exegesis: Problems of Method and Exercises in Reading (Genesis 22 and Luke 15).* Published under the direction of François Bovon and Grégoire Rouiller. Translated by Donald G. Miller. Pittsburgh: Pickwick, 1978.

Bradbrook, Muriel C. *The Growth and Structure of Elizabethan Comedy.* New edition. London: Chatto and Windus, 1973.

Bradshaw, John. *Homecoming: Reclaiming and Campioning Your Inner Child.* New York: Bantam, 1990.

Brooke, C. F. Tucker. *The Tudor Drama: A History of English National Drama to the Retirement of Shakespeare.* Boston: Houghton, 1911.

Brown, Cecil. "Interview with Tennessee Williams." *Partisan Review* 45 (1978): 276–305.

Brustein, Robert. *The Theatre of Revolt: An Approach to Modern Drama.* Boston: Atlantic Monthly-Little, 1962.

Carter, Lawson A. *Zola and the Theater.* Westport, Conn.: Greenwood, 1963.

Carter, Nancy Corson. "The Prodigal Daughter: A Parable Re-Visioned." *Soundings* 68 (1985): 88–105.

Case, Sue-Ellen. *Feminism and Theatre.* New York: Methuen, 1988.

———. ed. *Performing Feminisms: Feminist Critical Theory and Theatre.* Baltimore: Johns Hopkins University Press, 1990.

Cheesman, Tom. "The Return of the Transformed Son: A Popular Ballad Complex and Cultural History, Germany 1500–1900." *Oxford German Studies* 18/19 (1990): 60–91.

Cixous, Hélène. "Aller à la mer." *Modern Drama* 27 (1984): 546–48.

Clark, Suzanne. *Sentimental Modernism: Women Writers and the Revolution of the Word*. Bloomington: Indiana University Press, 1991.

Crane, R. S. "Suggestions Toward a Genealogy of the 'Man of Feeling.'" In *The Idea of the Humanities and Other Essays Critical and Historical*. Vol. 1. Chicago: University of Chicago Press, 1967.

Crichton, Sarah. "Sexual Correctness: Has It Gone Too Far?" *Newsweek*, 25 October 1993, 52–56.

Degler, Carl N. *At Odds: Women and the Family in America from the Revolution to the Present*. New York: Oxford University Press, 1980.

Denzin, Norman K. *Hollywood Shot by Shot: Alcoholism in American Cinema*. New York: Aldine de Gruyter, 1991.

———. *Interpretive Biography*. Vol. 17. Qualitative Research Methods. Newbury Park: Sage, 1989.

Derrett, J. Duncan M. "Law in the New Testament: The Parable of the Prodigal Son." *New Testament Studies* 14 (1967): 56–74.

Doebler, John. "Beaumont's *The Knight of the Burning Pestle* and the Prodigal Son Plays." *Studies in English Literature: 1500–1900* 5 (1965): 333–44.

Douglas, Ann. *The Feminization of American Culture*. New York: Anchor Press, Doubleday, 1988.

Eaton, William J. "Kennedy Admits Personal 'Frailties,' Vows to Fight On." *Los Angeles Times*, 26 October 1991, sec. A, p. 1.

Ehreneich, Barbara. *The Hearts of Men: American Dreams and the Flight from Commitment*. Garden City, N.Y.: Anchor-Doubleday, 1983.

Eisenbichler, Konrad. «From *Sacra Rappresentazione* to *Commedia Spirituale*. Three 'Prodigal Son' Plays.» *Bibliothèque d'Humanisme et Renaissance* 45 (1983): 107–13.

Elam, Keir. *The Semiotics of Theatre and Drama*. London: Methuen, 1980.

Epstein, Barbara Leslie. *The Politics of Domesticity: Women, Evangelism, and Temperance in Nineteenth-Century America*. Middletown, Ct.: Wesleyan University Press, 1981.

Esslin, Martin. "'*Dead!* and *never* called me mother!' The Missing Dimension in American Drama." *Studies in the Literary Imagination* 21 no. 2 (1988): 23–33.

Ewing, John A., and Beatrice A. Rouse. "Drinks, Drinkers, and Drinking." In *Drinking in American Society—Issues and Current Research*. Edited by John A. Ewing and Beatrice A. Rouse. Chicago: Nelson-Hall, 1978.

Feldman, A. Bronson. "Ghaphaeus in England." *Modern Language Notes* 67 (1952): 325–28.

Fiedler, Leslie A. *Love and Death in the American Novel*. 3d ed. New York: Scarborough Book-Stein and Day, 1966.

Fliegelman, Jay. *Prodigals and Pilgrims: The American Revolution Against Patriarchal Authority, 1750–1800*. Cambridge: Cambridge University Press, 1982.

Foucault, Michel. "Rarity, Exteriority, Accumulation." In *The Archaeology of Knowledge and the Discourse on Language*. Translated by A. M. Sheridan Smith. New York: Pantheon Books, 1972.

Freedman, Barbara. *Staging the Gaze: Postmodernism, Psychoanalysis, and Shakespearean Comedy*. Ithaca: Cornell University Press, 1991.

Frick, John W. "'He Drank from the Poisoned Cup.'" *Journal of American Drama and Theatre* 4 no. 2 (1992): 21–41.

Fried, Michael. *Absorption and Theatricalilty: Painting and the Beholder in the Age of Diderot.* Berkeley: University of California Press, 1980.

Friedman, Sharon. "Feminism as Theme in Twentieth-Century American Women's Drama." *American Studies* 25 no. 1 (1984): 69–89.

Frye, Northrop. *The Anatomy of Criticism.* Princeton: Princeton University Press, 1957.

Fuchs, Elinor. "Presence and the Revenge of Writing: Re-thinking Theatre after Derrida." *Performing Arts Journal 26/27* 9 no. 2 and 9 no. 3 (1985): 163–73.

Garvey, Sheila Hickey. "Recreating a Myth: *The Iceman Cometh* in Washington, 1985." *The Eugene O'Neill Newsletter* 9 no. 3 (1985): 17–23.

Gilmore, Thomas B. *Equivocal Spirits: Alcoholism and Drinking in Twentieth-Century Literature.* Chapel Hill: University of North Carolina Press, 1987.

Girard, René. *Violence and the Sacred.* Translated by Patrick Gregory. Baltimore: Johns Hopkins University Press, 1972.

Goodwin, Donald W. "O'Neill: Alcohol and the Irish." In *Alcohol and the Writer.* Kansas City: Andrews and McMeel, 1988.

Gusfield, Joseph R. *The Symbolic Crusade: Status Politics and the American Temperance Movement.* Urbana: University of Illinois Press, 1963.

Hadomi, Leah. *The Homecoming Theme in Modern Literature: The Return of the Prodigal, "Guilt to Be on Your Side."* Lewiston, N.Y.: Edwin Mellen Press, 1992.

Halewood, William H. *Six Subjects of Reformation Art: A Preface to Rembrandt.* Toronto: University of Toronto Press, 1982.

Hallam, Clifford. "The Double as Incomplete Self: Toward a Definition of Doppelgänger." In *Fearful Symmetry: Double and Doubling in Literature and Film.* Edited by Eugene J. Cook. Papers from the Fifth Annual Florida State University Conference on Literature and Film. Tallahassee: University Presses of Florida, 1981.

Harwin, Judith, and Shirley Otto. "Women, Alcohol and the Screen." In *Images of Alcoholism.* Edited by Jim Cook and Mike Lewington. London: British Film Institute and Alcohol Education Centre, 1979.

Hapgood, Robert, and Robert Y. Turner. "Dramatic Conventions in *All's Well That Ends Well.*" *Publications of the Modern Language Association of America* 79 (1964): 177–82.

Herford, Charles H. *Studies in the Literary Relations of England and Germany in the Sixteenth Century.* Cambridge: Cambridge University Press, 1886.

Herrick, Marvin T. *Tragicomedy: Its Origin and Development in Italy, France, and England.* Illinois Studies in Language and Literature 39. Urbana: University of Illinois Press, 1955.

Hillman, James. "On Psychological Feminity." In *The Myth of Analysis: Three Essays in Archetypal Psychology.* Evanston, Ill.: Northwestern University Press, 1972.

Hixon, Don L., and Don A. Hennessee. *Nineteenth-Century American Drama: A Finding Guide.* Metuchen, N.J.: Scarecrow Press, 1977.

Hyde, Mary Crapo. *Playwriting for Elizabethans: 1600–1605.* New York: Columbia University Press, 1949.

Jackson, Joan K. "Alcoholism and the Family." In *Society, Culture, and Drinking Patterns.* Edited by David J. Pittman and Charles R. Snyder. New York: John Wiley, 1962.

James, William. *The Varieties of Religious Experience: A Study in Human Nature.* London: Collier-Macmillian, 1961.

Johnson, Vernon E. *I'll Quit Tomorrow.* Rev. ed. San Francisco: Harper and Row, 1980.

Kaminer, Wendy. *I'm Dysfunctional, You're Dysfunctional:The Recovery Movement and Other Self-Help Fashions.* New York: Vintage-Random, 1993.

Kane, Patricia. "The Prodigal Daughter in Alice Walker's "Everyday Use." *Notes on Contemporary Literature* 15 (1985): 7.

Kasl, Charlotte Davis. *Women, Sex, and Addiction: A Search for Love and Power.* New York: Ticknor and Fields, 1989.

Kelly, Genevieve. "The Drama of Student Life in the German Renaissance." *Educational Theatre Journal* 26 (1974): 291–307.

Keppler, C. F. *The Literature of the Second Self.* Tucson: University of Arizona Press, 1972.

Kolb, Deborah S. "The Rise and Fall of the New Woman in American Drama." *Educational Theatre Journal* 27 (1975): 149–60.

Kostelanetz, Richard C. "*The Connection:* Heroin as Existential Choice." *Texas Quarterly* 5 (Winter 1962): 159–62.

Kunzle, David. *History of the Comic Strip,* Vol. I: *The Early Comic Strip, Narrative Strips and Picture Stories in the European Broadsheet from c. 1450 to 1825.* Berkeley: University of California Press, 1973.

Lender, Mark Edward, and James Kirby Martin. *Drinking in America: A History.* New York: Free Press, 1982.

Levine, Harry Gene. "The Alcohol Problem in America: From Temperance to Alcoholism." *British Journal of Addiction* 79 (1984): 109–19.

Lieblein, Leanore. "Thomas Middleton's Prodigal Play." *Comparative Drama* 10 (1976): 54–60.

Linker, Kate. "Representation and Sexuality." In *Art after Modernism: Rethinking Representation.* Edited by Brian Wallis. New York: New Museum of Contemporary Art, 1984.

Longmate, Norman. *The Waterdrinkers: A History of Temperance.* London: Hamish Hamilton, 1968.

Lyons, Charles. "Character and Criticism." Paper for the Speech Communications Association. Denver, November 1985.

———. "Some Variations of *Kindermord* as Dramatic Archetype." *Comparative Drama* 1 (1967): 56–71.

Mâle, Emile. *Religious Art in France: The Thirteenth Century, A Study of Medieval Iconography and Its Sources.* Bollingen Series, no. 90. Princeton: Princeton University Press, 1984.

Mandl, Bette. "Absence as Presence: The Second Sex in *The Iceman Cometh.*" *The Eugene O'Neill Newsletter* 6 no. 2 (1982): 10–15.

Manheim, Michael. *Eugene O'Neill's New Language of Kinship.* Syracuse, N.Y.: Syracuse University Press, 1982.

Marranca, Bonnie. "Robert Wilson: Byrd Hoffman School for Byrds." In *The Theatre of Images.* New York: Drama Book Specialists, 1977.

Marshall, David. *The Surprising Effects of Sympathy: Marivaux, Diderot, Rousseau, and Mary Shelley.* Chicago: University of Chicago Press, 1988.

Matthaei, Julie A. *An Economic History of Women in America: Women's Work, the Sexual Division of Labor, and the Development of Capitalism.* New York: Schocken, 1982.

May, James E., and Calhoun Winton. "The 'Prodigal Son' at Bartholomew Fair: A New Document." *Theatre Survey: The American Journal of Theatre History* 21 no. 1 (1980): 63–72.

McArthur, Judith N. "Demon Rum on the Boards: Temperance Melodrama and the Tradition of Antebellum Reform." *Journal of the Early Republic* 9 (1989): 517–40.

McClelland, David C., William R. Davis, Rudolf Kalin, and Eric Wanner. *The Drinking Man.* New York: Free Press, 1972.

Mintz, Steven, and Susan Kellogg. *Domestic Revolutions: A Social History of American Life.* New York: Free Press-Macmillan, 1988.

Moody, Richard. Introduction to *The Drunkard, or the Fallen Saved.* In *Dramas from the American Theatre: 1762–1909.* Cleveland, Ohio: World, 1969.

Nightingale, Benedict. *Fifth Row Center: A Critic's Year On and Off Broadway.* New York: Times Books-Random, 1986.

Noble, Richmond. *Shakespeare's Biblical Knowledge.* London: SPCK, 1935.

Owens, Craig. "The Discourse of Others: Feminists and Postmodernism." In *The Anti-Aesthetic: Essays on Postmodern Culture.* Edited by Hal Foster. Seattle, Wash.: Bay Press, 1983.

Park, Jeannie, and Robin Micheli. "Falling Down . . . and Getting Up Again." *People,* 29 January 1990, 56–61.

Parnell, Paul. "The Sentimental Mask." *Publications of the Modern Language Associations of America* 78 (1963): 529–35.

Proehl, Geoffrey. "Foucault on Discourse: O'Neill as Discourse: *LDJN* (4: 125–154) Tyrone and Edmund." *Journal of Dramatic Theory and Criticism* 4 no. 2 (1990): 51–62.

Quinn, Arthur Hobson. Introduction. *The Faire Maide of Bristow.* Publications of the University of Pennsylvania, Series in Philology and Literature 8.1. Philadelphia: Ginn, 1902.

Rahill, Frank. "The Delirium Tremens Drama." In *The World of Melodrama.* University Park: Pennsylvania State University Press, 1965.

Raleigh, John Henry. *The Plays of Eugene O'Neill.* Carbondale: Southern Illinois University Press, 1965.

Rank, Otto. *The Double: A Psychoanalytic Study.* Translated by Harry Tucker, Jr. Chapel Hill: University of North Carolina Press, 1971.

Rayner, Alice. *Comic Persuasion: Moral Structure in British Comedy from Shakespeare to Stoppard.* Berkeley: University of California Press, 1987.

Reaver, J. Russell, compiler. *An O'Neill Concordance.* 3 vols. Detroit: Gale, 1969.

Robbins, Jill. "The Prodigal Son and Elder Brother: The Example of Augustine's *Confessions.*" *Genre* 16 (1983): 317–33.

Rogers, Robert. *A Psychoanalytic Study of the Double in Literature.* Detroit: Wayne State University Press, 1970.

Romana, Carlin. "Daddy Was the Playboy." *Philadelphia Inquirer,* 19 June 1994, sec. M., p. 1.

Room, Robin. "A 'Reverence for Strong Drink': The Lost Generation and the Elevation of Alcohol in American Culture." *Journal of Studies in Alcohol* 45 (1984): 540–45.

Rorabaugh, W. J. *The Alcoholic Republic: An American Tradition.* New York: Oxford University Press, 1979.

Rosenfield, Claire. "The Conscious and the Unconscious Use of the Double." *Stories of the Double*. Edited by Albert J. Guerard. Philadelphia: Lippincott, 1967.

Scanlan, Tom. *Family, Drama, and American Dreams*. Contributions in American Studies, no. 35. Westport, Conn.: Greenwood, 1978.

Schelling, Felix E. *Elizabethan Drama: 1558–1642*. 2 vols. Boston: Houghton, 1908.

Shafer, Yvonne B. "The Liberated Woman in American Plays of the Past." *Players* 49 (1974): 95–100.

Sheaffer, Louis. *O'Neill: Son and Artist*. Boston: Little, 1973.

"Shekana Youth Chapel." Narr. Lynn Neary. *All Things Considered*. National Public Radio. WHYY, Philadelphia. 27 June 1994.

Silverman, Kaja. *The Subject of Semiotics*. New York: Oxford University Press, 1983.

Sizer, Sandra S. *Gospel Hymns and Social Religion: The Rhetoric of Nineteenth-Century Revivalism*. Philadelphia: Temple University Press, 1978.

Skinner, Maud, and Otis Skinner. *One Man in His Time: The Adventures of H. Watkins, Strolling Player, 1854–1863, from His Journal*. Philadelphia: University of Pennsylvania Press, 1938.

Slim, H. Colin. *The Prodigal Son at the Whores': Music, Art and Drama*. Distinguished Faculty Lecture: 1975–76. Irvine: University of California, 1976.

Snyder, Susan. "*King Lear* and the Prodigal Son." *Shakespeare Quarterly* 17 (1966): 361–96.

Spieker, Joseph B. "The Theme of the Prodigal Son in XVII Century Spanish Art and Letters." *Hispanic Journal* 5 (1984): 29–49.

Spoto, Donald. *The Kindness of Strangers: The Life of Tennessee Williams*. Boston: Little, 1985.

Stivers, Richard. *A Hair of the Dog: Irish Drinking and American Stereotype*. University Park: Pennsylvania State University Press, 1976.

Stowell, Sheila. "Rehabilitating Realism." *Journal of Dramatic Theory and Criticism* 6 no. 2 (1992): 81–88.

Tippens, Daryl. "Shakespeare and the Prodigal Son Tradition." *Explorations in Renaissance Culture* 14 (1988): 57–77.

Thompson, Stith. *Motif-Index of Folk-Literature: A Classification of Narrative Elements in Folktales, Ballads, Myths, Fables, Mediaeval Romances, Exempla, Fabliaux, Jest-Books, and Local Legends*. Rev. and enl. edition. 6 vols. Bloomington: Indiana University Press, [1955-1958].

Thompson, Will L. "Softly and Tenderly Jesus Is Calling." No. 178. *The Sunday School Hymnal with Office of Devotion*. Philadelphia: Heidelberg, 1902.

Tiusanen, Timo. *O'Neill's Scenic Images*. Princeton: Princeton University Press, 1968.

Todd, Janet. *Sensibility: An Introduction*. London: Methuen, 1986.

Tompkins, Jane. *Sensational Designs: The Cultural Work of American Fiction, 1790–1860*. New York: Oxford University Press, 1985.

———. *West of Everything: The Inner Life of Westerns*. New York: Oxford University Press, 1992.

Törnqvist, Egil. *A Drama of Souls: Studies in O'Neill's Supernaturalistic Technique*. Uppsala, Sweden: Almqvist and Wiksells, 1968.

Turner, Robert Y. "Dramatic Conventions in *All's Well That Ends Well*." *Publications of the Modern Language Association of America* 75 (1960): 497–502.

Turner, Victor. "Liminal to Liminoid, in Play, Flow, and Ritual: An Essay in Comparative Symbology." In *From Ritual to Theatre: The Human Seriousness of Play*. New York: Performing Arts Journal, 1982.

Watt, Stephen. "O'Neill and Otto Rank: Doubles, 'Death Instincts,' and the Trauma of Birth." *Comparative Drama* 20 (1986): 211–30.

Wellwarth, George E. "Hope Deferred—The New American Drama: Reflections on Edward Albee, Jack Richardson, Jack Gelber, and Arthur Kopit." *Literary Review: An International Journal of Contemporary Writing* 7 no. 1 (1963): 7–26.

Wertheim, Albert. "Eugene O'Neill's *Days Without End* and the Tradition of the Split Character in Modern American and British Drama." *The Eugene O'Neill Newsletter* 6 no. 3 (1982): 5–9.

White, Hayden. "The Absurdist Moment in Contemporary Literary Theory." In *Tropics of Discourse: Essays in Cultural Criticism*. Baltimore: Johns Hopkins University Press, 1978.

Whitman, Robert F. "O'Neill's Search for a 'Language of the Theatre.'" In *O'Neill: A Collection of Critical Essays*. Edited by John Gassner. Englewood Cliffs, N.J.: Prentice, 1964.

Wolf, Edwin, II. "The *Prodigal Son* in England and America: A Century of Change." In *Eighteenth-Century Prints in Colonial America: To Educate and Decorate*. Edited by Joan D. Dolmetsch. Williamsburg, Va.: Colonial Williamsburg Foundation, 1979.

Young, Alan R. *The English Prodigal Son Plays: A Theatrical Fashion of the Sixteenth and Seventeenth Centuries*. Jacobean Drama Studies 89. Salzburg: Institut für Anglistik und Amerikanistik, 1979.

Zeitlin, Froma I. "Playing the Other: Theater, Theatricality, and the Feminine in Greek Drama." In *Nothing to Do with Dionysos?* Edited by John J. Winkler and Froma I. Zeitlin. Princeton: Princeton University Press, 1990.

Index

217